THE MEDIAEVAL MYSTICS

OF ENGLAND

ELMER O'BRIEN, s.j.
General Editor

The Mediæval Mystics
of England

Edited and with an Introduction by
ERIC COLLEDGE
DEPARTMENT OF ENGLISH,
THE UNIVERSITY OF LIVERPOOL

JOHN MURRAY
Fifty Albemarle Street London

First published in Great Britain 1962

The decorative symbols on the title page and on the part-titles are from
SYMBOLISM IN LITURGICAL ART by LeRoy H. Appleton, Stephen Bridges and
Maurice Lavanoux. Copyright © 1959 LeRoy H. Appleton, Stephen Bridges
and Maurice Lavanoux. Used by permission of Charles Scribner's Sons.

Copyright © 1961 Charles Scribner's Sons.

*Printed in Great Britain by Butler & Tanner Ltd, Frome and London
and published by John Murray (Publishers) Ltd*

Ave Crux, Spes Unica

PREFACE

Whilst this anthology has been in preparation, all the library authorities and publishers who have been asked for permission to use their manuscript or published material have been most helpful. The editor would also like to thank those scholars who have given him information and advice, many of whom have most generously allowed him access to their work before its publication: Mrs. Rosemary Dorward, Mr. A.I. Doyle, Revd. Professor T.P. Dunning, C.M., Dom Hugh Farmer, O.S.B., Dr. Helen Gardner, Mr. S.S. Hussey, Miss Clare Kirchberger, Fr. Conrad Pepler, O.P., Sister Anna Maria Reynolds, C.P., Miss Joy Russell-Smith, Dr. C.H. Talbot, Fr. James Walsh, S.J., and Professor R.M. Wilson.

E. C.

CONTENTS

A*

THE MEDIAEVAL MYSTICS

OF ENGLAND

INTRODUCTION

From the foundations of the world, men have caught sight of God's invisible nature, His eternal power and His divineness, as they are known through His creatures. Here in the first chapter, the prologue of his *Epistle to the Romans,* the greatest of all the Christian mystics says with perfect simplicity what so many scholars in modern times have thought that they by devious enquiry and private illumination have discovered, that in every great religion of which we have knowledge there were those who speculated upon God's mysteries as they are presented to us in the one supreme mystery of His own nature: that their speculations followed the same order, man's observation first of his own self, then of the rest of the visible natural order, leading him to deductions concerning creation's Creator: and that these deductions, which represent the limits beyond which human intellect cannot proceed, have led to many similar conclusions, confirmed and augmented by knowledge, wisdom and vision infused, it may be, through God's grace, reached independently by inspired seekers, Christian and non-Christian. But before those who arrive at this point proceed from it to assert that in the resemblances between the teachings of the world's great Christian and pagan mystics we have some highest common denominator which renders negligible their differences, they would do well to read on in St. Paul, to note that he is led directly from this to his statement that hitherto such speculation upon the divine mysteries has too

In the notes to this Introduction, the numbers in heavy type correspond with those in the list, *Printed Works and Manuscripts Consulted* on pages 91-102.

3

often resulted in doctrinal error and moral perversion of the worst kind.

He is here speaking of pre-Christian religious history, but we know well that his words have been confirmed again and again during the Christian era; and it is to St. Paul that the teachers of the Church have constantly turned when their charges have asked that most pertinent question, how we can know if the mystics, those who claim to have received immediate and private revelations of God's nature and works, are true or false? By their nature, by their works, by their fruits, as Christ Himself has taught us: and in the writings which treat of *probatio,* of "testing," of the analysis for truth or falsehood of the claims and teachings of such seers, we shall often find St. Paul's classic enumeration of the attributes and tokens of divine love appealed to as authoritative. What he taught of the fruits of the good tree in his *First Epistle to the Corinthians* has its counterpart, in the *Epistle to the Romans,* in the list of the marks which those led into error and falsehood will bear. The true lovers of God will be patient and kind, the false full of ill-will and spite, without pity or love. One will feel no envy, will never be perverse, the others will be avaricious back-biters and slanderers, inventive in wickedness. Love is never proud, never insolent, but hatred is vainglorious, insolent, haughty. Love does not claim rights or brood over its wrongs, hatred is contentious. Love cannot be provoked, hatred is murderous. Love takes no pleasure in wrong-doing, hatred is known by its knavery, impurity, it is deceitful and depraved. God's love teaches man to rejoice in truth's victory, but these others are His enemies, disobedient and unnatural children: they have not honour or prudence or loyalty, but His children endure and sustain, hope and believe to the end. From the foundations of the world it has been so, and is now fully revealed in the new dispensation: man may possess every other kind of gift, natural and supernatural, but such gifts are of no use unless men are given the grace of divine love, so that their fruits are recognizably good.

We need not wonder that the intellectual and spiritual history of almost every great Christian mystic traces for us how he has been brought to recognize God's nature and Christ's Redemption by the help of Paul's preaching, how he has seen, with wonder and joy, his own secret intimations of the truth of the divine mysteries confirmed and enlarged for him by the Apostle who tells of the ways of abandonment and utter desolation, of knowing rapture and self-oblivion, of experiencing and embracing the impenetrable secrets by which his spirit became united in God, secrets which often he hints at in paradoxes more daring than those who have learned from him ever employed. So Augustine was his pupil, so Aelred of Rievaulx, so deeply influenced by Augustine's *Confessions,* was led back to him, so Walter Hilton, whose *Scale of Perfection* is so much the child of Aelred's *Mirror of Love,* found in St. Paul his perfect exemplar. Few more moving or powerful tributes to Paul the mystic have ever been written than St. Aelred's: "Mightiest champion, most faithful witness, great disputator, in whom Christ speaks, who died each day for Christ, who suffered every tribulation . . . I see him now, with great tribulation and anguish of heart writing to others through his tears, I see him bewailing those who have sinned and who do no penance, I see him rejoicing with the joyous, weeping with the sad . . . and was it not he, stirred by a wonderful sweetness and borne up into Christ's embrace, who said 'I long to be dissolved, to be with Christ, which is far better'? . . . Was it not he, drunken with the wondrous love of Christ, who renounced every glory, 'except in the Cross of my Lord Jesus Christ', who, moved by the fervour of a great love, said 'Let him who does not love our Lord Jesus Christ be anathema'?"[1] Aelred's language here is calculated, and he is telling us that he has perceived for himself out of his own experience that though St. Paul's writings are no ordered scientific treatise on the mystical way of prayer and contemplation and union with God, though they are written for all Christians, by few of whom that way will be known or travelled, still they are written because he has travelled that way and reached that goal, which every mystical writer after him has attempted to describe, and that the goal can only be Christ Crucified.

To mention St. Aelred's *Mirror of Love* here may seem like beginning an account of the mystics of mediaeval England in the middle. He was born in the year 1109, the year in which died St. Anselm, whose works contributed so much to Aelred's that even now scholars are not sure which of the two is the author of some of them; and Anselm and Aelred are both the heirs and debtors of many of their precursors in the Anglo-Saxon Church. Yet the truth is that we still know very little about spirituality and mysticism in England before the Norman Conquest. The Anglo-Saxons had produced, in the seventh century, one scholar, teacher and saint not unworthy, as all the Western world came to acknowledge, to be ranked after the foremost fathers and doctors of the Church, the great Bede. His life had been passed in the kingdom of Northumbria, in a peace and security rare in those days, and he was spared any great ecclesiastical office, devoting all his time to study and writing. Yet he, the

[1] 8 coll. 550-551.

famous chronicler of the ardours of the first years when St. Gregory's missionaries won England and the English for Christ, inherited some of their labours and cares: St. Cuthbert has left for us to read his account of Bede's struggles on his death-bed to finish his translation of St. John's Gospel, of his deep concern, a century and a half after St. Augustine of Canterbury's coming, for the rudimentary education of the clergy. "I do not wish my sons to read a lie". These are the words of a man who had used learning and solitude and quiet for toil, not for ease; and his work had been done in a setting for which his own description of Augustine's first monastic foundation at Canterbury can serve. "They began to imitate the apostolic life of the primitive Church, in continual prayers, vigils and fasts, preaching the Word of Life to all who would hear it, despising the riches of this world": this is the life which every mystic extols, and in Bede, we cannot doubt, we have a saint far advanced in contemplative prayer. When he comments on the verse from the Canticles, "Behold, this is he who comes leaping among the mountains, overstriding the hills", he says that in the spiritual sense these mountains and hills are the souls who surpass others in a singular purity, and rise above the desire of base things to make themselves more fit for contemplating things which are supernal. This, however, they do not do through their own power: such contemplation is not open to men to choose, but is inspired by God's grace as He wills, and it will come to the saints, with whom God constantly dwells, by faith, by love, and by the help of His grace. Yet "the sweetness of inward contemplation, just as it is deep, by knowledge of celestial things, so it is short and rare because of the heaviness of the spirit, chained still by the bonds of the flesh. But God appears still more clearly from time to time to those who are

yet more exalted, and this comes as and when He will".
This comes after a great labour of purification of the heart,
which, though it does not produce contemplation, disposes
towards it[2]. He uses the same language elsewhere, in his
comment on St. Luke x 38-42[3]. The contemplative, freed
from the cares of the world, and lamenting the load of
corruptible flesh which he still must bear, yearns for union
with Christ, so far as human infirmity permits, for that
unique and single theology which is the contemplation of
God, "to the merit of which every merit of justification, each
practice of virtue is inferior". To attain to this is granted
only to a very small number; and though this contemplative
life is begun on earth, its fulfillment and perfection will be
in our heavenly home.

Here we are shown in a singularly pure form many
essential teachings concerning mystical theology. Bede recog-
nizes progress in the life of contemplation—it can be
"exalted", "more exalted" and "most exalted"—and those
who achieve it will do so more by grace divinely infused
than by their own efforts. It will be marked by *charismata,*
by tokens of God's love at the nature of which he merely
hints, but such tokens will be rare and brief: and because
this is so, because the contemplative knows that the union
with God of which he is in this life allowed a mere glimpse
can be achieved perfectly only in heaven, he will long for
dissolution. (We cannot doubt that the unknown Anglo-
Saxon poet of *The Debate between Soul and Body* had
Bede's words in his mind when he made the soul say to
its body

[2] 20, coll. 1107-9: and see 22.
[3] 21, coll. 470-2: and see 22.

I dwelt within you,	could not depart from you,
your carcase's captive,	ever accursed
by sins you sought.	To me it often seemed
well thirty thousand	weary years
waiting for you to die).	

Finally, Bede meaningfully insists, such contemplation is an exceptional way, not to be achieved or even desired by most Christians.

We should also notice here what Bede does not say about the states and the attributes of such contemplation. Though he plainly understands a progress from state to state which will culminate in "a quite extraordinary state of union with God in prayer" (these words are by Dom Knowles, in his remarkable handbook)[4], he makes no mention of either "theological mysticism" (this term also is Dom Knowles's, and he defines it as "the drawing out of Christian truth and doctrine beyond the limit of revelation") or, specifically, of any miraculous accompaniments to this supernatural mysticism. To quote again the same authority, "for the moment there is no question of visions, voices, sensible favours or the power of working signs and wonders": we may indeed remember here how Bede in the *Ecclesiastical History* quoted from Gregory's letter to Augustine at Canterbury, warning him not to find happiness or pride in any such miracles which might be worked through him, and we may observe how often the claims that a mystic's life has been marked by such miraculous events are made not by him but by others, generally after his death, and often out of base motives. One has good authority, among the mystics themselves and among many other spiritually-minded mediaeval men, for deploring such insistence upon the miraculous and the "psychical

[4] 103, pp. 20-21.

phenomena of mysticism", and it will not be found in this book.

What were the sources on which Bede drew to nourish in himself the spiritual life and to help him to write as a master upon it? The Benedictine Simeon of Durham, a faithful student of his works, writing about the year 1130 and justifying his reliance, a well-placed reliance, on Bede's historical records, says that nowadays some can hardly believe that "a man living in a remote corner of the world, who had never gone overseas to study, or frequented the philosophers' schools" could have acquired Bede's international reputation as a scholar: but Simeon explains that Bede was brought up in a community of six hundred holy and learned monks, and that Archbishop Theodore of Canterbury and his contemporaries had provided in England such excellent religious and secular educational facilities and, from Rome and elsewhere, so many books, that Bede could say that in his day these provisions still bore fruit in scholars who knew Greek and Latin as if they were their native tongues.[5] He was above all a monk, seeking the Benedictines' *Pax:* in one of his homilies intended for preaching at mass he says that their house has been furnished from overseas with the treasures of salvation "so that we . . . may be at rest within the cloister and serve Christ in perfect freedom".[6] But he used this freedom for the most intensive studies and enquiries. We know from recent investigations that when he needed exact information on questions which could not be answered in this country, he caused research to be done in Rome on his behalf: and we still have some of the collections which he made of texts from the Fathers, including

[5] See 88.
[6] PL 94 228, and see 22.

St. Augustine on St. Paul. Their thoughts, and his, we shall presently see as they reappeared and grew in later centuries: but we should now remark one aspect of his spirituality of which we shall often need to take account and which can well be described as it is found in Bede and his influence, the constant interplay between "pure" mysticism and affective, devotional feeling, thinking and writing. This should be mentioned, because we undoubtedly have in Bede one of the early makers of the devotions to our Lord's Passion and to His Sacred Heart which we associate with later ages, and because his contributions to these devotions were the products of the "pure" mysticism which he had learned from the Fathers. We owe a clearer view of this matter to a recent study by the Italian Stigmatine Father, Ignazio Bonetti[7]: readers of the *Ancrene Riwle,* presently to be discussed as an English spiritual classic of the early thirteenth century, will have observed that it possibly anticipates the words of the prayer *Anima Christi* when its author writes "The prophet says, *Go into the rock, hide yourself in the ditch dug from the earth,* that is, in the wounds of our Lord's flesh, which was as it were dug with the blunt nails, as God in the Psalter long ago foretold: *They made holes in My feet and My hands*"[8], and that St. Bernard in his Sermon 61 on the Canticles similarly expounds a text there which the *Ancrene Riwle* goes on to use, *My dove in the clefts of the rock, in the crannies of the wall, show me your face.* St. Bernard writes "One expositor says that these clefts of the rock are the wounds of Christ", and then continues "And where in truth can there be safe and sure hiding and rest for the afflicted but in the wounds of our Saviour?"[9] The commen-

[7] See 96.
[8] 12, p. 131.
[9] PL 183 1071-2.

tator on whom St. Bernard here relies is Bede, in his *Allegorical Exposition of the Canticles*, where he writes "If, according to St. Paul, *Christ was the rock*, what are the clefts of the rock but the wounds which Christ received for our salvation? The dove settles there and builds her nest when any one meek spirit or the whole Church confides her sole hope of salvation in our Lord's Passion";[10] and although Vernet had already observed how much Bede drew in this *Exposition* on the Fathers, notably St. Gregory, this spiritual interpretation of the "dove" and the "rock" was taken by him from the writings of the sixth-century Spanish bishop, St. Justus of Urgel, as Bonetti shows us, going on to trace the history of Bede's potent influence through this one comment on later spiritual writers.[11] He also makes the cogent remark that although for St. Anthony of Padua, a true Franciscan "affective", the wounds remain in Christ's glorified body primarily to evoke compassion in us, Bede, who seems to have been the first to deal with this question, has doctrine here for us more complex, subtle and mystical, for he teaches that this was and is so as to reform in the disciples true faith in the Resurrection, to strengthen our Lord's own intercession before the Father, to show the blessed the marks of the love by which they have been redeemed and the damned the justice of their condemnation.[12]

Bonetti then leads us to a further point, vital to the consideration of the sources and spread of Anglo-Saxon mysticism and devotion, when he observes how closely Bede's thought on the Sacred Wounds corresponds to the feeling of such devotional manuals as the Book of Cerne and

[10] 20, col. 1111.
[11] PL 67 972: and see 96, pp. 62, 90-91.
[12] 21, col. 630: and see 96, pp. 79-84.

the Book of Nunnaminster. The prayer "Of the Lord's Side" in this second manual illustrates this even better than those quoted by Bonetti: "O wonderful dispenser of divine medicine, You Who suffered Your side to be opened by the lance, open, I beg, to me who knock at the gate of life, that entering by it I may give praise to You. By the wound of Your side, by the cure of Your mercy, heal all the wounds of my wickedness, that I, though unworthy to receive them, may never be guilty of Your body and blood"[13]. "Here we have the conceit", Bonetti remarks, "found in St. Augustine and commonly among the Fathers, that the wounds which were fatal to Christ are healing to the soul: but the novelty here is that such a conceit has found expression in an emotional formula"[14]: and we now know, thanks chiefly to the immense learning and labours of the French Benedictine, Louis Gougaud, that in the Cerne and Nunnaminster manuals, hardly to be paralleled in the ninth century on the European continent for their purely devotional fervour, we have the clearest signs of another strong influence upon Bede and all other Anglo-Saxons in the development of their spirituality, that of the Celtic Church in Ireland and Scotland.[15] St. Patrick and his followers, we shall find, gave more to the formation of the thought and feeling out of which mediaeval English mysticism was to grow than the English knew or cared to acknowledge, although Bede himself pays tribute to the learning, asceticism and sanctity of the Irish monks, to whom pupils flocked from England, Scotland and even more distant lands.[16]

The interplay which we can see here, pure contemplation

[13] 95, p. 77.
[14] 96, p. 88.
[15] 101, p. 274.
[16] 101, p. 257.

being inspired by affective devotion, and in its turn being re-interpreted in terms of affective devotion for souls not advanced in contemplation, is a process which will be observed at work in every age. It is true that we shall find that almost all mystics teach that there is a certain conflict in the spiritual life between contemplation and devotion, but the most enlightened instructors among them, such as Hilton in *The Scale,* came to see that this conflict will differ according to the abilities and needs of different men and the grace given to them, and that it will never be satisfactorily resolved by the complete neglect of devotion for contemplation. Often today in the writings of scholars we discover an almost snobbish stressing of the superiority of "pure" mysticism, free of every taint, as they consider it, of affective devotion, or philosophy, or psychology: but this is a modern view, encouraged usually by partial or inattentive reading or by a narrow preoccupation with single authors, and at variance with what the mystics themselves learned from their own experience and from the great guides whom they followed. One such guide, or, better, guide-book, used from the earliest days in England as throughout the Western Church, and a most powerful factor in the development of mystical doctrine, is the famous "Conversations with the Desert Fathers", the *Collationes* of the Western monk John Cassian, who towards the end of the fourth century went first to the Holy Land and then to Egypt, to sit at the feet of the hermits there and learn from them a more perfect way of life. Let us for a moment examine what they taught him, and he the West, about "pure mysticism."

For them there was no question of men remaining in the world and striving to find perfection there. They are specialists, teaching those who wish to specialize, in a spiritual

school of advanced study, the hermit settlements of the
Theban desert: the beginning of these studies must be a
two-fold renunciation, of material possessions and of every
habit, passion and vice which can impede the soul, and the
end is St. Paul's end, illumination, absorption, recognition,
in that light which is Christ, of the soul's closeness to God.
Here, for instance, is Abbot Daniel, teaching a seemingly
very "pure" mysticism: "Sometimes it happens that God's
grace does not disdain to visit the negligent and abandoned,
through a holy inspiration, and with abundance of spiritual
thoughts it inspires the unworthy, it wakens the sleeping
and enlightens those shrouded in the darkness of ignorance,
mercifully reproving and chastising us and filling our hearts,
so that by its merest touch we are roused from our slothful
dreams. And often in these sudden visitations we are filled by
odours of a sweetness surpassing every earthly perfume, so
that the mind, established in this joy, is ravished and carried
out of itself, forgetting that it lives still in the flesh."[17] Yet
here we have as it were a prospectus of the instruction which
Cassian and Germanus were to receive from Daniel and his
colleagues. They will be concerned with human psychology,
with man's unworthiness, his struggles against the world,
the flesh, and the devil (like so many ideas which have become for us almost meaningless commonplaces, this particular formula must have had a startling clarity and novelty
for the first students of the "Conversations"), with the impossibility of constant attention but the imperative necessity
of constant intention, with the incomprehensibility of God
Who can yet be contemplated, and with "discretion", the
knowing of true from false of every kind, true seclusion, true
mortification, true inspiration. They must be taught philoso-

[17] PL 49 col. 589.

phy: did God create evil? they are asked by Abbot Theodore, and Abbot Serenus expounds to them the truth concerning grace and free will. But psychology and philosophy are mere manifestations of the intellect; and the intellect and the will must be trained. It is not enough, Abbot Moses tells them, to know who are the enemies of the soul: they must learn to fight them; and his teaching leads to Abbot Chaeremon's long discussions of perfection and chastity. Then, when the soul is freed, it must be taught to mount towards God: and so we have Abbot Isaac's two famous conversations on prayer. This prayer, as Abbot Daniel has shown, will be accompanied sometimes by *charismata* (one of the many Greek technical terms which gained currency in Latin through Cassian): and Abbot Nestor teaches what tokens of divine grace and favour, some of them miraculous, perfected men have received. And this prayer and devotion will lead to a greater mastery of "spiritual science", one part of which, Abbot Nestor shows, is what he called "spiritual intelligence", what came to bear the name of "contemplation." Finally, we must remember that this prospectus covers only half the course, for every virtue has its opposing vice, every operation of the Holy Spirit will be combated by the devil; and these same didactic methods are used to teach young monks how to recognize and fight against every manifestation of evil.

It is worth dwelling at this length on the contents and scheme of the *Collationes,* firstly because it is a work the authority and effects of which grew as the Middle Ages advanced, so that we shall hardly treat of one English mystic who cannot be shown to have learned from it: secondly, because one sees how alien from the lives of the Desert Fathers, and from all who followed their monastic way of life, were any aspirations for a mysticism unmixed with devotion, asceticism and constant intellectual exercise; and, thirdly, because we can understand very clearly from its attractive picture of these two young students from the West, patiently and humbly sitting, day after day, submitting to questioning and exposition and exhortation, how true it is that the monasteries inherited the techniques of Greek and Roman pedagogy and kept them alive. We shall never understand the Christian mystics unless we remember that they were ardent and gifted teachers, possessed by their calling to the work of education, knowing, as all experienced instructors learn, that one can never go back too often to the beginnings and retrace the steps which lead to the point which one has now reached: the frequency with which we find contemplative works combined with didactic, catechetic material, or with such material interpolated, sometimes as an afterthought by their own authors (as in the case of the *Ancrene Riwle* and St. Edmund's *Mirror of Holy Church*), shows the preoccupation of mediaeval spiritual writers with the ceaseless work of elementary religious instruction, without which higher studies would be impossible.

Bede, as we have seen, was such a teacher, in his life and works in every way a worthy successor to the Desert Fathers, and rewarded as they were by a living experience in his own soul of "spiritual science"; and in his turn he bequeathed his patrimony, enlarged and enriched, to those in England who followed him. There is not space here to speak of the spirituality of such men as Boniface and Alcuin or of their contribution to the learning and sanctity of the Western world, nor yet of some of the anonymous, vernacular literature, such as *The Dream of the Rood,* which testifies to the flowering in devotion among the people of the spirit engendered by saintly scholars. Yet it must be conceded that such scholars and such works of piety are rarer in the later centuries of the Anglo-Saxon era; and when William the Conqueror entrusted the English Church to the rule of Norman prelates, they found for the most part that in the short respite which the country had enjoyed after the ruinous centuries of war with the Scandinavians, much sloth and many evil ways had developed which needed urgent reform. How these reforms were put in hand is strikingly shown by the lives of the first two great mystics of the post-Conquest era, St. Anselm of Canterbury and St. Aelred of Rievaulx.

Although we may rightly claim St. Anselm as an English mystic, his authority in England as prelate, teacher and saint was enhanced because, when he succeeded his old teacher Lanfranc at Canterbury in 1093, he was welcomed by the people not as the representative of an alien, usurping power, but as a truly international figure, a Benedictine whose Italian birth and Norman upbringing made him the more ready to greet the English as his children in God: and the last years of his life established the pattern of exile and persecution which others after him were to suffer for fighting against the Crown for the Church and the people. When he was named archbishop he gave every sign, not of the ritual show of humility and reluctance expected of successful contestants for the Church's richest prizes, but of deep sorrow that he must accept this burden. As a boy in Piedmont he had first been drawn to the solitary way of a hermit, but had then decided to enter monastic life, and, plainly, had found in it, despite its many cares and distractions, fulfilment of his spiritual wants. Many of his letters testify to this, few better than that which he wrote from the abbey of Bec, where he had been trained and early became prior, to a young man named Lanzo, a dear friend and possibly another Piedmontese, who had recently been professed at Cluny.[18] Lanzo, it would seem, found himself wishing for a stricter rule and a life more filled with private devotion than he found there, and his abbot, not knowing how to counsel him, had asked for Anselm's help. His answer is important and significant, for it repeats the counsel of the Fathers and applies it to a situation which we shall find often recurring in the spiritual lives of those whom the ,later mystics had to direct. Lanzo must build, Anselm tells him, on the one sound foundation of obedience to his rule, and he must also treat with great caution his desires for a greater fervour than monastic life can give him, for this may be nothing but a subtle diabolic temptation.

This letter to Lanzo, written in a Latin of exquisite simplicity and filled with a wisdom as gentle as it is firm, shows us Anselm's finest qualities. He was an inspired teacher, as we can see from other works of his, such as the treatise *On Grammar*,[19] which is a series of elementary logical exercises composed in dialogue form, one of the most lively and entertaining accounts which have survived to us of an instructor at work in the monastic schools. He was a devoted superior: the Englishman Eadmer, in his loving life of the saint,[20] says that as prior of Bec he was "a father to the healthy, a mother to the sick". Yet at all times, at Bec and in the great responsibilities of Canterbury, his rule was marked by that effortless command of obedience only given to those who perfectly command themselves and their affections: his entire life was outstanding for what Dom Vernet truly called his "manly piety."[21]

In some of the great works on theology, such as *The*

[18] 15, vol. III pp. 144-8.
[19] 15, vol. I pp. 145-168.
[20] 16.
[21] 107, p. 17.

Incarnation of the Word and *Why God Became Man,* for which he is now most often remembered, Anselm undertook a wider task of instruction, addressed to the whole Church; and he was one of the foremost speculative thinkers of his time. Eadmer tells us that at Bec he became obsessed by the problem of how to demonstrate by one single short proof that God is all which is believed and taught about Him, and that the obsession destroyed his health and disorganized his religious life, until at last the solution was revealed to him which, after a strange series of misadventures, he put forward in the celebrated *Proslogion.*[22] The validity of this ontological proof was challenged in Anselm's own day, as it later was to be by St. Thomas: but its opening has for us in this present work great interest. "How wretched was the lot of man, when he lost that for which he was made, how hard, how terrible was then his state! Alas, what did he lose, what did he find, and what departed from him, what remained to him! He lost the blessedness for which he was created, and found the misery for which he was not made: that departed from him without which happiness cannot be, misery's own self remained to him. Once man ate the bread of angels, which now he hungers for, now he eats the bread of sorrow which once he did not know . . ."[23] So the prologue begins, and it ends: "I praise You, Lord, and I give You thanks, that You created in me Your image, that, remembering You, I might think of You and love You. But that image in me is so worn away by the friction of vices, so blackened with the smoke of sins, that it cannot do that for which it was made unless You renew it and form it again". In this prologue we have very clear marks of the trans-

[22] The *Proslogion* is edited in 15, vol. I pp. 97-122.
[23] 15, vol. I p. 98.

mission and fusion in Anselm's thought of several doctrines
which informed and formed much of later English mystical
teaching. In the first place, he manifestly has learned from
Augustine the idea of the *regio dissimilitudinis,* of "the land
of unlikeness", which Augustine developed from the Chris-
tion Platonist Plotinus, as Plotinus had adapted it from
Plato, who in the *Politics* says that God's guidance is needed
if the earth is not to plunge into the "region" (which seems
to be a better reading than the variant "ocean") of "unlikeness". Plotinus teaches that the soul in its lapse from virtue
into vice falls into this "region of unlikeness", and that the
soul must travel towards God through its "likeness" to
Him. For Augustine, the soul's likeness to God has been
restored in the Incarnate Word. In Genesis i 26, God said
that He would make man in His image and likeness, and
Augustine teaches that the soul is God's image through its
reason, His likeness through its intelligence.[24] And when
Anselm says that the soul's image of God is "worn away by
the friction of vices", he seems to be using that figurative
illustration, comparing the soul with a coin, stamped with
a representation of its maker but losing the representation as
it becomes worn down, first found in St. Augustine, then in
Bede, borrowed from Bede by St. Bernard and from St.
Bernard by Tauler and Ruysbroek.[25] In Bede and Anselm we
have two early and influential propagators in England of
what has come to be known as "image theology".

The short quotations just cited from the *Proslogion* also
show us another facet of St. Anselm's personality, one of the
secrets of his power over his contemporaries and his authority throughout the Middle Ages as a spiritual writer, the

[24] See **99** and **100**.
[25] See **105**.

markedly affective quality even of his scientific theological books and of his correspondence: and this is yet more apparent in his purely devotional works, which are distinguished by an absorption in the Passion of our Lord and a love of His Mother, expressed in language as ardent as it is controlled and refined. Dom Wilmart showed what were Anselm's own additions, representing the growth of his doctrine and devotion, to his third great prayer addressed to the Blessed Virgin, in which Mary's "love" (*pietas*) becomes her "propitiation", and where a passage is added to celebrate her pre-eminence among the human race (. . "No-one is Mary's equal, no-one, except God, Mary's better . ."), which, though Wilmart did not remark this, is strongly reminiscent of the praises of the Virgin in the *Dream of the Rood*.[26] Here are some phrases from the so-called *Sermon of the Lord's Passion* (in reality a long prayer which might serve as conclusion to such a sermon): "Make me a sharer in Your glory, You Who drank the bitter cup for me: Your pains torment my conscience, Your torments are my memory's cross, for the drink of which You have drunk I dreaded, the sins for which You suffered were mine, I was the disobedient slave who earned the blows which You endured . . ."[27]. Here is the opening of the famous *Prayer before a Crucifix*,[28] so strongly recalling the literary ancestors of the Anglo-Saxon *Dream of the Rood,* and that honour for the *lignum Domini,* the True Cross, for which England had been famous since King Alfred's days: "Holy cross, through which is brought to our mind the Cross on which our Lord Jesus Christ by His death called us back from that everlasting death to which we wretches were all bound, into that ever-

[26] See 17.
[27] PL 158 coll. 675-6.
[28] 15, vol. III p. 11.

lasting life which we by our sins had lost: I adore, I venerate, I glorify in you the Cross which you recall for us, and in the Cross Him, our merciful Lord, and those benefits which He in mercy gave to us through it. O lovely Cross, in which we find our health, our life, our resurrection! O precious wood, by which we have been succoured and set free! O sign for us to venerate, which God has signed us with, a glorious Cross in which alone we should have glory!" Lastly, here is a passage from the *Meditation on the Dread of Judgment*,[29] a passage which was later to be quoted many times by Richard Rolle and others who paid special honour to the Holy Name: "Who shall save me from the hands of God? Where shall I find counsel, what shall heal me? Who is it who is called 'Messenger of good counsel', who is called 'Saviour', that I may call upon his name? It is He, it is He, Jesus: He is the judge, between Whose hands I tremble; so look up, sinner, look up, do not despair, hope in Him Whom you fear, flee to Him from Whom you fled. Call aloud to Him Whom in your pride you have offended: 'Jesus, Jesus, for Your name's sake be to me what Your name promises. Jesus, Jesus, forget how in my pride I angered You, and look on me in my wretchedness imploring You. Sweet name, loveable name, name of good hope and consolation to sinners! For what is "Jesus" but "Saviour"? So, therefore, Jesus, for Your own sake be to me a "Jesus": You Who made me, let me not perish, You Who redeemed me, do not condemn me, You Who in Your goodness created me, do not let Your work be destroyed because of my wickedness . . .'" All these sentiments are easily to be understood by the simplest man who hears them, but they are inspired by the purest mystical passion.

[29] **15**, vol. III, p. 79.

B

The work of Lanfranc and Anselm as reformers of the easygoing Anglo-Saxon ways of the English monasteries has been mentioned: and in the next great English mystic, St. Aelred of Rievaulx, we have a remarkable example of the results of the changes, brought about in the eleventh century, which led to the ardours and enthusiasm of the twelfth. Aelred's father, Eilaf son of Eilaf, was in effect the hereditary priest of Hexham in Northumberland: Professor Powicke writes of his family as "a long line of married priests, learned, respectable, conscientious". But during Eilaf's incumbency, many reforms and innovations came from the south: old monastic foundations were restored, and in 1113 he was replaced at Hexham by Austin canons. Though he was able to retain a title to his office and income, he renounced these in 1138, and, significantly, ended his days as an inmate of the great new Benedictine house at Durham which the Norman bishop William of St. Carileph had built.[30] Walter Daniel, Aelred's biographer, fellow-monk and dear friend, tells us that he was given an education, partly at the Scottish royal court, which might have been expected to fit him for a secular career, and Aelred somewhat ruefully says, in the Prologue to *The Mirror of Love,* that he was never given a proper academic training, entering religion not from a monastic school but out of a kitchen; yet he was one of the first Englishmen to respond to the call of a new way of life, newer even than Lanfranc and Anselm had promoted by their internal reorganizations of their order. Some of St. Bernard's first emissaries to England had established at Rievaulx in Yorkshire a house, the very simplicity and humility of whose brethren, as Powicke observes, were promoting unrest and discord in Northern England.[31] The

---

[30] 9, pp. xxxiv-vi.
[31] 9, pp. xxxvi-vii.

Cistercians were zealous in their agitation against such secular priests as Eilaf who married: and they were not guiltless of meddling, though with entirely worthy and selfless motives, in the country's politics. If high ecclesiastical appointments had to be opposed, it was well that such opposition should be led by an order the whole tone of which, as dictated by Bernard himself, was against seeking any kind of distinction, hierarchical or intellectual. The ties between Rievaulx and Bernard were very close: William, the first abbot, had served as his amanuensis: and we now know that the work a part of which has been chosen to represent St. Aelred in this anthology, *The Mirror of Love,* was written, or, at least, finished and published, at the instigation of Bernard.[32] There is a prefatory letter to the *Mirror* which had been mistakenly ascribed to an "Abbot Gervase", until T.E. Harvey drew attention to an early manuscript in the British Museum in which St. Bernard is named as the author. This finding was investigated and confirmed by no less an authority than Wilmart, who began his study of the question by pointing out that the *Mirror,* so plainly a record of Aelred's educational programme for the Rievaulx novices, might well never have been completed, at least by its author, since his period of office as novice-master was very brief. He was appointed in 1141, on his return from Rome, but in 1142 he was transferred to the new community at Revesby as its head. Bernard says that he has asked, indeed ordered, Aelred to write something to help those who are seeking for perfection, and, though Aelred has made various excuses, he is now commanded in obedience to put aside his humility, to overcome his difficulties, and not to fear the jealousy or the charges of presumption which such a work may inspire. He is to write at once about the excellence, the fruits and the

[32] 10.

applications of *caritas,* what it is, what sweetness it brings, how it opposes *cupiditas,* how discretion should govern its practice. The work is to be called *Speculum Caritatis, The Mirror of Love,* and it is to be issued with this letter as preface.

It is quite clear that Aelred had told Bernard, doubtless in answer to his questions, of the course of lectures on mystical theology which he intended to deliver as novice-master: and we may well now consider how much Aelred's theology and his works were influenced by Bernard. On this point, too much seems to have been assumed. In the first place, like all other great mediaeval teachers, Bernard and Aelred enjoyed a common heritage: Wilmart observes that one feature of the scheme outlined in Bernard's preface, the opposition between *caritas,* divine love, and *cupiditas,* self-love, is characteristically Augustinian; and we shall indeed see that Augustine was perhaps the most potent influence of all upon Aelred. He was, it is true, proud to borrow openly from Bernard. The long and beautiful lament (not translated in this anthology) for the monk Simon, the dear friend who had died in his absence from England, is an undisguised reminiscence of Bernard's eulogy of his dead brother Gerard, in his Sermon 26 on the Canticles,[33] and Dr. C. H. Talbot observes that in Aelred's Candlemass Sermon, where for once he does make a very discreet use of the Bernardine analogy of an espousal between the Word and the perfected soul, we also find, in his description of the soul's impatience for union wih God—"When will He come, when will the Word be born, when shall I see Him, can I endure till then?"—that he is remembering and paraphrasing Bernard's words,

---

[33] 23, pp. 169-181: the borrowing was pointed out to the present writer by Miss Clare Kirchberger.

in the tenth chapter of *De diligendo Deo,* about the soul's longing for what he there specifically names as "deification".[34] But when Vernet calls Aelred Bernard's most notable successor,[35] there is much left unsaid which should be stated.

In the first place, there is far more in Aelred than in Bernard of "manly piety": and Aelred, with a very few minor exceptions such as that noted by Talbot, is free of what we today may look on as Bernard's chief contribution to spirituality, his *Brautmystik,* his affection for the analogies between carnal and divine love, his use, for spiritual and Christian purposes, of the ideas and images of mediaeval secular romantic literature. When Etienne Gilson says that "the mystical literature of the twelfth century is the harmonious fulfilment and the crown of the secular literature which soon it was to form again in its own image"[36], he is thinking only of mystical literature harmonious with Bernard's thought and imagery, he is ignoring the deep mistrust which many mystics had for secular literature and for the philosophies and the theology which seemed to reflect it. We can see this mistrust clearly stated in a passage in the second book of *The Mirror of Love,* in a colloquy between Aelred and a novice who expresses some surprise and disillusionment that in the monastic life he has so far experienced only a lessening of the fervours which he used to know. Aelred sets out to show him that in the world he had lived in a constant state of ill-directed enthusiasm, whereas now he is committed to a sober, steady pursuit of purely spiritual ends. "At these words he blushed for shame, and hung his head, and kept his eyes to the ground. 'It is too true', he answered, 'too true: I can remember sometimes being moved to tears

[34] 7, pp. 47-52.
[35] 107, p. 22.
[36] 24, p. 14.

by some worldly tale or other about Arthur' "[37]. Aelred here is merely saying what St. John Chrysostom and many another had already said, what his English precursor Alcuin had stated with especial distinctness for the benefit of the monks of Lindisfarne: "Let the Word of God be read when they are at meals: they should listen to the lector, not the harpist, to the works of the Fathers, not the songs of the pagans. What has Ingeld to do with Christ? Your house is small, there is not room for them both, the King of Heaven will not keep company with so-called kings who were pagans and are lost. Let the voices of readers be heard in your halls, not the ribald laughter of the streets"[38]. In his *Rule for Anchoresses,* Aelred shows a similar disapproval of pious art-objects used merely for adornment: the anchoress's altar is to be vested in plain linen, and she is to content herself with a representation of the Crucifixion, because her oratory is for prayer, not for aesthetic pleasure.[39]

If today we esteem the mediaeval mystics because we think them characteristic of the Middle Ages, or, to be more exact, of what we imagine the mediaeval world to have been like, if in our minds we associate mystical literature with the painting and sculpture and architecture and music of the epoch, with the ballads and romances and plays, if we begin calling the mystics "the troubadours of God" and that sort of thing, we fail to understand their first common quality, their fundamental rejection of the earthly society which surrounded them but in which they would not live. They were indifferent to man-made beauty, and many of them feared it and would have destroyed it. So we may justly contrast Aelred's logic and sobriety with Bernard's emotional exub-

[37] 8, col. 565.
[38] *Alcuini Epistolae* (Monumenta Germaniae Historica, Berlin, 1895), p. 183.
[39] 6, col. 1463.

erance, Bernard's mastery of style and form with Aelred's indifference to literary graces. Bernard is beyond doubt a powerful influence upon the affective and devotional literature of mediaeval England: but we can find a stronger influence upon Aelred in Bernard's contemporary and friend William of St-Thierry, whose whole mind and temper are much nearer to what Aelred has to say of the spiritual life[40]. William's famous *Epistle to the Brethren of Mont-Dieu,* generally ascribed in mediaeval times to St. Bernard, but now restored to its rightful author,[41] is one of the most significant and characteristic documents of the "new spirituality" of the twelfth century, and in his exhortations and encouragement to the little band of Carthusians who had just settled at Mont-Dieu, praising their "desert", the life of prayer and contemplation in solitude, he is preaching a very pure mysticism closely akin to the doctrine of *The Mirror of Love.* "It is not enough for you to be satisfied with what is required of all Christians, merely to keep God's commandments. You must try to anticipate His wishes, to find out what is good and pleasing and perfect according to His will. Let others live to serve God: you must have no other life than God. Let others believe in Him, learn about Him, love Him, reverence Him: you must taste and comprehend Him, know Him, delight in Him"[42].

If any intermediary were needed, Aelred would also find in William even more than in Bernard that dependence on the thought and language of Augustine which is so marked a feature of *The Mirror of Love.* Walter Daniel tells us that Aelred's especial devotion to the *Confessions* never failed:

---

[40] We may shortly expect a full-scale study of Aelred by Fr. Aelred Squire, O.P., in which this influence will be examined.
[41] 92.
[42] 90, col. 311.

towards the end of his life, crippled and tormented by arthritis, he had a cell made for him near the infirmary, and an oratory with "a kind of grave" sunk in the floor, where he would sit and read and weep and pray, "and more than any other books he had Augustine's *Confessions* in his hands, for they had been his guide when he was turned from the world"[43]. No-one who knows the *Confessions* can fail to hear its echoes in every chapter of Aelred's *Mirror*, though one example must here be sufficient: when, in the first book, chapter 28, Aelred writes "Vilui ipse mihi in his verbis, saepe, et flebam aliquando amarissima contentione animae" ("But as I prayed I often saw my own worthlessness, and sometimes I wept for this most bitter struggle in my soul"), he is remembering Augustine's words as he tells, in Book VIII chapter 12 of the *Confessions,* of his violent and bitter struggles before his conversion: "Dicebam haec, et flebam amarissima contritione cordis mei"[44]. And as we read Aelred's words on memory, on the threefold power of the soul, on the "reforming of the image", on the peace of the Sabbath, on the Psalms and St. Paul and the Desert Fathers, we can see how well and constantly he had indeed been guided by Augustine's great spiritual autobiography.

Aelred is however no intellectual antiquarian: what he writes in Book I chapter 8 of the *Mirror,* a chapter which was to affect Hilton deeply, the very moving development of Augustine's theme, telling how the soul, wearied and disgusted by the world, becomes free from the world, not loving or envying or fearing it, and so approaching to its Sabbath, where it will find its rest in the contemplation of God, shows, in the "spiritual" interpretation of "Sabbath"

---

[43] 9, pp. 39-40, 50.
[44] 8, col. 532: 18, col. 762.

and in much else, the tastes and manners of Aelred's own
times: to read this chapter is inevitably to be reminded of
O quanta qualia, Peter Abelard's great hymn to the soul's
true rest in God. Aelred can also look forward: we find, for
example, in Book II chapter 5 a defence of "mixed life", a
demonstration that the external works of love and "inward
sweetness" are not incompatible, which again must wait for
development and acceptance until the fourteenth century and
Walter Hilton. The *Mirror* reflects the passion of Aelred's
age, a passion to which the revival of Hebrew studies contributed, for the spiritual re-interpretation of the Old Law
in the light of the new dispensation and of mystical experience. Today we may find some of Aelred's concern for the
synagogue and the Sabbath heavy-handed, but we must remember that we come to such expositions weighed down
with the fatigue of many centuries of the mechanical application of this technique. In the twelfth century, such scholars
as William of St-Thierry and the Victorines had made it new
again, and a direct source of revelation of divine wisdom.

Nor must we think of Aelred, in his life or in his influence,
as remote or self-sufficient. He could show deep sympathy for
forms of spirituality entirely foreign to him: it was he who
first suggested to the Benedictine monk Reginald of Durham,
whilst St. Godric of Finchale was still alive, that Reginald
should begin to prepare that biography of Godric which
is today so priceless a witness to the beginnings, in England,
of a secular and unlearned holiness of which Aelred himself
had experienced little or nothing.[45] Then, too, in Aelred's
Rule for Anchoresses (this Latin work was given various
titles, of which Wilmart preferred that confirmed by Walter
Daniel, *De institutione inclusarum*) we have some of the

[45] 41, p. 403, using 40.

B*

earliest surviving evidence for yet another form of mediaeval spirituality, closely related in its origins and development to the awakening aspirations of humble and unlearned laymen to a higher form of life, the call of women to the solitary and enclosed life of anchoresses. Such women, and their need for spiritual guidance, occasioned some of our greatest mediaeval spiritual classics, including the famous *Ancrene Riwle* (the mediaeval English title will be used here to avoid confusion with Aelred's work): and in *A Rule for Anchoresses* we have a precursor of the *Riwle* (Aelred died in 1167, and in its very earliest form the *Riwle* cannot have been written long before 1200—the present writer is, indeed, disposed to date it later) which has many superficial resemblances to it. Gossipping, chattering women at the window of the anchorhold, the sin of possessions and notably of anchoresses keeping cattle, scandalous "hospitality", the advisability of appointing an old, grave confessor: all these are features common to both treatises.

The *Riwle* is not, as has often been claimed for it, a work of mysticism; but still it remains a text essential to the study of mediaeval English mysticism, because in it we have an account, detailed and living as few others are, of the enclosed, solitary life in which mysticism could and did flourish. There are many technical questions concerning the *Riwle* which we need not here seek to answer—many of them seem still to be unanswerable—but it is now becoming clearer that even if it be not of Dominican authorship, it is filled with the spirituality which, everywhere in Europe, the Dominicans and Franciscans would soon assimilate and make their own,[46] and that, especially in its "second edition", the *Ancrene Wisse,* which we know to have been made after the

[46] See particularly 14.

friars had arrived in this country in the 1220's, we have tantalizingly inscrutable witness of the beginnings in England of a popular devotional movement, rooted no doubt in mysticism but characterised by affective fervour, a movement fostered and practised by devout women which we may compare with the great *Frauenbewegung* which was sweeping through the Rhineland and the Low Countries, a movement which, however, was lost and came to nothing in England. In one of the most important additions which the editor of the *Wisse* made to his original, he writes of the anachoritic way of life led by his readers as beginning to spread throughout England, as characterised by "singularity" (which we today would call "enthusiasm"), and as needing discipline and rule.[47] We must be reminded by this of the early struggles of communities of devout German and Dutch women for monastic incorporation and recognition: but it is most significant that whereas overseas these struggles led to a great foundation of Dominican nunneries from the source to the estuary of the Rhine and across the great German plain, and the appearance under Dominican sponsorship of some of the greatest of the mediaeval women mystics, in England the order had merely a single house of nuns, and our one great woman mystic lived in an earthly as in a spiritual solitude.

Aelred too, in his *Rule,* shows that care for and understanding of all levels of intellectual attainment which we may expect from a prelate who could say, in his beautiful Pastoral Prayer: "My God, You know how unwise I am . . . but I do not ask from You, sweet Lord, gold or silver or precious stones: give me wisdom, let me know how to rule Your people. You Who are the source of wisdom, send some

[47] 13, pp. 112-113.

to me from the throne of Your greatness, to be and toil and work with me, to speak through me, to order my thoughts and my words and all my deeds and my counsels, according to Your will, to the honour of Your name, for my children's benefit and my salvation."[48] The *Rule* is written for some of his youngest children, anchoresses who probably could not even read,[49] and for their benefit he includes a series of "meditations on the mysteries of Christ," highly emotional reconstructions and amplifications of the Gospel narrative, in which they are urged to regard themselves as participants. "See how He stands before the judgement seat, head bowed, eyes cast down, face calm, saying little, ready for insults, prepared for blows. Now I know that you can endure no more, you cannot bear to watch how His delicate back is torn with scourges, His face slapped, His adorable head crowned with thorns, His right hand which holds up heaven and earth made ludicrous with a reed. See Him now led out, scourged, wearing His thorns as a crown and His purple garment, and Pilate says 'This is the man!' Of course He is a man—who can doubt it, when the proofs are the rods' weals, His bruises, and His face defouled with spittle . . ."[50] We have Walter Daniel's assurance that Aelred was the author of this *Rule,* but it is not remarkable that it has so often been attributed to Anselm, since it closely follows the method and recaptures the highly emotional manner of some of Anselm's own meditations: these two mystical writers were to popularize in England a form of spiritual exercise which greatly influenced authors and visionaries such as Rolle, Julian and Margery Kempe, and which, in England as

[48] 11, p. 294.
[49] For a discussion of the problems caused by illiterate or Latinless women religious in the Middle Ages, sec 25, pp. 66-78.
[50] 6, col. 1469.

overseas, produced many later examples characterized by a morbidity and near-hysteria as little to the taste of the twentieth century as are many medieval representations of our Lord's Passion in other forms of art. Yet we may perhaps view them with more understanding if we will remember that bloodshed and violent death were then common sights, and that this art was produced for the benefit of those to whom most of our aids to devotion were denied, since, whether laity or religious, they could read neither in Latin nor the vernacular.

In Anglo-Saxon times there was a tradition that some nuns, at least, should learn Latin. In the early eighth century the nun Liota, who was to die abbess of Bischofheim on the Anglo-Saxon mission to Germany, sent samples of her not very original verses, which she had learned to compose from her mistress, Abbess Eadburg of Thanet, "who never wearies of turning God's law into verse," to St. Boniface.[51] We may guess that Boniface had told her to work hard at her Latin. The tradition seems to have persisted in some nunneries after the Conquest. In the reign of William Rufus, the Conqueror's son, the nun Muriel of the Benedictine house of Wilton made a great reputation as a Latin poetess, and the French bishop Hildebert of Lavardin addresses her as

> Wise virgin who watches and prays, your least word
> Men prize above all the works of the poets of old:
> You live to praise God, and your praises shall live for all time
> To His glory Whose wisdom the whole world admires in
> your song.[52]

Yet today we should not know of Muriel, were it not for Hildebert's lines, all that survives to tell of her fame. She

---

[51] *S. Bonifatii Epistolae* (Monumenta Germaniae Historica, Berlin, 1892), p. 281.
[52] See **73**.

was still alive at the abbey at the time of the profession of another learned sister, Eva of Wilton, born in England of a Danish father and a Lorraine mother and sent to school there with the nuns as a very young child. We know of her through the "Book of Consolation," *Liber Confortatorius,* which was addressed to her by the monk Goscelin, a Frenchman settled in England, when, some time after the year 1102, she left the abbey for a stricter way of life, went to France and was established at Angers as one of a number of recluses, among them the saintly Herve, to whom she acted as domestic servant, their piety apparently saving them from every taint of scandal. Despite its title, Goscelin's treatise to her begins with a passionate declaration of his grief when he discovered that she had departed. This opening must remind us of the Abelard-Heloise correspondence, and doubtless owes as much to contemporary literary fashions. Gradually the work develops into admonitions on her conduct of the enclosed life. She is to be constant in her study of the Bible, the Fathers, the *Lives,* the *Confessions,* the *Civitas Dei:* Goscelin imagines her with her window filled with bookshelves. And there is much which anticipates Aelred's *Rule* and the *Ancrene Riwle:* at the canonical hours she is to meditate upon the Passion, and there are the beginnings of formal devotion to the Five Wounds.[53]

Eva, in leaving the land of her birth to find a greater solitude overseas, became one of the many men and women known as "pilgrims," *peregrini,* the term being used not in its modern sense but to designate those who, in the words of an Anglo-Saxon chronicler, "wanted to live among strangers for the love of God."[54] Many of these "pilgrims," we

[53] See 35.
[54] The fullest account of such "pilgrims", especially from Ireland, is in 101.

know, came to sad ends overseas, and others returned, having seen the world and its wonders: yet to perhaps the most
famous English exile of the Middle Ages, William Flete,
the hermit of Leccetto, his expatriation was a harsh austerity
and the remembrance of his homeland a tormenting grief.[55]
But we find a somewhat different pattern in the life of the
great ecstatic and hermit Godric of Finchale, a contemporary of Muriel and Eva who died, in extreme old age, in
1170.[56] The child of very humble, very pious East Anglian
parents, he had received no schooling whatever, but as a
boy distinguished himself as a keen and intrepid pedlar.
Wherever he went on business, to Scotland, Rome and elsewhere, he visited the great shrines. He could say the Creed
and the 'Our Father,' and as he journeyed he used to meditate on the mysteries of the Faith. Then he gave up trade,
took the Cross and went to Jerusalem, and a second time
to Rome, accompanied by his mother, on foot, and, out of
devotion, barefoot. When they returned, he gave away all
his possessions, and set out, with his parents' blessing, to
seek solitude in a strange land as the most perfect way of
life. For a time he lived at Carlisle, near the Scottish border;
and he seems here to have begun with the help of others
to learn "St. Jerome's Psalter," as it was called, an arrange-
ment of Latin verses from the psalms abbreviated for the
use of the laity. When he was an old man his biographer
Reginald of Durham asked him why his forefinger was
twisted into his palm, and Godric laughed and said that
Jerome would be able to recognize him by this mark on the
Day of Judgement, for his finger had become twisted through
carrying around his psalter, "for he loved the book so much

[55] See **39**.
[56] See **40**.

that he carried it about when he laboured as well as when he rested, praying as well as working, secured by this finger."[57] Fleeing the popular esteem which his piety excited in the town of Carlisle, he lived as a wanderer, and then as servant and companion to a hermit Aelfric who had a cell at Wolsingham in Durham. Aelfric had been educated among the monks at Durham, and until his death he acted as tutor as well as spiritual mentor to Godric. One significant remark shows us the kind of conversation they must have enjoyed. Reginald writes that when Godric was asked "by one of our brethren" (that is, by a Benedictine monk from Durham) for an account of his vision of Aelfric's spirit departing from his body at the moment of death, he finished the narrative by saying that he could not doubt whose spirit it was, "even though I did not understand the 'discretion of spirits.' "[58] Aelfric and he must have discussed *discretio, probatio,* that branch of "spiritual science," so important to the mediaeval contemplative, which taught how to distinguish true union with God in prayer and contemplation, and the favours which such union may bring, from the wiles and frauds of the devil[59]; and he would certainly speak to Godric, in this and other connexions, of John Cassian and the Desert Fathers. He was supernaturally admonished, soon after Aelfric's death, to go on pilgrimage a second time to Jerusalem, and then, returning, to seek a habitation for himself at Finchale near Durham. This he did, seeking out every place in the Holy Land where our Lord had walked, praying throughout whole nights upon the mountains, visiting the Holy Sepulchre with untellable devotion. He seemed there to suffer rapture, and on recovery to

[57] 40, p. 200.
[58] 40, p. 51.
[59] For a discussion of the classical literature on this subject, see 25, pp. 61-65.

be as it were a different man, filled with amazing joy. His words, as Reginald reports them, tell of the traditional, ever-recurrent marks of mystical rapture: "in his heart there was a gentleness greater than anything else, in his mouth a sweetness sweeter than honey or the honeycomb, and his ears were filled with the melody of a great jubilation . . ."[60] After he had bathed in Jordan he returned to Jerusalem and remained there for several months, ministering to the sick, visiting the Holy Places with much devotion, seeking out holy, solitary men and commending himself to their prayers: and then, returning to England, he presently went to Durham itself, showing much reverence for St. Cuthbert's shrine, and furthering his religious education. He now learned to recite the whole Latin Psalter, and attended the school attached to St. Mary's church below the castle, sitting in the church when the youngest boys were reciting their first Latin lessons, so that in a short time he had command of certain canticles, hymns and prayers, "enough, as he thought, to suffice him."[61] Then, having so equipped himself for a solitary, contemplative life, he settled near Durham at Finchale, in a spot thought uninhabitable, so wild and inclement and infested with wild beasts was it. But his spiritual director at Durham gave him leave, and he was helped by the great Norman prince-bishop, Ralph Flambard, part of whose hunting forest the land was. Then begins the last long chapter in his life, which cannot here be described in detail: heroic fastings and penances, horrifying diabolical apparitions and temptations, consoling visions of God and His Mother, the saints and eternal blessedness, and more and more, the veneration and care of the Durham monks, who

[60] 40, pp. 55-56.
[61] 40, p. 60.

were not alone—we have already seen that Aelred regarded
Godric as a saint in the making—in realizing that the simple,
humble wanderer who had put himself under their protection, who still regarded himself as the vilest of sinners, a
Latinless layman not fit to touch the sacred objects in his
oratory, was in truth the master of them all in holiness of
life and in his powerful prayer. And we owe to Aelred's
prompting and Reginald's diligence a record, in Godric's
own English, of the one or two short hymns which he composed and used to sing for his consolation. One of them we
may render as:

> Holy Mary, Virgin clean,
> Mother of the Nazarene,
> For help Godric thy child does cry:
> Bring him with thee to God on high.

> Holy Mary, Christ's own bower,
> Of maidens purest, of mothers flower,
> My queen, my champion, grant me this:
> Bring me at last to heaven's bliss.[62]

It may seem that an excessive time has been spent on an
obscure hermit whose only contribution to English religious
literature is a few short verses: but Reginald's *Life* documents for us better than any other earlier English source a
type of spirituality which was to inspire many of the later
mystical classics. Uneducated, with no proper knowledge
of Latin, a layman, Godric still saw that the strictest and
most arduous vocation known to the Church, the solitary
life, was his true call; and his faith and assiduity did remove
the mountains which lay between him and some form of par-
ticipation in the sacred liturgy, which he had recognized
from afar as the work most pleasing to God. Any technical

---

[62] For a critical text of the original English, see 41.

study of the means which he employed to overcome his obstacles—his learning by heart, the ecclesiastical *lingua franca*
which he mastered and which Reginald is careful to call
lingua Romana, not "Latin," his use of pictures as an aid to
meditation—must await another occasion, but enough has
been said here to show that he represents something new and
most important in English spiritual history. It is good also
to be able to record that his fame survived until the sixteenth
century, not merely as a thaumaturge, but also as a lover of
the Mother of God. Not long before the Dissolution, the
Carthusian Richard Methley in his *Epistle of Solitary Life,*
addressed simply "to Hugh, hermit," recommends Godric's
prayer to our Lady as a solace when Hugh is overtaken by
weariness.[63]

To those who love these simple saints it must always be a
moving circumstance when happy accident has preserved
some words of theirs, not transformed into mellifluous yet
impersonal Latin, but as they spoke them so many centuries
ago. We have Godric of Finchale's hymns, we have St. Edmund Rich's interjection into the elegant French in which
The Mirror of Holy Church was preached of the popular
English quatrain, well-known to his hearers, which Carleton
Brown so justly entitled *Sunset on Calvary*—

> Now sinks the sun behind the wood apace:
> I sorrow, Mary, for thy lovely face.
> Now sinks the sun behind the tree:
> I sorrow, Mary, for thy Son and thee.[64]

and the anonymous monk of St. Albans who composed the
Latin biography of another great ascetic and visionary of
the twelfth century, Christina of Markyate, evidently judged

[63] See 72.
[64] This occurs in one of the passages omitted in the translation of *The Mirror of Holy Church* in this anthology. A text of the original English will be found in 97, p. 1.

that his reader would be touched when he quoted the English term of endearment used by her spiritual father, another hermit Godric, who, when he recalled the fullness of grace which had brought her safe through fearful trials and hardships, used to call her "my Sunday's daughter."[65] If we are disposed to think of mediaeval England as a gentler climate, in which piety and devotion and mystical rapture could come unchecked and unscathed to their full flowering, we shall do well to read what this "Sunday's child" had to suffer before she gained the peace and security of the monastic life to which she had vowed herself as a young girl. Her wealthy and ambitious parents were determined not to contract out of the advantageous marriage which they had made for her—Christina preserved her virginity even though married in the church and brought to bed with her young husband—and they were helped to hinder her in the search for God by a succession of venal and unscrupulous prelates, not least Bishop Ralph Flambard of Durham, who, though he was a benevolent patron towards Godric of Finchale, played a most lewd and scandalous part in the unhappy Christina's early life. Though she also has no place in the catalogue of mystical writers, she lived according to their precepts and experienced their transports, and her *Life* is an important document for the growth in the twelfth century of devotion to the eremitical life so favourable to mysticism. Of the hermit Godric, her first great friend and counsellor, we know nothing beyond what her anonymous biographer tells us: yet even that makes him a figure worthy to be compared with his namesake of Finchale. He in his "desert" near Dunstable, and his contemporary, the famous and holy West Country anchorite St. Wulfric of Haselbury,[66]

[65] See 26.
[66] See 94.

were doubtless only two of many solitaries who at this time drew to themselves others, men and women, wishing to learn and to practise a life of complete seclusion from the world, who might say with the Psalmist and Christina of Markyate "What is there in Heaven for me but You? What should I ask on earth but You?" It is no wonder that the *Ancrene Riwle* is only one, though the most famous, of a number of treatises composed in the early thirteenth century which not only lay down rules for the daily, external observances of the solitary life, but concern themselves with higher spiritual aspirations, as these might be experienced and realised by those whose lack of formal education deprived them of easy access to spiritual literature. One such treatise, remarkable because it does not bother at all about external rules, but goes straight to contemplation, is the brief *Threefold Exercise* by Stephen, abbot of the Cistercian house of Sawley in the West Riding of Yorkshire, c.1200-1230.[67] Stephen begins by emphasizing that his tract is not a learned work, but is for the edification of the simple. Whenever one is in solitude and at leisure, one must drive out of the heart all corporeal imaginations, and lift one's spirit up to one supreme principle, the Creator of all things, God, Father and Son and Holy Spirit, not seeking to understand by a laborious use of the intellect but to love by faith, giving thanks to Him for all His benefits, special and general, and thanking Him for what He is in Himself, all-good, all-blessed, all-powerful, all-felicitous. One should remember the blessedness of man's first state, his wretched fall and sins: and then one's own particular shortcomings, one's individual sins against God. Let each man by such meditation move himself to tears, bewailing his offences and looking to God for mercy. In his second meditation, let him in confidence approach the throne of the

[67] See 89.

Mother of Mercy: and in his third, let him consider how gloriously the city of Jerusalem is set on high, and the joy and happiness of delighting in the presence of God. It is for this that we should long, to this that we should set all our thoughts and hearts: and these meditations are to be performed not with intellectual subtlety (*curiose*) but "sweetly and simply," looking above all to God and to the Blessed Virgin for help.

Despite this simplicity of intention and execution, Stephen's *Threefold Exercise* is a modern work, aware of new developments in the science of the spiritual life. Perhaps we can hear, in Stephen's counsel that his "meditations" are to be accomplished not with the intellect but with the heart and with faith, an early allusion to the great hymn to Jesus and His Holy Name, *Dulcis Iesu Memoria,* already being copied and sent around England before it could have been composed by St. Bernard, to whom so many of its later devotees ascribed it[68]; and we are not far from the *via negativa,* the way to God by acknowledging that the most which our finite human intellects can achieve is the knowledge that we cannot know what He is Who is infinite, the way which in English spiritual literature has its supreme expositor in *The Cloud of Unknowing* in the fourteenth century, the way which is now inseparably associated with the works of the great Greek mystical theologian, "pseudo-Dionysius."

Some modern scholars are at a loss to account for the great prestige which "Dionysius" enjoyed in Western Europe from the twelfth century until the time of St. John of the Cross. Certainly, no mediaeval scholar questioned the author's identity with the Athenian, mentioned in chapter xvii of the Acts of the Apostles, converted by St. Paul, and it is hard to avoid

[68] See **108.**

the conclusion that "Dionysius" himself wished this to be thought, whereas we know today that he must have been a Syrian religious trained in Alexandria, and writing there about the year 500. But his works were revered in the West, not only because they were believed to be as old as the New Testament itself, but also because they expressed, in a novel and powerful form, ideas concerning the process and nature of the soul's union with God which transformed and advanced the speculations of Western contemplatives upon mystical theory. It is also true that many of the Dionysian doctrines (for example, his "angelology," his teaching that mystical phenomena, knowledge of the Word comes to man through the ministry of angels, teaching found in many great mystics, such as Bernard and Walter Hilton)[69] and metaphors, such as the famous "dark cloud," had found their way already from Dionysius's sources, Christian and pagan Greek followers of Platonic philosophy, into Latin works, and could be discovered scattered through the writings of such authorities as St. Gregory the Great and St. Augustine. But this did not lessen the impact of the *Celestial Hierarchy,* the *Mystical Theology* and the other Dionysian works upon Western minds: rather, they found for the first time in a single body of treatises, short by mediaeval standards, confirmation of the many isolated, tantalizing hints which had preceded them of God's nature, and of His union with the soul. We can see Dionysian doctrine, and its effects, very clearly in a work written probably a few years earlier than Stephen's *Threefold Exercise,* the *Fourfold Exercise of the Cell* by the celebrated Premonstratension abbot turned Carthusian, Adam of Dryburgh.[70] Adam's "eighth stage of meditation"

[69] See **45**, Appendix.
[70] See 2 and 3.

deals with mystical union, and he writes: "We wish to talk about God, but we cannot say what He is, because we are unable to understand it, and what we cannot comprehend with our minds it follows that we cannot express in words. Undoubtedly, everything which is, is either God or the creatures which He has created: but the being of His creatures is so far removed from His being that one might say, in a certain sense, that His creatures are not, but only He is. It was in this sense that the holy man Job spoke when he said 'He only is, and no man can avert His thoughts; and His Spirit has done whatever It wished'; and the apostle says 'To Him alone immortality belongs.' How indeed could He not alone have immortality, He Who is alone? He is indeed alone, He Who alone has being: for He is the being of Himself and of all things. But what is He, He Who is alone, to Whom alone immortality belongs? Not one of those things which He made is He, because He exists not in time but from eternity: He is the maker of all His creatures, and therefore, because He is not made, He is always alike. I know how to tell you what God is not, but how should I tell you what He is? This is what the holy man Dionysius says on this matter in the second chapter of his *Celestial Hierarchy:* 'Sometimes the Scriptures, teaching us mystical doctrine, praise the blessedness of the superessential Godhead by calling it "reason" and "intellect" and "essence" . . .' ";[71] and Adam then quotes a long passage, in the Latin translation by John Scotus Eriugena,[72] on the "negative way." Wilmart called Adam a "bold innovator" for this quotation, which probably is the first use in England of the passage,[73] but there were those already anxious for knowledge of these

[71] 1, col. 855.
[72] See 30, 31 and 32.
[73] See 4.

Greek classics. Adam wrote his work during his years as a Carthusian, that is between 1188 and 1212: but the famous English scholar John of Salisbury in 1167 had written to his friend John Sarrazin complaining that there was no-one in England who could tell him the meaning of Greek technical theological terms,[74] and in the same year Sarrazin undertook his revision of Eriugena's Dionysius translations, a revision which he made at the request of John of Salisbury.[75] Another circumstance which must be remembered in accounting, not only for the sudden popularity of Dionysius but also for many new departures in mystical thought and teaching in England, is that by this time the writings of the two chief scholars from the Abbey of St. Victor in Paris, Hugh of St. Victor (died 1141) and Richard of St. Victor (died 1173) were circulating here.

The origins and the spectacular growth of the Victorine order,[76] and the contributions of its members to every field of international scholarship, more especially to Biblical studies[77] in the twelfth century, illustrate well the need which was then felt throughout the West for more arduous ways of life and wider curricula of studies than the older religious communities could provide, and also for the textbooks which such studies demanded. Any gifted theologian and teacher in the monastic schools, such as "Master" Anselm, St. Anselm's pupil from Bec, at Laon, might find himself frequented by large numbers of students: and in the Biblical gloss which Master Anselm and his department produced we have one of the earliest of the great compendia of knowledge which were to appear as aids to study in what soon

[74] PL 16 col. 842; and 32, p. 367.
[75] 32, p. 368.
[76] See 78, pp. 15-20.
[77] *See* 106.

would be recognizable as the first universities.[78] In Paris, William of Champeaux gave up his lecturing in 1108, since scandalous quarrels with his former pupil, Peter Abelard, had made life insupportable: he intended to live as a hermit, but instead found himself first besieged by students anxious to study under him, and then, before he was promoted bishop, head of a new order at St. Victor, which was to be the mother house to many others.

Its fame for science and spirituality drew men from every land: Hugh, whatever his origins, came to Paris from Saxony, and Richard was an Irishman or Scot. Although Hugh was probably dead before Richard entered St. Victor, they were formed by the same traditions: and modern scholars sometimes deplore the insistence on their achievements as mystical theologians, at the expense of the rest of their works. Yet doubtless the later Middle Ages, in praising them as mystical writers, remembered them as they would have wished, for in their systematization of spiritual science, what we today call "infused contemplation" comes last and is the highest step in the progress of the soul towards eternal life. So Hugh in his *Didascalion* (a "Students' Guide" or "Prospectus of Studies") teaches that there are four steps or degrees which prepare the soul for future blessedness—study, prayer, meditation and works—and a fifth, in which we have as it were a foretaste of that blessedness, which he here calls "contemplation"[79] (Vernet[80] points out some of the pecularities of Hugh's terminology, that "mystic" for him means "allegorical" or "symbolical," and that what we call "mysticism" is for him "contemplation"; although this is not invariable, and we can find places, *De Arca Noe Morali* II iv, for example,[81] where

[78] See **78**, p. 25.
[79] **59**, col. 772.
[80] **60**.
[81] **59**, cols. 637-8.

"contemplation" means merely "acquired" contemplation
or "speculation").

It is not surprising that Hugh should have been best remembered as a mystic, since he wrote, in some of his
short treatises, descriptions of rapture, strongly influenced
by pseudo-Dionysius, which later anthologists and devotional
writers never wearied of quoting. Perhaps the most famous
is the following one: "But see now what joy, and what cause
for joy, is brought by the blessed presence of our Lord! When
He comes, the soul grows light and joyful, the conscience is
clear and in great rest, the spirits, which were dull and dead,
are quickened and ready for labour, and everything which
seemed hard and painful and impossible becomes soft and
sweet, and every kind of exercise such as fasting and vigils
and all good works are turned into pleasure. The soul in its
great desire and love for Him is filled with charity and perfect purity, and it is fed with spiritual sweetness, and has such
delight in this spiritual food that all external things are almost forgotten . . ." A most rewarding if laborious study
would be to trace the path of this famous passage through
European ascetic and devotional literature in the later Middle
Ages: the English used here is a modernization of that in
the huge compendium *Disce Mori,* made in the late fifteenth
century, probably in Syon Abbey: *Disce Mori* borrows it
from *The Chastising of God's Children,* the *Chastising* borrows it from Blessed Henry Suso's *Horologium Sapientiae,*
and whether Suso took it direct from its ultimate source,
Hugh's *De Arrha Animae,* we do not know.[82]

Richard of St. Victor widened and advanced Hugh's work:
and, especially when he is concerned with the psychology of
contemplation and mystical prayer, as in *Benjamin Minor,*

[82] 59 col. 970: 25, pp. 99-100, 264-265; and see 98.

Benjamin Major[83] and *The Four Degrees of Passionate Charity*,[84] he was to be a potent influence upon English mysticism, notably in the work of the two greatest fourteenth-century writers, Walter Hilton and the author of *The Cloud of Unknowing*. But already in the thirteenth century, we can see very clearly the changes in vision and in emphasis brought about by pseudo-Dionysius and the Victorines, in St. Edmund Rich's *Mirror of Holy Church*.

There are several outward resemblances between *The Mirror of Love* and *The Mirror of Holy Church*. Each is the record of instruction to novices or young monks: this makes them both of particular value, since mediaeval English mystical literature is on the whole deficient in this respect. If there was any English teacher of spiritual doctrine of the same stature as a preacher as Tauler or St. Vincent Ferrer, neither his fame nor his sermons have survived. But there are also considerable differences between Aelred's *Mirror* and that of Edmund. It is clear that Aelred was addressing an audience of a high educational standard, capable of following refined doctrine and literary allusion: and it is something of a paradox that Aelred's work, in its lack of general plan and its many digressions, should in places betray that lack of formal schooling which he himself confessed and deplored, whereas in the superficially more elementary discourse of Edmund we see a subtle and highly trained mind at work. As a youth Edmund had studied at Paris: when he returned to Oxford, soon after the year 1200, he held the master's degree, that is, the university's licence to accept pupils and lecture, in arts, and had taught in the university. Innocent III, himself an old student of Paris, had decreed through

[83] See **78.**
[84] See **77.**

his legate's statutes that to obtain the degree a man must have studied for six years and be twenty-one years of age. Edmund may have been the first Oxford teacher to hold the degree: and Roger Bacon, recalling his own studies there, says that Edmund was the first to lecture systematically on Aristotelian logic. Later Edmund was promoted to public lecturing on theology, but his abilities led him to various high church offices, and finally, in 1233, to the see of Canterbury.[85] The constitution of the see made the archbishop, if he chose to exercise this office, the "abbot," the father in God of the Benedictine monks of Christ Church: and Edmund was one who followed Lanfranc and Anselm in his devotion to this part of his duties. He also followed Anselm and St. Thomas a Becket into exile, and it seems that *The Mirror of Holy Church* was published during his stay at Pontigny, but internal evidence—notably the English verses, already mentioned, which he quotes as well-known to his audience—shows that these discourses were first preached in England, almost certainly at Canterbury. That they were preached by an Englishman in French need not surprise us: we are still in the age of the long struggle between the two languages for supremacy, and as late as the fourteenth century we find Benedictine "customaries" which follow the old tradition of assuming that French will be the common vernacular tongue.[86] But *The Mirror of Holy Church* gives us no impression of its audience as a social or intellectual elite. It is very moving to read, as we see the tender solicitude of this great scholar and prelate for the simple and awkward young men to whom he is speaking, his compassionate understanding of their bewilderment in their new life, their grief for the

[85] See 34.
[86] See 25, pp. 66-7.

homes and families they have relinquished, and their struggles to overcome their handicaps. Often we may be reminded of Hugh of St. Victor's *De Institutione Novitiorum* by *The Mirror:* but Edmund is breaking new ground when he deals with the problems set by seeking to present the highest spiritual ideals to the uninstructed, Latinless, illiterate. For him Victorine method and Dionysian theology solve these problems, and he teaches of three forms of contemplation, the first two (of "created things" and of "Scripture," that is, the Bible and the Fathers) an acquired contemplation, the third and last and highest an infused contemplation which will lead us along the *via negativa.* "Put every corporeal image outside your heart, and let your naked intention fly up above all human reasoning, and there you shall find such great sweetness and such great secrets that without special grace there is no-one who can think of it, except only him who has experienced it": and St. Edmund then goes on, in words of great humility, to confess that he is one of these. The simplicity and clarity of this exposition may well recall for us, as they were so often to be recalled, his dying words: "Lord, I have believed in You, preached You, taught You: and You are my witness that here on earth I have sought nothing else than You."[87]

The Mirror of Holy Church gained much celebrity and wide circulation, being translated into both Latin and English: and a long section from it, as Professor E.J. Arnould among others has observed, was incorporated into the famous French theological compendium, *Le Manuel des Péchés.*[88] As might be expected, however, the mediaeval anthologies quote Edmund as a catechist and a devotional writer: for

[87] For sources, see the quotation in 36, p. 202.
[88] See 71, p. 238.

his speculative mysticism we have to consult his own work; and the present writer has pointed out, in one of the footnotes to the extracts from his *Mirror,* that many scribes who copied this text were not certain that they had the author's true translation of St. Augustine before them, so that in the surviving manuscripts we have several garbled versions of "God became man to make man God. . . ." Though Edmund only glances at the doctrine of "deification," and carefully states it in Augustine's words and with his authority, it would present no difficulties to so skilled a theologian, and, in any case, it had not yet in England acquired its undesirable associations with Pelagian heresy. Though Edmund must have known from his years in Paris, where the University was called upon to be especially active in their condemnation and combat, of such errors as that which taught that man can "become God," not as an experience of grace, a supernatural operation of the Divinity, but by his own powers and natural potentiality, the author of the *Ancrene Riwle* could at about this time still write "Thanks be to God, there is no heresy prevalent in England";[89] and this happy state was to persist for another century and a half. Robert Grosseteste, the great bishop of Lincoln, the fervent lover of St. Francis and loyal friend to the first English Franciscans, who in learning, sanctity and pastoral devotion is well fitted to be named with St. Edmund, could write to the Pope at Lyons in 1250, when Christendom was riven with internal dissensions, that the shepherd's office was "the teaching of the living truth:" and Dr. W.A. Pantin has observed how essentially "Dionysian" his ideas on the cure of souls and the teaching of the gospel were, "the purgation and illumination of souls, their 'deification,' their assimilation and

[89] 12, p. 35.

union as far as possible with God, their 'perfect and incon-
vertible recession' from what is evil.' "[90] We gather these
ideas about Grosseteste's spirituality from his letters and
other registered official transactions: it is a thousand pities
that, with so few exceptions, his allocutions were never
recorded.

The fifty years or so after Grosseteste's death produced no
one great name in mystical writing, but it was not a time of
inactivity or decline, and several writers followed the path
explored by the author of the *Ancrene Riwle,* experimenting
with English as a literary language which could be adapted
to the needs which Latin could no longer serve, since pastoral
devotion and interest in speculative religious thought was on
the increase among the unlearned and the laity. John Peck-
ham, the Franciscan archbishop of Canterbury, composed
his exquisite song of divine love, the *Philomena,* in Latin:
but his precursor in the Order, Thomas of Hales, wrote his
Love-Rune in English,[91] "at the request of a virgin vowed to
God," as the Latin rubric to the manuscript tells us. Thomas
must have flourished about the middle of the thirteenth century: Adam Marsh, his confrere, who died in 1257 or 1258,
mentions him as a personal friend.[92] The two final stanzas
tell the maiden for whom it is written to learn it off by heart
and use it as a devotional exercise when she is unoccupied:
and this leisurely poem, with its insistence on *Brautmystik,*
the analogy between human and divine love, and its essentially "Christocentric" devotion, its concentration upon the
humanity and Passion of our Lord, has many qualities in
common with a similar exercise, *The Wooing of Our Lord,*
one of a group of long "meditations," all fashioned in a
highly rhythmic prose—the *Wooing* further has a recurring

[90] 42, pp. 179-80.
[91] A text is in 97, pp. 68-74.
[92] 97, p. 198.

petition used as a refrain—and all of them composed under the influence of the *Ancrene Riwle*. A recent editor of these tracts has gone so far as to claim for the *Wooing* "that it was written by a gifted woman,"[93] but his argument loses most of its force, since it is based upon the misapprehension of an earlier scholar, who thought that the passage in the *Riwle,* which says to the three anchoresses for whom it was written "concerning these joys (of divine love), you have it written down for you in another place," means "you have written about it in another place."[94] There is nothing in the *Wooing,* or in its conclusion, "Pray for me, my dear sister. I have written this for you so that these words may often gladden your heart and move it to think of our Lord: so when you are at leisure speak to Jesus, and say these words, and imagine that He hangs beside you, bleeding upon the Cross," to distinguish it from the many other spiritual aids written for anchoresses (as the recipient of the *Wooing* seems to have been) or nuns by their spiritual directors. But though the same editor goes too far in claiming for this elementary though edifying devotional work that its author was a "true mystic," the *Wooing,* like Thomas of Hales' *Love-Rune,* is of importance for the study of mystical literature: both show the popularity, especially among women religious, of the simple and not always wise fervours of *Brautmystik,* and both show what was being achieved in the thirteenth century towards making English an adequate medium, both in verse and prose, for the recording of mystical experience. It is tentative and not always successful experiments such as these which made possible, in the next century, the successes of Richard Rolle and his great followers.

It is easy to account for the exceptional popularity which

[93] 93, p. xxiv.
[94] 12, p. 187: see 13, p. 181, where it is correctly translated.

C

Rolle enjoyed in the fourteenth and fifteenth centuries: soon after he died in the terrible Black Death of 1349, his grave was the object of pilgrimages, and he was accorded popular veneration as a saint; and the manuscript copies of his works still exist in profusion. One can also well understand why this popularity has been so revived in the present century. He has been better served by academic scholars than any other of the English mystics: and it is part of the contribution of Dr. Hope Allen to this field that her investigations, which set out first merely to disprove the mediaeval ascription to Rolle of the long didactic poem, *The Prick of Conscience*,[95] have also furnished us with a masterly collection of the material needed for the study of his life and works,[96] and with an edition of his chief English writings.[97] We have for long had published editions of his Latin *Incendium Amoris*[98] and of the fifteenth-century English translations of this work and of his Latin *Emendatio Vitae;*[99] and now Professor Arnould, to whom we already owed the refutation of two further misapprehensions concerning Rolle, that he had studied in Paris and that as a young man he had been in conflict with episcopal authority, has completed his labour of editing the Latin *Melos Amoris*.[100] For modern as for mediaeval readers, his life and his works—the *Melos* apart—present few difficulties and many attractive, popular traits. We, in judging him, must always remember that we look back to him through the achievements of Hilton and *The Cloud*, and may therefore be disposed to think the esteem which he has enjoyed exaggerated; but he was the first English mystic to make use

[95] See 83.
[96] See 84.
[97] See 81.
[98] See 80.
[99] See 79.
[100] See 82.

of his own language for a series of works communicating his experience, and the later mystics of the fourteenth century, however little they may have thought of his doctrine and his influence, were his followers in their use of their native tongue for their literary purposes. He is best represented by such a short English treatise as the one chosen for this anthology, *Ego Dormio,* in which he makes an expert use of both prose and verse to convey his messages in plain and easy terms: but what we can easily forget is how much of the style and the vocabulary which we take for granted in reading him and his contemporaries is Rolle's own contribution to his subject: in *Ego Dormio,* for instance, we find such English "Dionysian" terms as "dominate," "hierarchy," "principate," "potestate," used apparently by him for the first time.[101] And in one respect Rolle had neither rival nor successor: the ease and spontaneity with which he passes in the English treatises from prose to verse, and his mastery of traditional verse-forms, requiring, in their use of alliteration and internal as well as end-rhyme, a high degree of skill, when often he is very closely translating his own earlier Latin works, make him unique. Only his contemporary Ruysbroek, writing in Dutch, is in this respect to be compared with him; but Rolle achieved a reputation as a writer of religious lyrics which Ruysbroek with his utilitarian verses never aimed at.

All this is to be recorded to Rolle's credit, as are also his deep sincerity, the depth of his fervour in devotion to the Holy Name of Jesus and to the Mother of God, the passion with which he describes his own *canor, calor, dulcor,* the physical and psychical phenomena with which, as so many before him, he was visited, and, above all, his constant level

[101] See 85.

of "jubilation," his joy in the presence of God which is seldom long absent from his writings. Yet his knowledge of
mysticism, and his capacity for communicating his knowledge, are limited, if we compare him with his masters or his
greater successors: to take one example only, Miss Kirchberger has recently shown[102] that the categories of love which
we find described in *The Form of Living*,[103] love wounded
and insuperable, found in meditation, love binding and inseparable, found in contemplation, and love, unsatisfied except by love, and singular, found in jubilation, are taken from
Richard of St. Victor's *Four Degrees of Passionate Charity*,[104]
but that Rolle stops short before the Victorine's last and
highest category, the "love of compassion," insatiable and
unsatisfied even in love. And other mediaeval English mystics, and some modern critics, have seen elements in Rolle's
writing which are not entirely praiseworthy. On the merely
literary and psychological levels, there is the problem presented by the *Melos,* a freakish performance worthy of comparison with the notorious *Latinitas Hisperica* which
Gougaud described as "fantastic, inflated, enigmatical, and
indeed for the most part absolutely unintelligible."[105] Few
scholars had read the *Melos* in manuscript: one of these, Dr.
Allen, was disposed to write it off, indulgently, as a juvenile
work, the product of Rolle's earliest years as a hermit, when,
fresh from his studies, he might have wished still to gain for
himself a reputation in learned literary circles. In her view,
the sobriety of the *Incendium Amoris* and the simplicity of
the English works mark Rolle's progress towards intellectual maturity. Professor Arnould challenges this in his edition

---

[102] 78, p. 222 and n.1.
[103] 87, pp. 85-119.
[104] 77, and 78, pp. 213-233.
[105] 101, p. 250.

of the *Melos,* which he claims as a later work: the present writer can only say that he thinks that Dr. Allen is nearer to the probable truth. But there are features of the *Melos,* which we may find disagreeable, which are to be found throughout the Rolle canon: a rancorous preoccupation with "enemies" and "persecutors" (though in his pursuit of his solitary vocation he appears to have suffered little real opposition or hardship), recurrent descriptions of the torments of eternal damnation which such opponents would suffer, a prospect which seems to have afforded him more consolation than we today would consider seemly or healthy, and a naive self-approbation which in any age must have shown a lack of true humility. The Church in her wisdom has made place and given scope to many kinds of vocation: and it is hard to imagine the hermit of Hampole as a succesful parish priest or member of a religious house. His qualities and his defects must often put us in mind of his German Dominican contemporary, Blessed Henry Suso: and had Rolle joined an order, he would very probably have shared Suso's unhappy experiences. In both men there is a very saintly pursuit of perfection, wholehearted, uncompromising: but they both show a too human lack of kindliness towards those who will not do as they do. Suso and Rolle may well put us in mind of Ruysbroek's famous description of "spiritual drunkenness" (a description modernized here from its translation in the second chapter of *The Chastising*): "This kind of drunkenness makes some men sing and give glory to God in the fullness of their joy. Some weep copiously, some are agitated in all their limbs, so that they have to skip or run or dance. Some clap their hands in joy, some shout aloud, some are silent and cannot speak. Sometimes they think that everyone acts like this: some of them are amazed that everyone does not act as they do. Often they think that what they feel will last forever; but some of them think that no-one has ever felt what they feel."[106] Ruysbroek is here writing not without a certain irony, recalling, it may be, his own early experiences of mystical transport, and seeing them as very early steps upon a very long path.

In their different ways, Walter Hilton and the author of *The Cloud of Unknowing* show that they, in the next generation, found Rolle immature and his influence in some ways harmful. One feature which their doctrine has in common is that they both share the point of view of their contemporary, the "learned Carthusian" to whom the hermit Thomas Bassett had addressed his *Defence against the Detractors of Richard,* and who had said that Rolle's teaching had led simple men to a superstitious veneration of the physical phenomena of mysticism, and had "destroyed as many men as it had saved."[107] Here is *The Cloud's* distinction between "acquisition" and "infusion," a distinction obviously inspired by its author's impatience with such a remark as Rolle's "Some say that men burn in Christ's love, because they see them made free by their zeal and their scorn of the world to God's service; but just as anyone putting his finger in the fire would feel a sensible heat, so the soul which is on fire with love feels a burning not to be mistaken . . . :"[108] "Sometimes God will inflame the body of some devout servant of His here in this life with very wonderful sweetness and consolations, not once or twice, but, it may be, again and again, as He pleases. And some of such consolations do not come from outside into our bodies through the windows of the senses, but from within, rising and springing out

[106] 25, p. 103.
[107] 84, pp. 335, 529-537.
[108] 80, pp. 145-6.

of an abundance of spiritual joy and true spiritual devotion. We need not suspect such sweetness and consolations, nor, I think, need he who experiences it. But, I beg you, do not trust all the other consolations, melodies, rejoicings and sweetnesses that enter you suddenly from outside, from you have no idea where. They may be good, they may be evil . . ."[109] Hilton in his Latin tract, *Of Reading, Intention and Prayer,* similarly writes: "It is Christ Who sends fire into the hearts of men, a fire which is Himself, a fire which no other fire is like"[110], and we cannot miss the direction in which his disparaging remarks in Book I of *The Scale* are aimed: ". . . not noises in your ears nor a sweet taste in your mouth, nor any such physical sensation . . ."[111], ". . . all the visions and the revelations brought by angels, all the songs and sounds, the savours and scents, the burnings and the delectable bodily sensations . . ."[112] And whereas Rolle in the *Melos,* as in many other places, writes of his raptures, his *canor, calor, dulcor* as ineffable—"Sighing for the solace of the Saviour, I am inflamed from on high, begging for the kiss of His divine sweetness, I see the sign of the song of His love. Whilst I live there shall descend to me that singing which shall eternally be silent to fleshly men, that it may heal me of the hurt of my harms: and lifting up my lips to His most joyful praise, I savour that song of glory which the angels wonder at . . ."[113], Hilton more prudently says, in *Of Angels' Song:* "Such touching and speaking is spiritual and not physical: for when the soul is lifted and ravished beyond its powers of physical perception, and out of its recol-

[109] **27**, pp. 90-91.
[110] **52**, f. 121ʳ.
[111] Chapter 12.
[112] Chapter 47.
[113] **82**, p. 9.

lection of all earthly things, it may, if our Lord pleases, in its great fervour of love for Him and light from Him hear and feel heavenly sounds which the angels make to the glory of God. But this song of the angels is not the soul's greatest joy. . . . its greatest and its living joy is in God's love of Himself alone, and any vision of angels and spiritual beings, any communing with them, is a secondary delight"[114].

Many such allusions show that Walter Hilton and the author of *The Cloud of Unknowing* had had time to see the effects of Rolle's popularity upon indiscreet enthusiasts. We have, for Walter Hilton, a little precise biographical information. He seems to have been trained in a university, though the tradition that this was at Paris has little to support it.[115] Evelyn Underhill[116] thought that his learning was slight: she seemed quite shocked that he failed to understand, in his translation of St. John ii 9 in Book I chapter 4 of *The Scale,* that the Latin word *architriclinus* (itself a borrowing from Greek) is not a proper name: but this misinterpretation of a rare and exotic word was common everywhere in the West before Hilton's day, and is often found in mediaeval English Biblical versions. We can date one of Hilton's early works, the *Epistola Aurea* or "Golden Letter", about the year 1375, since it is addressed to his friend Adam Horsley when he was proposing to renounce the world for religious life, and we know that in that year Horsley was still an official of the Exchequer.[117] In the *Epistola,* and in other as yet unpublished Latin works, *De Imagine Peccati,* "Of the Image of Sin," and *De Utilitate et Prerogatiuis Religionis,* "Of the Profit and Prerogatives of Religious Life",

[114] 50, p. 178.
[115] See 57, pp. 204-205.
[116] See 44.
[117] 53, p. 144: and 57, p. 181 and n.4.

Hilton speaks of himself as living as a hermit, and Dr. Helen Gardner observes that both works "convey a strong impression of his own personal unhappiness.[118] He says, in the *Epistola,* that Horsley may ask why he, Hilton, does not enter religion, since he so greatly praises it: he longs indeed to do so, but feels himself unworthy, and believes that as yet he is following God's will in his present solitary life.[119] Some critics have doubted if these references to "solitude" are more than metaphorical, since thereafter Hilton joined the Augustinian canons regular, a procedure which would not be permitted by canon law to one vowed to the harder, stricter life of a hermit: but we have an exact parallel in the case of Ruysbroek and his companions, who abandoned their secular benefices in Brussels, retired to a "desert" outside the city, but finally also became Austin canons, and, like them, Hilton was probably never professed as a solitary but merely tried, unsuccessfully, his vocation. In the 1380's we know that he held office at Thurgarton; and the date of his death is given as 1395 or 1396.

We probably do not yet know all Hilton's surviving works. In addition to those already mentioned, and to his masterpiece, *The Scale of Perfection,* there are the five shorter English treatises contained in Dorothy Jones's modernized edition,[120] *On Mixed Life, Eight Chapters on Perfection,*[121] and the expositions of *"Qui Habitat,"*[122] *"Bonum Est"*[122] and *"Benodictus"*. MS British Museum Royal 6 E III, which contains a text of *The Profit and Prerogatives of Religious Life,* also has *Ad Quemdam Solitarium de Leccione, In-*

---

[118] 55, p. 110, and 57, pp. 186 n.20, 199.
[119] 55, pp. 111-112.
[120] 46.
[121] See also 48.
[122] See also 47.

tencione, Oracione et Aliis, "Of Reading, Intention and Prayer"[123], *Ad Quemdam Seculo Renunciare Volentem,* "To One Wishing to renounce the World"[124]; and a related English epistle, *To a Christian Friend,* is in MS British Museum Add.33971.[125] There is the Latin tract, *In Defence of the Veneration of Images,* which Miss Joy Russell-Smith has described[126]; and Miss Kirchberger has shown how highly probable it is that the English translation of James of Milan's *Stimulus Amoris,* with its many original interpolations, is also Hilton's work.[127] This list, incomplete though it may be, shows us how wide his interests were and how varied his activities, ranging from the active repression of heresy, through practical counsel to those seeking the religious vocation, to the purest mystical speculation.

One most vexed question, which must be mentioned though it cannot be adequately dealt with, is whether Hilton is also the author of *The Cloud of Unknowing.*[128] The English Carthusians, outstanding in their zeal for mystical studies, thought so in the late fifteenth century: and at least two of the manuscript records which state this are in the hand of that famous scribe-editor, James Greenhalgh of Sheen Charterhouse.[129] But these records were made a century or so after Hilton's death; and even the Carthusians were not infallible. They also originated the false ascriptions to Hilton of Books I-III of *The Imitation of Christ,*[130] and to Ruysbroek of *The Mirror of Simple Souls.*[131] When all

[123] See **57**, p. 190 n.34.
[124] See **57**, p. 186 n.20.
[125] *Ibid.*
[126] **57**.
[127] **49**.
[128] On this, see especially **56** and **58**.
[129] For a description of Greenhalgh's activities, see **87**.
[130] **53**, p. 134.
[131] See **87**.

the evidence has been sifted (and many of the points raised by supporters and opponents of this theory of common authorship are trivial, and serve only to obscure the issue), two facts remain. The author of *The Cloud,* and of the other treatises which he acknowledges as his, cannot help, as he writes, drawing for us a living self portrait, and we see him as a quizzical and humorous observer of his fellow-men, vivacious to the point of eccentricity, deeply engrossed with the psychological processes involved in speculation and the attainment of mystical illumination: and this man is as different as well can be from Walter Hilton, as we know him in his works. Then, too, even though these men share a common background of learning and reading, and sometimes use language very similar, though not always meaning by the same words precisely the same thing, what they teach about man's knowledge of God is quite different. If we were to accept the theory—and the present writer does not —that *The Cloud* and its allied tracts are the work of the young Hilton, we must accept the hypothetical case of a mystic, totally engrossed by Dionysian theology, and experiencing and teaching a non-cognitive union, who later came to teach that such union is something else, is cognitive. This hypothesis seems essentially improbable.

As we see how the present state of the text of *The Scale of Perfection* evolved, we surely see that the author of *The Cloud of Unknowing* had no hand in this. Evelyn Underhill, even though she consulted only a few manuscripts for her 1923 edition of *The Scale,* put forward a theory about its development which has stood the tests which later and more learned students have applied. It is now generally accepted that Books I and II were written as separate works: Miss Gardner has said that their present title is inappropriate to them[132]; and in two manuscripts the whole work is called, more appropriately, it may be thought, "Of the Nobility of the Soul," *De Nobilitate Animae*.[133] The first book was originally complete in itself, and was addressed to a female recluse: in chapter 16, it will be seen, Hilton says to her ". . . that is why you are shut up in a house alone." It is surely this, the fact either that she could not read, or, more probably, that she could read no Latin, which explains his remarks (in a chapter not translated in this anthology) that she cannot very well read the Bible: when Evelyn Underhill suggests that between writing Books I and II Hilton's views on Bible-reading underwent a change, and that he was, finally, "the first English religious writer to recommend the reading of the Scriptures to the laity"[134], her remarks require so much explanation and qualification that it must here be sufficient simply to say that they are not well founded. But Miss Gardner's study of a great number of manuscripts, of the mediaeval Latin translation as well as of Hilton's English, led her to decide that Evelyn Underhill was right in her next conclusion, that Hilton himself was probably responsible for the two main versions of Book I which can be distinguished, and that the outstanding feature of the "first edition", a long, most movingly written passage on devotion to the Holy Name of Jesus which is lost in the second version of chapter 44, is probably by Hilton himself. Its disappearance, Miss Gardner observes, causes a break in the sequence of sense between chapters 44 and 45: and indeed chapter 46 (included in this anthology) logically follows from this once disputed passage.

The remarkable characteristic of the "second edition" of Book I is what Evelyn Underhill called the "Christocentric

[132] 54, p. 15.
[133] 57, p. 209 and n.14.
[134] 44, p. xvi.

additions." Miss Gardner thought that this term exaggerated their importance, and, unlike Evelyn Underhill, she doubted their authenticity, being disposed to regard them, on what appear to the present writer very dubious grounds, as additions emanating from fifteenth-century Carthusian editorial work. But Miss Gardner might have been disposed to conclude differently, had Miss Kirchberger already published her arresting study of Hilton's translation—for his it plainly seems to be—of James of Milan's *Stimulus Amoris*,[135] where we find precisely the same kind of "Christocentric addition". Here is one such passage, in which the italicized words are Hilton's additions to James's text: "Whoever presumes to attain to the contemplation of Christ, and does not enter by this door (of devotion to the Passion), *nor by this way, and by knowing the bitterness He knew and the compassion He showed in His humanity,* is but a thief and a robber: *for when he presumes to have entered this contemplation, he is still far outside. How can a man come to Christ, and see Him, and have Him, without Christ? This is impossible, for He Himself says: 'I am the way, the truth, and the life'; so therefore follow Him along the way of His humanity, so that you may come to the life of His divinity.*"[136] As Miss Kirchberger observes, we can see throughout Hilton's translation of the *Stimulus* and the "second edition" of Book I of *The Scale* the same process at work, the identification of earlier references to "God" with "Jesus Christ" or "our Lord," and the addition of many short passages of allusion or devotion to Christ's manhood on earth. As we shall see when we consider *The Cloud,* this is something different from the theology of its author.

Book II of *The Scale* shows no such process of revision,

[135] 49.
[136] 49, p. 143.

because, scholars suggest, it never required revision. Miss Gardner found it marked by "spiritual maturity and surety" which she associated with the end of Hilton's career; and Miss Kirchberger has seen in it traces of the influence of his work on the *Stimulus*. It is of interest to compare the two books with the unpublished Latin tract, *Of Reading, Intention and Prayer*.[137] Like *The Scale,* Book I, this was addressed originally to a single recipient, a priest vowed to the solitary life. Internal evidence suggests that it was written in the same period of Hilton's life as Book I, perhaps slightly earlier. At times the Latin and English texts say almost the same thing: in *Of Reading,* dealing with the necessity of a professed religious preserving a constant intention towards God, even in times of enforced cessation of spiritual exercise, the author writes: "You must not say 'I am willing to serve God in prayer and meditation for so long or for so many hours, and then after that I want the rest of the day free' "[138]. This is precisely what he says in *The Scale,* I 22: but there he elaborates his arguments against "recreations" as a desirable thing. Some of the problems dealt with are special to the priest addressed: he has been "led astray into a certain error through the secret judgments of God,"[139] and he is condemned for "eccentricity": "You go to much trouble to tell me what you feel, how wonderful it all seems, how there is rarely anyone who can understand it . . . Whenever there spring up in you . . . impulses born of false exaltation, wilful eccentricity, conceit, or undue intellectual curiosity, to flourish as would barren weeds, cut them down with the sickle of self-knowledge and self-accusation"[140]. Yet we see applied

[137] 52.
[138] 52, f.121ᵛ.
[139] f.120ᵛ.
[140] f.120ᵛ.

to this special case the same teaching as in *The Scale:* "Nor must you accept any opinion or fantasy or strange idea which represents itself as a greater form of sanctity . . . if it be contrary to the smallest ordinance or to the general teaching of all Holy Church"[141], or, elsewhere "Say every day: 'What am I?', and judge no man"[142].

Of Reading suggests a further basis of comparison between *The Scale,* Books I and II. Though the style of Hilton's English composition in Book I is better than the turgid and academic language and manner of this Latin tract, for he does in his early English works at least try to say simply and directly what he has to say, as soon as one begins on Book II it leaps to the eye that here, compared with Book I, we have the work of a skilled writer who has gained a greater command of English style, and who uses, with great art, a variety of literary devices, not for their own sake but to further his ends. Consider, for example, the sparing repetitions and the subtle variation on the "refrain", "I am nothing, I have nothing . . ."; and observe how superior Hilton's employment of his "pilgrimage" allegory is to most of the heavy-handed uses of that device found in *Piers Plowman.* (The formal resemblance to be found between Book II and that poem are incidental and quite superficial: and Evelyn Underhill's suggestion that the idea of this allegory was found in the *Confessions* XIII 9 was barely worth making). Altogether, the second part of *The Scale* creates the impression of being the work of a man who has addressed himself seriously to the business of writing, and who now commands a wider and more cultivated audience, in addressing whom he need no longer use the traditional form

---

[141] *The Scale* I chapter 21.
[142] I Chapter 16.

of the brief and pithy paragraph-chapter, five or at the most ten minutes' reading aloud. Instead he can now write at his leisure, at sermon-length if need be.

Yet Hilton's later style is still something very different from that of *The Cloud's* author, who, in *The Book of Privy Counsel* too, contrives always to maintain, by the use of artifices extraordinary in a mediaeval religious writer in the vernacular, the perfect illusion of intimate and personal discourse with a single hearer: whereas in the periods of the "Jerusalem" chapters, *The Scale* is very much a public performance in the grand manner.

When we come to consider Hilton's doctrine, we find that he, like all mediaeval mystics, is much in the debt of his precursors; and yet there is much which is his own unique contribution to the subject. Even his vocabulary is traditional. For him, as for the Victorines, "contemplation" is mysticism. That is why, in Book I of *The Scale,* he can distinguish between three stages in "contemplation", intellectual, affective, and the highest stage which is both cognitive and affective, a stage of "contemplation" which will be fulfilled affectively in rapture, cognitively in illumination; and this is also why he can say, of the illuminative as compared with the affective way, "this is contemplation" (we should today say "pure mysticism") "and the other is not". We must keep these distinctions in mind, if we are properly to understand, for example, his praise, in Book I chapter 63, of the virtues of humility and love: here humility, according to his view of the psychology of mysticism, is "transformed," an idea developed more fully in II 21. "Intellectual contemplation", a perception of the divine order and of man's place in it which is merely rational, untouched by grace, available alike to Christian, heretic and pagan, may bring with it a cold and formal practice of virtue: but it is in affective mysticism that the "transformation of virtues" is achieved, when what was done rationally and unfeelingly becomes enlivened by grace into a loving fostering of virtue. In this insistence upon humility and love, and their inter-action, Hilton is developing what is to be found, perhaps most explicitly, in Richard of St. Victor's *Four Degrees of Passionate Charity:* but whereas at times we may find Richard a little too schematic and ingenious in his adroit manipulation of his categories, Hilton seems always to be considering more closely not an abstract pattern of the human mind and soul, but individual cases, above all his own, as he has known and observed them. He takes the view propounded by Hugh of St. Victor that in Adam's fall man lost his natural capacity for the mystical vision of God: he makes this clear, for example, in *Of Reading.*[143] But it is characteristic of Hilton, and of his essentially cognitive conception of mystical vision, that he describes it in terms of "true light", and that for him "darkness" is the symbol of sin, of ignorance, or, at best, of a period of trial and rest in which the soul waits for light. If one's intention is wholly directed towards God, He will draw the intellect and affections to Him, and fill them with His light.[144] In *Of Reading,* he can speak of "choosing rather to sleep for a while in the shade of the Faith than to wake in the dim light of the intellect"[145], and he goes on to relate this "sleeping in the shade" to "darkness", the "dark night", the times when God will hide Himself from the soul.

There is not space here to dwell on Hilton's other salient characteristics as a mystical teacher: on his insistence upon the necessity of self-knowledge, the "straight high road" to

[143] 52, f.120ʳ.
[144] 52, f.121ᵛ: and compare *The Scale,* II chapter 24.
[145] 52, f.121ʳ.

mystical communion,[146] on the clarity of his distinction between acquired and infused contemplation,[147] on his doctrine
of the reforming of the image of the soul in the image of
God, with its startling use, so reminiscent of the imagery of
Julian of Norwich, of the figure of the image of sin, the
sorrow, pain, blindness, darkness, the "nothing" which must
be endured, "because inside this nothing, Jesus is hidden in
all His joy"[148]. Nor can we here deal with the very difficult
question of how far Hilton in such doctrine was influenced
by mystical writers abroad. Those who know Ruysbroek and
Tauler will have no difficulty in following Hilton on the
reforming of the image of the soul, those who know Hade-
wijch of Antwerp and her followers will be reminded of
them by Hilton's "nothing"; but we cannot say that Hilton
knew Eckhart and his followers in Germany and the Low
Countries, because we lack the necessary evidence. We know
that Ruysbroek's works were circulating in England in the
late fourteenth century,[149] but we cannot be sure that Hilton
and Julian had read them. Nor is it necessary here to insist
on the magnitude of Hilton's contribution to English spirituality in his counsels on the technique of prayer: chapters
27-36 of Book I of *The Scale* are in themselves sufficient
witness to this. In his learning, his piety and his sanity, he
was able to bring to a situation more troubled and distressed
than ever before advice which was moderate, healing and in-
spiring. Though *The Scale* shows that he had deep sympathy
and understanding for the needs and the potentialities of the
simple folk, the *idiotae,* he himself was a thorough-going
academic in his approach to spiritual problems. "I say to you:
'They have Moses and the prophets: let them hear them.'

[146] *The Scale* I chapter 41.
[147] E.g. *The Scale* I chapter 25.
[148] *The Scale,* I chapters 51-53.
[149] See **25** and **87**.

You have Holy Scripture for a foundation, you have Bernard and Richard and others who know all these matters well. Search their books, diligently and humbly, add up for yourself from their writings what they felt, what they thought, what they did, and then you need not fear that you may go astray"[150]. He is very much an Evangelical, a man of the Bible; and he is above all a very faithful, very humble son of Holy Church: "You must turn to Christ and to the Faith of the Church, saying fervently: 'O Lord Jesus, be You my only hope, my only merit and my only reward. Whatever I may feel, whatever I may think, whatever I may say, always I will be subject to the Faith of the Church"[151].

In *The Cloud of Unknowing* and its author's other acknowledged works, though there are many allusions to "heretics" and "hypocrites", there is no active concern with the Lollard heresy as such. The author, in comparison with Hilton, appears as a man totally engrossed in his private affairs—it is characteristic that Hilton praised the "mixed life" of action and contemplation, and taught that contemplatives required by their office to perform public duties could turn these seeming distractions into aids to contemplation,[152] whereas the *Cloud* author shows little or no concern for the spiritual needs of "Marthas"—and his private affairs consist in the teaching of the technique of unitive prayer. He confesses himself a convinced "Dionysian": in chapter 70 of *The Cloud* he writes "Whoever will consult the works of Dionysius will find that his words plainly support everything which I have said, from the beginning of this treatise to the end"[153]; and the Western, later theologians who can be seen to have influenced him most are in general those sympathetic

---

[150] 52, ff.120ᵛ-121ʳ.
[151] 52, f.121ʳ.
[152] *On Mixed Life*, in 46.
[153] 27, p. 125.

to Dionysius's ideas, notably the Victorines and John of
Kastle in *De Adhaerendo Deo*. Apart from several allusions
to Dionysius, the author gives the sources of his teaching less
often even than the usual mediaeval theologian: and he goes
on, in chapter 70 of *The Cloud*, to explain this abstention.
The practice of adducing authority for one's every statement,
he says, which originated in a modest diffidence, has nowadays degenerated into pedantry and ostentation, and he will
have nothing to do with it. This makes it the more remarkable that he should go out of his way, in chapter 35 of *The
Cloud*, to say that since the disciple for whom the treatise
is written already has, in "another book, writen by another
man, on Reading, Thinking and Praying", a better exposition of these three aids to contemplation than he can attempt,
there is no need for him to touch upon the subject.[154] He
gives no further hint in this chapter which would help to
identify this work, and Dom Noetinger and Abbot McCann
suggested several older spiritual classics in parts of which the
topic is discussed: but the author seems to suggest that this
is the work's name and sole topic, and the resemblance to the
title of Hilton's *Of Reading, Intention and Prayer* is surely
remarkable. Furthermore, when in chapter 48 he writes "And
I do not propose to tell you now how you can know whether
other spiritual consolations and sounds and sweetnesses are
good or evil, for I do not think it necessary, because you can
find it written, a thousand times better than I can say or
write it, elsewhere in another man's work"[155], he may well
be alluding again to *Of Reading,* which has a long section
on "discretion" in the assessment of such consolations.[156]
Perhaps the marginal note against this second passage, "Hil-

[154] 27, p. 71.
[155] 27, p. 91.
[156] 52, f.121.

ton's", in MS University College Oxford 14[157] was made by someone who knew *Of Reading* and recognized the allusion.

But many of the speculations concerning the inter-relations between *The Cloud* and *The Scale* are vitiated by being based on the assumption that their resemblances of thought and their occasional identity of language[158] must show direct borrowing by one writer or the other. The same scholars who have shown us that Hilton and the *Cloud* author shared a common esteem for some of their precursors, and a common distrust of others, fail to allow for this in their search for points of contact between the two men: nor have they always remembered the possibility that their ideas and their language were commonplaces in the intellectual circles in which they moved. There must be many today who are familiar with, and on occasion use, the phrase "To do the right thing for the wrong reason", who have never read *Murder in the Cathedral:* and there can be few who would be prepared to say who first wrote of "Making a virtue of necessity". When we read several contemporary authors on one given topic—for example, *The Cloud* chapters 51-52, *The Scale* I chapter 28, *The Chastising of God's Children* chapter 2-5, and *The Chastising's* source, Ruysbroek's *Spiritual Espousals,* all on the dangers to physical health and mental balance of impetuosity in mysticism—we can surely see that they resemble each other chiefly because they reflect a common experience. The theory, in particular, that *The Cloud* is earlier than *The Scale,* so that "borrowings" were by Hilton, rests ultimately only on Dom Noetinger's argument[159] that Hilton's greater zeal against the Lollards shows

[157] **27**, p. 198.
[158] See, e.g., **58**.
[159] See **53**, p. 146.

that *The Cloud* is pre-Lollard: but a different explanation of this has already been suggested.

Even when they do treat of similar topics in similar language, Hilton and the *Cloud* author often think very differently. We have seen what are Hilton's views on devotion to the Passion, meditation upon the Passion: yet in *The Cloud,* chapter 7 introduces the idea of a "psychomachia", a war in the soul between thought and intelligence, productive of devotion, and love, productive of mystical union (this derives from the concept, already explained in chapter 4, of the "two operative powers" of the soul, the one cognitive, to which God is incomprehensible, the other affective, to which He is comprehensible). In this conflict, the author says, recollection of the Passion can be a distraction in prayer. He then has to qualify this: ". . . any man or woman who tries to attain to mystical prayer without first experiencing many such sweet meditations upon their own wretchedness, the Passion, the compassion and the great goodness and the glory of God, will undoubtedly go astray and fail in their intention. But it is still necessary for a man or woman who has practised such meditations for a long time to give them up entirely, and to suppress them under the cloud of oblivion, if they are ever to pierce the cloud of unknowing between them and their God"[160]. In chapter 8 he tells us that thought is by its own nature good, "a ray from the image of God"; but it can be evil if it leads to intellectual vanity, or if it impedes "the higher part of contemplation". This theme, the hindrances to mystical prayer which may come of recollection of the Passion, is somewhat repetitiously insisted on in *The Cloud* —in chapters 12 and 21, for instance—and in *The Book of Privy Counsel* there is a long section containing the same

[160] **27**, pp. 27-28.

doctrine, where we are told that "whoever does not come by this way (of meditation on the Passion) does not come by the true way". These are practically Hilton's words, as we have seen in the gloss quoted from the *Stimulus Amoris*, but if he had been writing *The Book of Privy Counsel*, he would have begun the treatise, in logical fashion, with these "first steps." Introduced as they are here and in *The Cloud*, they have very much the appearance of concessions and after-thoughts. Particularly in *The Book*, they lack logic: he begins by deploring intellectual meditation on the Passion, and ends by saying that those who neglect the humanity of Christ are trying to attain to mysticism by purely intellectual means.

It must, of course, be conceded that in *The Cloud* and *The Book* the author is attempting something much more difficult than Hilton in *The Scale*. This is doubtless what was in Dr. Gardner's mind when she wrote that "*The Cloud* is a work of genius, *The Scale*, though beautiful, is not"[161]; and although we may think it truer to say that they display different kinds of genius, the achievement, particularly, of *The Book of Privy Counsel* is unique. It avoids many of the traits of *The Cloud* which a modern reader may find un-prepossessing: the presentation of the two works may justly be compared with the differences, already observed, between Books I and II of *The Scale*. *The Cloud* is permitted to digress, to wander from topic to topic, but *The Book*, perhaps because it was written for a more particular occasion, the need of a disciple for explanation of some of the "dark sayings" of *The Cloud*, shows many signs of having been more carefully planned in advance, and it gains in consequence by greater concision. It lacks, too, some of the author's rhe-

[161] 56, p. 41.

torical devices so lavishly displayed in his earlier work: at no time, it has been observed, does he show Hilton's love of traditional metaphors, but in *The Cloud* he shows great fondness for jolting, arresting colloquialisms which he can only use metaphorically. Such figures of speech as "applying God as a plaster to one's sick self" are not really very helpful, especially when the author then has to come back to them and explain them in ordinary theological language, but this example is one of only a few to be found in *The Book*. Nor do we find there the somewhat tedious reiterations of *The Cloud* upon such topics as the profits of ejaculatory prayer or the eccentricities of enthusiasts.

In the second paragraph, as it is edited in this anthology, of *The Book*, the author comes direct to his matter, and illustrates there an essential difficulty and paradox inherent in all his writing. He proposes to write of what his German contemporaries were calling *isticheit*, of "isness", "beingness", of unitive prayer which must form itself around our feeling of God's being, that He is. But as soon as the author suggests what should be the reader's disposition to "the prayer of quiet"—"What I am, Lord, I offer to You . ."—he is forced to have recourse to forms of words, the very thing he is counselling his readers to avoid. Later we shall find further illustrations of this same dilemma, as when, "pampering the intellect," advancing intellectual proofs of the excellence of his spiritual exercise, he can only say that it is beyond intellectual comprehension. This is the paradox which he has seen and so well exploited already in *The Cloud*—" 'How shall I think about God, and what He is?', to which I can only reply, 'I have no idea' "[162]—and Fr. Conrad Pepler has recently reminded us, very aptly, of St. Teresa's advocacy

[162] 27, p. 25.

of meditation, the "work of the intellect", in case people should "drive themselves silly by trying to think of nothing at all"[163].

The Book is as much in the debt of earlier authority as is *The Cloud.* There are plain indications of the author's study of Richard of St. Victor: when he writes "By Benjamin we understand contemplation, by Rachel reason", he is following *Benjamin Minor,* a work which he himself translated into English[164]. And the concluding paragraphs, moving though they are, yet owe much to the famous passage, already quoted, on "the play of love" by Hugh of St. Victor.

How popular and how widely circulated in mediaeval England the works of the *Cloud* author became, it is hard to judge. Professor Hodgson shows what she considers evidence for great popularity, and she is prepared to discount the author's prohibitions in *The Cloud* of indiscriminate circulation of his works, saying that such protests are "frequent in mystical writings"[165]. Dr. Gardner asks for evidence of such frequency, outside the Dionysian canon itself[166], and doubts whether *The Cloud* and the rest ever became widely known. The case most nearly parallel which is known to the present writer is Ruysbroek's veto on publication of *The Spiritual Espousals*[167]. In spite of this, the work was smuggled out of his convent, and his perturbation on discovering this, with the result that he had feared, bewilderment and misinterpretation from readers for whom it was not intended, seems genuine. We may compare the occasion of the writing of his explanatory glosses, *The Little Book of Enlightenment,* with the relations between *The Cloud* and *The Book of*

---

[163] 104, pp. 231-232.
[164] See 28.
[165] 27, p. 180.
[166] 56, p. 38 n.4.
[167] See 29, pp. 13-14.

Privy Counsel, and remember that in England in the late fourteenth century, as a little earlier in the Low Countries, there was real danger of misinterpretation, both by simple devotees and by the "worldly gossips, those sick with self-love and hatred of others, whisperers and tale-bearers and cavillers of every kind"[168] who are castigated in the Prologue to *The Cloud.* Whoever the author was, both *The Cloud* and *The Book* show that he had much to suffer from harsh and adverse criticism: and *The Book* especially, in its angry denunciation of those "half-humbled, logic-chopping souls" who listen every day of their lives to the Scriptures and the Fathers being read aloud, and yet refuse to accept the evidence of their ears that mystical prayer has always been extolled as the highest form of spiritual life, contains several indications that the author's chief critics are in constant touch with him, probably members of his own order. The editor must here content himself with saying that he thinks that the evidence against the author being a religious is negligible—in the often-quoted passage from chapter 10 of *The Cloud,* all that he is doing is to stress that even seculars and the laity have their own obligations to obedience, and in chapter 23, where he says that "we" are dependent on other men's casual charity for the necessities of "our" existence, the "we" seems to refer not particularly to him and his disciple, but to religious in general, the subject of the whole discussion on patrimony here. But, unless proof could be found to show that in the Carthusian order in England in the author's day there was such a division on the merits of mystical prayer—and that would be very surprising—it would seem that he was not a Carthusian. None the less, he took their device for his motto, and he has kept, over five centuries, the secret of his name to himself.

[168] 27, p. 2.

Fifteenth-century Carthusian students of mysticism such as James Greenhalgh and Richard Methley were apt to credit their Order with even more than its great services in this field. Methley believed that *The Cloud* was written by a confrere[169], and the false statement that Ruysbroek was a Carthusian prior was generally accepted in Greenhalgh's circle[170]. But of course the other religious orders had continued to produce men outstanding in prayer and contemplation, though such writers as Methley were probably close to the truth when, calling the Carthusians the "modern hermits", they associated opportunity to produce writings on the spiritual life with solitude and freedom from worldly preoccupations. Three men in their different ways all devoted to the pursuit of sanctity can in this connexion be contrasted, the Benedictine "Monk-Solitary" of Farne[171], the Augustinian friar William Flete[172], and the secular priest Richard Caister, vicar of St. Stephen's, Norwich. The Farne hermit, who seems from allusions in his writings to have composed them while the terrible events of the mid-fourteenth century, the Black Death and the succeeding pestilences, were still recent, was able to take advantage of the provisions made by his Order for those of its brethren who aspired to a solitary life: and he has bequeathed us a most edifying memorial of his years as hermit on the lonely little island off the Northumberland coast, since England's first Christian days a dwelling for saints, in his "Meditations", learned yet simple, and in places vivified by shy allusions to his own experiences of illumination and rapture. Though he seems to have known Rolle's writings, he had no idea of emulating him, of gaining

169 27, p. 183.
170 See 87.
171 See 36 and 37.
172 See 39.

any reputation for himself. Until the nineteenth century there were probably few outside his own Order who knew of his life or his writings. William Flete was probably a contemporary of the Farne hermit, and his desire for solitude led him to follow the ancient paths of the *peregrini*. With the blessing of their superiors, he and other English companions went to Italy in 1359, and Flete was assigned by the prior-general of the Order to their house at Lecceto near Siena, where Flete, as other friars before him, was permitted to live in great retirement. But his reputation for sanctity and his great gifts as a spiritual director partly defeated his object in leaving his own country, for he was drawn into the circle of St. Catherine of Siena, he was soon regarded by her as the head of her spiritual "family", and in spite of himself he became involved with her in the political campaigns to bring the Pope back from Avignon to Rome. Though Flete and Catherine were in the most intimate communion—it was to him that she dictated her famous *Spiritual Document*—his own writings which have survived contain no work of mysticism. He seems to have wanted to play no part in the world of literature or the world of affairs —his one quarrel with Catherine was over his refusal to leave his hermitage and go to Rome with her in 1378 to serve as guides and counsellors to the new Pope, Urban VI, and history has amply justified his refusal—and those few of his undisputed writings which survive comprise only letters written on specific occasions, and one ascetic treatise, which was known in England and translated into English[173]. We have, indeed, in William Flete a case typical of the many scholars who turned to contemplation and spirituality in fatigue and disgust at the frenzied competition for celebrity and pre-eminence in the universities and the religious orders.

[173] 38.

He, a Cambridge man, could write after decades of absence from such warfare to the "masters", the academic teaching staff of his order in England, comparing the atmosphere of their houses of higher study with that of a pot-house. And in Richard Caister, the Norwich parish priest who died in 1420[174], we have a man sought after in his lifetime and popularly venerated after his death as a saint—witness the extracts in this anthology from *The Book of Margery Kempe* —who wrote no word which is known to posterity. True, there is the very beautiful set of verses, "Jesus, Lord, that madest me, And with Thy Precious Blood hast bought . ."[175], but they are not wholly original, and their usual title, "Richard Caister's Hymn", suggests that it was the piety of the East Anglian people which preserved them.

We have often been reminded of this East Anglian piety, in recent years almost to the point of weariness, and many suggestions have been made concerning its special suscepti- bility to the influences of Continental mysticism, because of the constant traffic of the thriving merchant towns between the Thames and Humber estuaries with the Low Countries, a traffic to which Margery Kempe's biography is so interest- ing a witness. But there is rarely positive evidence to support these suggestions, merely an accumulation of detail showing possibility and suggesting probability; and usually facts, when these can be found, show that Continental mystical writings, when they did become known in England, came in Latin versions brought by members of the religious orders. We know that the Carthusians, in particular, were very active in this work of dissemination[176]. Without doubt Julian of Norwich, of whom we must think most in con-

---

[174] **69**, p. 320.
[175] Carleton Brown and Rossell Hope Robbins, *Index of Middle English Verse*, New York, 1943, no. 1727.
[176] See **87**.

sidering East Anglian piety, was helped by the words of others in the formation of her extraordinary spirituality: but we know nothing of how she was helped, or by whom, and it is not necessary to argue that because she is the one English woman mystic and visionary, she must have had knowledge of her counterparts abroad such as Mechtild of Magdeburg or Bridget of Sweden. Part of Julian's greatness is her exceptional independence of such external influence, that her "Revelations" are a singularly pure distillation of her own experiences of mystical rapture, sanctified by long years of prayerful meditation. It is as impossible to do justice to Julian's stature as a spiritual writer in this brief mention as it is to represent her *Revelations* adequately in an anthology. Two recent studies of her whole work[177] have added to our understanding of her genius; and in the extract chosen to represent her, one single "revelation", that described in chapters 50 and 51 of the later, lengthened version which she wrote, has been selected because it illustrates very clearly the nature of her visions and the modes of thought imposed on her. The contemporaries with whom her name is always joined, Hilton and the *Cloud* author, were trained academics, widely read, proficient in Latin, their minds sharp and agile from constant discussion and disputation, their pens running quickly and easily. As they write, they can review the succession of great writers on their subject; and when they needed to refresh their memories or to enquire further, they had libraries to consult and colleagues to ask. Julian was an unlearned woman, though we shall never be sure what she meant by her statement that at the time of her revelations she "knew no letter". *Illiteratus* is commonly used by mediaeval writers to mean "knowing no Latin", and no-one

[177] **68**, and **104**, pp. 305-371.

has ever suggested that Julian was a Latin scholar, which
would in itself have been in fourteenth-century England so
extraordinary as not to have passed unremarked. On the
other hand, those who are unwilling to take her words literally forget those mediaeval spiritual works, showing familiarity with the text of the Scriptures and of other writings
and also a great command of language, which were dictated
by women who could neither read nor write—St. Catherine
of Siena, as we have seen, and, in England, Margery Kempe.
But Julian was an anchoress who lived most of her adult
life—she says that her revelations were granted to her in
1373, when she seems to have been about thirty years old,
and she was still living in 1416[178]—in enclosed solitude,
which obviously must have restricted her opportunities for
such spiritual conversations as Catherine and Margery enjoyed. But instead we can discern in her book the remarkable
qualities which so remarkable a way of life might well in-
duce. She begins with a succession of bright, clear images,
our Lord crowned with thorns, our Lady, still a young girl,
bearing her Son, a little thing, the size of a hazel-nut, in the
palm of her hand, which is Creation, and so on: and as she
describes each image, each revelation, she makes the details
as vivid for her readers, so that we who read them must
inevitably be reminded of the sacred art of Julian's times.
(Norwich's many churches were crowded with art objects
such as the pieta which produced such transports of grief
in Margery Kempe: the city was an important centre of
devotional painting and sculpture, and a surprisingly large
number of such works has survived). In her careful analysis,
in chapter 51, of the sequence in which she was granted
her revelations and her understanding of them, she stresses,

[178] 68, p. 7.

both by her analysis and her examples, their essentially visual first nature. After we have read this chapter we see plainly the personages and the action in the allegory of the lord seated in the desert and his toil-stained, running, falling servant: and if we wish to know how a painter of the late Middle Ages would have realised these scenes, described so minutely and with such an eye for colour and form, we should see the mysterious tablet of paintings, still preserved at the shrine of St. Nicholas of Flüe in Sachseln near Lucerne, which were executed to the specifications of the illiterate hermit-ecstatic to help him to contemplate the mysteries of the Faith[179]. Julian herself understood why the revelations were presented to her in this series of vivid images: she says that the images are still, after so many years, fresh and clear in her memory, and in them she was given "instruction which I can keep, as though it were a child's alphabet". These divine mysteries were revealed to her in just the same fashion as the main events of Holy Scripture were fixed in the recollection of the laity in the Middle Ages, by means of pictures. Yet, she says, at the very beginning she knew that there was to be a "double sight": she understood that what she saw was an allegory, and that, although some of its meaning was at once clear, she would later see it "more spiritually". When at last she came to record this vision in the longer version of her *Revelations,* full understanding had been given to her—Fr. Molinari here justly speaks of her "infused contemplation"—so that now without effort she can simultaneously recall both comprehensions, the first, "spiritual", and the second, "more spiritual".

To read her exposition of the "more spiritual" vision, even in this one chapter, is to perceive how completely at home she

[179] See 74.

had become in mystical speculation of the most refined kind, and how effortlessly she could translate such abstractions into homely, popular language. Her theology, in her description of the Son-servant who is at once Adam the gardener and the Redeemer, is that of Anselm and Hilton: but her imagery is that of popular pious verse, such as *I would be clad in Christes skin* and the concluding "visions" in *Piers Plowman*. She is thoroughly familiar with the idea of "fruition", and she tells us what it is, simply and easily, in her description of the lord's delight in his own being. Christ as the Word, the Father's Wisdom, the doctrine of the Mystical Body (she is as definite about this as Tauler or Hilton, much more so than *The Cloud*), the necessity of self-knowledge as a step towards our knowledge of God: all these are topics implicit in her treatment of this one revelation. And repeatedly she reverts to one of her great intellectual and emotional difficulties, the necessity for reconciling our vision of God as perfect love with the Church's teaching on eternal damnation. Fr. Conrad Pepler has some especially shrewd things to say about this difficulty as it presents itself to many mystics[180]—we may particularly remember Mechtild of Magdeburg here—and both he and Fr. Molinari[181] have gone to great pains to synthesize the entire *Revelations* and to exhibit the profundity and the perfect orthodoxy of Julian's whole mystical doctrine. We cannot doubt her sincerity when she says in commendation of her visions that they were "humble, common, necessary". It is touching evidence of her humility that she did not know how truly extraordinary they and she were.

In Margery Kempe, the last author represented in this

---

[180] **104**, pp. 322 e.s.
[181] **68**.

D

anthology, we have another extraordinary figure, but extraordinary for quite different reasons. Her *Book* occupies a place towards the end of our period comparable with that of the *Ancrene Riwle* two hundred years before: though many will question her genuineness and its claim to be considered as a work of mysticism, none the less it provides incomparable evidence of the literary and devotional sources of mysticism, of the exercises and preoccupations of those affected, at whatever distance it may be thought, by mysticism, and of the firm foundation in the Faith which even so volatile a character as Margery preserved. For this reason a number of extracts from her *Book* have been included. Her colloquies with Richard Caister and Julian are the only supplementary but first-hand testimony which we have to the characters and conversation of these two. Her accounts of her "meditations" show the best—and the worst—of the Anselmian exercises which the author of the *Cloud* calls the highway of all Christians to repentance and salvation, even as he warns chosen souls of the distractions and dangers which such "meditations" bring with them. Her story of the young priest who read to her is a rare and precious witness to the use to which the classics of English mystical literature were put; and in her reports of her triumphant emergence from her several contests with those who imputed heresy to her, we can observe how well the Church fulfilled its pastoral obligations to the humblest and simplest of its flock, when they had ears to hear her teaching.

Part of Margery's account of her pilgrimage to Rome is given here, because it shows the great esteem in which she held St. Bridget of Sweden. An account of mediaeval English spirituality would not be complete if it did not pay tribute to the work of the one house of Bridget's order, Syon, during the fifteenth century, in fostering study of the mystics, English and Continental alike. Yet among the many translators and commentators of that century—one thinks especially of Nicholas Love, prior of Mount Grace Charterhouse, and his *Mirror of the Blessed Life of Jesus Christ,* and of the anonymous Bridgittine translation of St. Catherine of Siena's *Dialogo, The Orchard of Syon*—no-one is found who can be considered together with the mystical writers of the past. The Middle Ages were drawing to their close: and probably no one event contributed more towards ending the whole mediaeval way of life than the dissolution of the religious houses, the total destruction in England of the organized life of prayer and contemplation and solitude in which mediaeval mysticism had flourished. The Church had known many centuries of peace and protection, and we shall do well to remember, as the historians arraign its members for their crimes, and count up the slothful and indifferent pastors, the worldly and rapacious prelates, that still there were such parish priests as Caister, such solitaries as Godric and Julian, religious like Hilton and bishops of the stamp of Grosseteste, *homines Deiformi* whose godliness is mediaeval England's greatest glory. But their day was now done, their whole world brought down in ruins, and their last great testimony to the Faith was not in the pitiful story of Elizabeth Barton, that unhappy pseudo-Catherine, pseudo-Bridget whose lost "Book," should any copy of it have survived Cromwell's zeal and be recovered, would undoubtedly reveal the basest counterfeit of any genuine rapture or revelation, but was enacted by that noble little company from St. Bridget's house of Syon and the Charterhouses, monasteries in which the mediaeval English mystics had always been read and revered, whom Blessed John Houghton led to Tyburn, on 4 May

1535, there to be the first to give their lives for the Church. To Houghton, whose last agonized words offered his bitter passion to his Lord, and to his fellow-sufferers, constant to the end in prayer, "as cheerfully going to their death as bridegrooms to their marriage", we may truly apply the immortal words on mystical prayer which Augustine long ago had written: "If to any man the tumult of the flesh be silent, if fantasies of earth and air and sea be silent also, if the poles of heaven be silent and the very soul of man be silent to itself, and by not thinking pass beyond itself, if all dreams be silent and all such things as be revealed by the imagination, if every tongue and every sign and every thing that hath its existence by passing-on be silent wholly unto any man. . . . if then He only speak, not by them but by Himself, that we may hear His word not by tongue of flesh nor voice of angel nor by the sound of a cloud that is broken by thunder nor by the dark riddle of a similitude, and we may hear Him, Whom in these things we love, Himself, apart from them. . . . and this alone might so transport and swallow up and wrap him who beheld it in those intrinsical joys, so that his life might be for all eternity such as was this moment of understanding . . . would not this be that whereof is written: 'Enter thou into the joy of thy Lord'?"[182]

[182] 19, pp. 225-226.

PRINTED WORKS
AND MANUSCRIPTS CONSULTED

This is not a bibliography of the subject, which would itself make a large volume: but many of the studies listed below contain valuable bibliographical information. The following abbreviations are used:

BM=British Museum.
DSAM=*Dictionnaire de Spiritualité et Ascétique médiévale,* Paris, 1937- .
EETS (OS)=Early English Text Society (Original Series).
PL=*Patrologia Latina,* ed. Migne, Paris, 1879- .
RB=Revue bénédictine.

I   *INDIVIDUAL AUTHORS AND TEXTS*

Adam the Carthusian

1. *De quadripartito exercitio cellae,* PL 153 coll. 799-884 (the original Latin, here ascribed to Guigo III)

2. *Eden's Fourfold River,* edited by a monk of Parkminster, London, 1927 (a much-abridged translation of 1, treating it as of unknown authorship and written at the Grande Chartreuse)

3. Bulloch, James: *Adam of Dryburgh,* London, 1958

4. Wilmart, André, O.S.B.: *Magister Adam Cartusiensis,* Mélanges Mandonnet 2, 1930, pp. 145-161 (an examination of the manuscript authority for attributing 1 to Adam)

Aelred of Rievaulx

5. *De spirituali amicitia,* PL 195 coll. 659-702 (the original Latin)

6. *De vita eremitica,* PL 32 coll. 1451-1474 (the original Latin, also attributed to Anselm)

7. *Sermones inediti,* ed. C.H. Talbot, Rome, 1952 (the original Latin)

8. *Speculum charitatis,* PL 195 coll. 501-658 (the original Latin)

9. Powicke, F.M., ed.: *The Life of Ailred of Rievaulx by Walter Daniel,* London, 1950 (the original Latin, with an English translation)

10. Wilmart, A.: *L'instigateur du 'Speculum Caritatis' d'Aelred abbé de Rievaulx,* Revue d'ascétique et mystique 14, 1933, pp. 369-394, 429

11. Wilmart, A.: *L'oraison pastorale de l'abbé Aelred,* in *Auteurs spirituels et textes dévots du Moyen Age latin,* Paris, 1932, pp. 287-298, reprinted from RB (a Latin text is given from MS Jesus College Cambridge 34, a "family heirloom" written at Rievaulx soon after A.D. 1200)

Ancrene Riwle

12. Day, Mabel, ed.: *The English Text of the "Ancrene Riwle" (MS B.M. Cotton Nero A. xiv),* EETS OS 225, 1952 (the original Middle English of the first version of the *Riwle*)

13. Salu, M.B.: *The Ancrene Riwle,* London, 1955 (a modern English translation not of the *Riwle,* but of its second version, the *Wisse*)

14. Kirchberger, Clare: *Some Notes on the "Ancrene Riwle,"* Dominican Studies 7, 1954, pp. 215-238

Anselm of Canterbury

15. Schmitt, F.S., O.S.B., ed.: *Opera Omnia,* Edinburgh, 5 voll., 1946-1951 (one further volume is to appear of this new critical edition of all the Latin works)

16. Eadmer of Canterbury: *Vita Sancti Anselmi,* PL 158 coll. 49-118 (the original Latin)

17. Wilmart, A.: *Les propres corrections de S. Anselme dans sa grande prière à la Vierge Marie,* Recherches de théologie ancienne et médiévale 2, 1930, pp. 189-204

Augustine of Hippo

18. *Confessiones,* PL 32 (the original Latin)
19. Hudleston, Roger, O.S.B. ed.: *The Confessions of St. Augustine, in the Translation of Sir Tobie Matthew, Kt.,* London, 1923

Bede

20. *In Cantica Canticorum allegorica expositio,* PL 91 coll. 1065-1236 (the original Latin)
21. *In Lucae evangelium expositio,* PL 92 coll. 301-634 (the original Latin)
22. Vernet, Felix, O.S.B.: *Bède le Vénérable,* DSAM

Bernard of Clairvaux

23. Leclercq, J., O.S.B., Talbot, C.H. and Rochais, H.M., O.S.B.: *Sermones super Cantica Canticorum, 1-35,* Rome 1957 (the first volume of a new critical edition of the whole Latin works)
24. Gilson, Etienne: *La théologie mystique de St Bernard,* Paris, 1934

The Chastising of God's Children

25. Bazire, Joyce, and Colledge, Eric, ed. *The Chastising of God's Children and The Treatise of Perfection of the Sons of God,* Oxford, 1957 (a critical edition, with introduction by E.C., of the original Middle English)

Christina of Markyate

26. Talbot, C.H., ed.: *The Life of Christina Markyate* (an edition of the unique Latin text in MS B.M. Cotton Tiberius E.i: Oxford, 1959)

The Cloud of Unknowing

27. Hodgson, Phyllis, ed.: *The Cloud of Unknowing and The Book of Privy Counselling*, EETS OS 218, 1944 (a critical edition of the original Middle English)

28. Hodgson, Phyllis, ed.: *"Deonise Hid Diuinite"*, *and other Treatises on Contemplative Prayer related to "The Cloud of Unknowing"*, EETS 231, 1955 (a critical edition of the original Middle English of *D.H.D.* (Pseudo-Dionysius, *De Mystica Theologia*), *A Treatise of the Study of Wisdom* (Richard of St. Victor, *Benjamin Minor*), *An Epistle of Prayer, An Epistle of Discretion in Stirrings, a Treatise of Discretion of Spirits*)

29. McCann, Justin, O.S.B., ed.: *The Cloud of Unknowing*, London, 1952 (a revised edition of Abbot McCann's modernized versions of 27 and *D.H.D.* (28), together with extracts from Augustine Baker's *Secretum,* a commentary on *The Cloud*)

Dionysius, Pseudo-

30. The Latin translations by John Scotus Eriugena (9th century), John Sarrazin (12th century) and Thomas of Vercelli (13th century) are all to be found, together with the commentaries of Denis the Carthusian (15th century) in *Dionysii Cartusiani Opera Omnia,* Tournai, 42 voll., 1896-1913, vol. 15 (*Celestial Hierarchy* and *Ecclesiastical Hierarchy*) and vol. 16 (*Divine Names, Mystical Theology, Letters*)

31. Théry, Gabriel, O.P.: *L'entrée du pseudo-Denys en Occident,* Melanges Mandonnet 2, 1930, pp. 23-30 (a brief description of the Latin manuscript tradition)

32. Théry, Gabriel, O.P.: *Jean Sarrazin, "traducteur" de Scot Erigène,* in *Studia Mediaevalia in honorem* . . . *Raymundi Josephi Martin,* Bruges, ? 1948, pp. 359-381 (a critical textual study of the mediaeval Latin translations)

Edmund Rich (Edmund of Canterbury)

33. Robbins, H.W., ed.: *Le Merure de Seinte Eglise,* Lewisburg, 1925 (a critical edition of the original Anglo-Norman)
34. Wallace, Wilfred, O.S.B.,: *The Life of St. Edmund of Canterbury,* London, 1893

Eva of Wilton

35. Wilmart, A.: *Eve et Goscelin,* RB 46, 1934, pp. 414-438, and 50, 1938, pp. 42-83

The Monk-Solitary of Farne

36. Farmer, Hugh, O.S.B.; ed.: *Meditaciones cuiusdam monachi apud Farneland quondam solitarii,* Studia Anselmiana 41, 1957, pp. 141-245 (the original Latin, with introduction and notes: an English version is in preparation by Dom Farmer and the Benedictines of Stanbrook)
37. Pantin, W.A.: *The Monk-Solitary of Farne: a fourteenth-century English Mystic,* English Historical Review 59, 1944, pp. 162-186

William Flete

38. *De remediis contra temptationes:* for the Latin text, MSS Bodley 43, Bodley Laud misc. 407, Cambridge University Library Ii.vi.30 and Trinity College Cambridge R.14.1 have been consulted; for the Middle English translation, MSS Bodley 131 (there wrongly ascribed to Walter Hilton) and B.M. Harley 2409 (Fr. Benedict Hackett and Eric Colledge hope to publish a critical edition of the Latin and Middle English texts)
39. Hackett, Benedict, O.S.A.: *William Flete, O.S.A. (c. 1325-1390) and St. Catherine of Siena,* unpublished Dublin National University of Ireland Ph.D. dissertation, 1955

D*

Godric of Finchale

40. Stevenson, Joseph, S.J., ed.: *Libellus de vita et miraculis S. Godrici, heremitae de Finchale,* Surtees Society, 1847 (the original Latin of Reginald of Durham's *Life*)

41. Zupitza, J.: *Cantus Beati Godrici,* Englische Studien 11, 1888, pp. 401-432 (a textual study of Godric's English hymns)

Robert Grosseteste

42. Callus, Daniel A., O.P., ed.: *Robert Grosseteste, Scholar and Bishop,* Oxford, 1955

Walter Hilton

43. Birts, Rosemary (Mrs. F.S. Dorward), ed.: *The Scale of Perfection, Book I Chapters 38-52,* unpublished Oxford dissertation

44. Underhill, Evelyn, ed.: *The Scale of Perfection,* London, 1923 (a modernized version made from MS B.M. Harley 6579, collated with nine other manuscripts)

45. Sitwell, Gerard, O.S.B., ed.: *The Scale of Perfection,* London, 1953 (a modernized version made from 44, collated with the Worde 1494 printed edition)

46. Jones, Dorothy, ed.: *Minor Works of Walter Hilton,* London, 1929 (modernized English versions, made from seven collated manuscripts, of *On Mixed Life, Eight Chapters on Perfection, Qui Habitat, Bonum Est* and *Benedictus*)

47. Wallner, Björn, ed.: *An Exposition of "Qui Habitat" and "Bonum Est" in English,* Lund and Copenhagen, 1954 (a critical text of the original Middle English)

48. Kuriyagawa, Fumio, ed.: *The Paris Manuscript of Walter Hilton's "Eight Chapters on Perfection",* Tokyo, 1958 (the original Middle English of MS Bibliothèque Nationale anglais 41)

49. Kirchberger, Clare, ed.: *The Goad of Love,* London, 1952 (a modernized English version, made from the manuscripts, of the Middle English translation of James of Milan's Latin *Stimulus Amoris*)

50. *Of Angels' Song,* in **102,** vol. 1, pp. 175-182 (the original Middle English, from two manuscripts)

51. Gardner, E.G., ed.: *The Cell of Self-Knowledge,* London, 1910 (modernized versions of **28** and **50,** together with extracts from **69**)

52. *Epistola ad quemdam solitarium de lectione, intentione, oratione et alii,* MS B.M. Royal 6 E III, ff. 120ʳ-123ʳ (the original Latin)

53. Gardner, Helen L.: *Walter Hilton and the Authorship of "The Cloud of Unknowing",* Review of English Studies 9, 1933, pp. 129-147

54. Gardner, Helen L.: *The Text of "The Scale of Perfection",* Medium Ævum 5, 1936, pp. 11-29

55. Gardner, Helen L.: *Walter Hilton and the Mystical Tradition in England,* Essays and Studies by Members of the English Association 22, 1937, pp. 103-127

56. Gardner, Helen L., review of **27,** Medium Ævum 16, 1947, pp. 36-42

57. Russell-Smith, Joy: *Walter Hilton and a Tract in Defence of the Veneration of Images,* Dominican Studies 7, 1954, pp. 180-214

58. Hodgson, Phyllis: *Walter Hilton and "The Cloud of Unknowing": A Problem of Authorship Reconsidered,* Modern Language Review 50, 1955, pp. 395-406

Hugh of St. Victor

59. *De Arca Noe Morali, Didascalion, De Arrha Animae,* PL 176, coll. 618-680, 741-838, 951-970 (the original Latin)

60. Vernet, F.: *Hugues de Saint-Victor,* Dictionnaire de théologie catholique

Julian of Norwich

61. MS B.M. Additional 37790 (the "Amherst Manuscript", 15th century, containing, ff. 97^r-115^r, Julian's shorter, earlier version of her *Revelations*)

62. MS B.M. Sloane 2499 (17th century: a copy of Julian's later, longer version)

63. MS B.M. Sloane 3705 (c. A.D. 1700: also the longer version)

64. MS Westminster Cathedral Library (a 15th-century anthology containing extracts from the *Revelations*—see 67—and *The Scale of Perfection*)

65. Hudleston, R., ed.: *Revelations of Divine Love*, London, 1927 (a modernized version of the longer text)

66. Reynolds, Anna Maria, C.P., ed.: *A Shewing of God's Love*, London, 1958 (a modernized version of 61)

67. Foucard, Betty, ed.: *A Cathedral Manuscript: Excerpts from the "Revelations of Divine Love" by Julian of Norwich*, Westminster Cathedral Chronicle, 1956 (a modernized version of 64)

68. Molinari, Paul, S.J.: *Julian of Norwich: the Teaching of a Fourteenth-Century Mystic*, London, 1957

Margery Kempe

69. Meech, S.B. and Allen, Hope Emily, edd.: *The Book of Margery Kempe*, EETS OS 212, 1940 (the original Middle English)

70. Butler-Bowdon, W., ed.: *The Book of Margery Kempe*, London, 1936 (a modernized English version)

Le Manuel des Péchés

71. Arnould, E.J.: *Le "Manuel des Péchés": Etude de littérature anglo-normande*, Paris, 1940

Richard Methley

72. *An Epistle of Solitary Life,* in *The Thought and Culture of the English Renaissance,* ed. Elizabeth M. Nugent, Cambridge, 1956

Muriel of Wilton

73. Wilmart, A.: *L'élégie d'Hildebert pour Muriel,* RB 49, 1937, pp. 376-380

Nicholas of Flüe

74. Hegglin, Georg Thomas, O.P.: *Das Visionsbild des hl. Niklaus von Flüe,* Lucerne, 1951 (the frontispiece a reproduction of the painted tablet mentioned in the Introduction)

Richard of St. Victor

75. *Opera omnia,* PL 196 (the original Latin)
76. Chatillon, Jean, and Tulloch, William Joseph, edd.: *Sermons et opuscules spirituals inédits,* Bruges, 1951 (a critical Latin text with modern French translations: the first volume of a projected new edition of the whole works)
77. Dumeige, Gervais, ed.: *Ives, Epître à Severin sur la charité, Richard de Saint-Victor, Les quâtre degrés de la violente charité,* Paris, 1955 (a critical Latin text with modern French translations)
78. Kirchberger, Clare, ed.: *Selected Writings on Contemplation,* London, 1957 (a modern English translation, from **75,** of extracts from *Benjamin Minor, Benjamin Major* and several minor works)

Richard Rolle

79. Harvey, Ralph, ed.: *The Fire of Love, and the Mending of Life or The Rule of Living,* EETS OS 106, 1896 (the Carmelite Richard Misyn's Middle English translations of

80 and the *Emendatio Vitae*)

80. Deanesly, Margaret, ed.: *The "Incendium Amoris" of Richard Rolle of Hampole,* Manchester, 1915 (the original Latin)

81. Allen, Hope Emily, ed.: *English Writings of Richard Rolle, Hermit of Hampole,* Oxford, 1931 (the original Middle English texts of the lyrics, prose tracts and four only of the commentaries on the Psalms)

82. Arnould, E.J., ed.: *The "Melos Amoris" of Richard Rolle of Hampole,* Oxford, 1957 (the original Latin)

83. Allen, Hope Emily: *The Authorship of "The Prick of Conscience",* Radcliffe College Monographs 15, 1910

84. Allen, Hope Emily: *Writings Ascribed to Richard Rolle, Hermit of Hampole, and Materials for his Biography,* London and New York, 1927

85. Gilmour, James: *Notes on the Vocabulary of Richard Rolle,* Notes and Queries 201, March 1956, pp. 94-95

John Ruysbroek

86. Colledge, Eric, ed.: *The Spiritual Espousals,* London, 1952 (a modern English translation)

87. Colledge, Eric: *"The Treatise of Perfection of the Sons of God": a Fifteenth-Century English Ruysbroek Translation,* English Studies 33, 1952, pp. 49-66

Simeon of Durham

88. *Letter to Hugh, dean of York,* in *Opera et Collectanea* (the original Latin of Simeon's works) vol. 1, Surtees Society 51, 1868

Stephen of Sawley

89. Wilmart, A., ed.: *Le Triple Exercise d'Etienne de Sallai,* Revue d'ascétique et mystique 11, 1930, pp. 355-374 (the original Latin)

William of St. Thierry

90. *Epistola ad fratres de Monte Dei*, PL 184 coll. 307-354 (the original Latin)

91. Willeumier-Schalij, J.M.: *Willem van St. Thierry's Epistel totten Bruederen vanden Berghe Godes*, Leyden, 1950

92. Wilmart, A.: *La préface de la lettre aux frères du Mont-Dieu*, RB 36, 1924, pp. 229-247

The Wooing of Our Lord

93. Thompson, W. Meredith: *The Wohunge of Ure Lauerd*, EETS 241, 1958 (the original Middle English)

Wulfric of Haselbury

94. Bell, Maurice, O.S.B.; ed.: *Wulfric of Haselbury, by John, Abbot of Ford*, Somerset Record Society 47, 1933 (the original Latin)

II   *OTHER STUDIES*

95. Birch, W. de G., ed.: *An Ancient Manuscript of the Eighth or Ninth Century*, London, 1889 (the Book of Nunnaminster: the original Latin)

96. Bonetti, Ignazio, *C.P.S.: Le Stimate della Passione: Dottrina e Storia della Devozione alle Cinque Piaghe*, Rovigo, 1952 (a modern Italian study of mediaeval European devotion to the Five Wounds)

97. Brown, Carleton, ed.: *English Lyrics of the Thirteenth Century*, Oxford, 1932

98. Colledge, Eric.: *The "Büchlein der ewigen Weisheit" and the "Horologium Sapientiae"*, Dominican Studies 6, 1953, pp. 77-89

99. Courcelle, Pierre: *Tradition néo-platonicienne et traditions chrétiennes de la "région de dissemblance,"* Archives d'histoire doctrinale et littéraire du Moyen Age 24, 1957, pp. 5-33

100. Gilson, Etienne: *"Regio Dissimilitudinis" de Platon à St Bernard de Clairvaux,* Mediaeval Studies 9, 1947, pp. 108-130

101. Gougaud, Louis, O.S.B.: *Christianity in Celtic Lands,* London, 1932

102. Horstman, Carl, ed.: *Richard Rolle of Hampole and his Followers,* London, 2 voll., 1895-1896 (an anthology of many late mediaeval English mystical texts in their original languages)

103. Knowles, David, O.S.B.: *The English Mystics,* London, 1927

104. Pepler, Conrad, O.P.: *The English Religious Heritage,* London, 1958

105. Reypens, L., S.J.: *De "Gulden Penning" bij Tauler en Ruusbroec,* Ons Geestelijk Erf 24, 1950, pp. 70-79

106. Smalley, Beryl: *The Study of the Bible in the Middle Ages,* second edition, Oxford, 1952

107. Vernet, F.: *Mediaeval Spirituality,* translated by the Benedictines of Talacre, London and St. Louis, 1930

108. Wilmart, A.: *Le 'Jubilus' sur le nom de Jésus dit de saint Bernard,* Ephemerides Liturgicae 57, 1943, pp. 3-285 (a critical Latin text)

ST. AELRED OF RIEVAULX

The Mirror of Love

Excerpts from Book I

These excerpts from Book I of THE MIRROR OF LOVE *have been translated from the text of St. Aelred's Latin printed in PL vol. 195.*

THE MIRROR OF LOVE

CHAPTER I: *That there is nothing more worthy than that the Creator be loved by man whom He created.*

You have spread out Your heaven, Lord, like a garment, and in the heavens You have placed the stars to lighten us in this night, the night in which the beasts of the forest rove, the young lions roaring for their prey and seeking to devour us. You have adorned the heights with springs, from which You send down secret torrents to water the plain of our hearts, that they may yield a harvest of wheat and wine and oil, that we need not sweat in vain to seek our bread, but seeking we may find, finding we may eat, and that we may taste Your sweetness, Lord. My soul, an arid soul, a sterile and fruitless soul, thirsts for the sweet drops of this rain, that it may see that heavenly bread which feeds the angels and which infants suck, that I may taste in my soul that divine food, and no more long for the fleshpots which I left in Egypt, where I had made bricks of clay when Pharaoh commanded that I be given no straw. May Your voice sound in my ears, dear Jesus, and teach me how my heart should love You, how my mind should love You, how the bowels of my soul should love You. May my inmost heart of hearts enclose You, my one and only true treasure, my sweet and lovely joy. But what is love, my God? If I am right, it is a strange delight of the spirit, ever sweeter

as it is chaster, ever gentler as it is truer, ever gladder as it is
wider: it is the savour of the heart which You inspire, for
You are sweet, it is the eye by which You see, for You are
good, it is a place that can contain You Who are everything.
For he who loves You knows what You are: and as he knows
You, so he loves You, for You are earthly love, You are
divine love.[1] These are the riches of Your house, with which
Your lovers are made drunk, losing knowledge of themselves
that they may come to You. How could they do this, Lord,
except by loving You? By loving You with all their hearts and
souls. Lord, I beseech You, let some fragment of this Your
great sweetness fall upon my soul, that the bread of my bitterness may be sweetened by it. Let it drink a drop as foretaste
of what it yearns for, what it desires, what it sighs for in its
wandering exile. Let it taste a morsel as it hungers, let it
drink as it thirsts. For those who feed upon You still will
hunger, those who drink of You will thirst again; but they
will be filled when Your glory shall appear, when the great
magnitude of Your sweetness shall be shown to those who
fear You but from whom You have hidden it, for not till
they love You will You make it known. Till then, O Lord,
I shall seek You, and I shall seek You in love: for the soul
that prospers in loving You is always seeking You, and the
soul that loves You perfectly is the soul which has already
found You. And what could be more fitting than that the
soul which You created should love You, for this was Your
gift to it, that it could love You? For those without reason
or sense cannot love You: that is not the nature of their
being. Such beings have each their own nature, their own
kind, their own order: and though they are not numbered

---

[1] In several places in this work the Latin synonyms for "love," *amor* and *caritas*,
have perforce been paraphrased in this way, since to translate *amor* by "love" and
caritas by "charity" would to a modern reader be misleading.

among the blessed and cannot have their being in love of You, they help through their beauty, their goodness, their order towards the glory of those who can be blessed because they can love You.

(CHAPTER 2: *Of the nature, kind and use which are given in common to all created things.*)

CHAPTER 3: *That man was made in the image of his Creator, that he might be capable of blessedness.*

So, THEREFORE, it was given to man at the creation of the universe not only to be created, nor yet, like the rest of created beings, merely to be good: not only to be beautiful or to be ordered, but, much more than this, to be blessed. But since no created thing exists by its own creating, nor has beauty or goodness of itself, but from Him Who is everything, Who is wholly good and wholly beautiful, it follows that the goodness of all good things, the beauty of all beautiful things must derive from Him Who is the cause of all existence, and therefore also that man's blessedness is not from man's self but from Him Who is wholly blessed and Who thus is the blessedness of all the blessed. Reasonable creatures alone are capable of this blessedness. Because they were made in the image of their Creator, it is seemly that they should cleave to Him in Whose image they are made: and this is the only good thing for the reasonable creature, as the holy David says: *It is good for me that I should cleave to God.* This "cleaving" or "clinging" plainly is nothing to do with the body, but with the mind, into which its Creator has put three powers of nature, which make it able to partake of God's eternity, to share in His wisdom, to taste of

His sweetness. These three I call memory, knowledge and love, or will. Memory can comprehend eternity, knowledge can comprehend wisdom, and love can comprehend sweetness. Man was made with these three powers in the likeness of the Trinity, of God Whom his memory keeps without forgetting, his knowledge knows without deceit, his love embraces without desire of anything else. And in this is man blessed.

(CHAPTER 4: *That the image of God in man becomes corrupted by sin.*)

CHAPTER 5: *That since the coming of the Saviour God's image in man is renewed: and that the perfection of this renewing is to be looked for not now but in the future life.*

YET A MEDIATOR came between God and men, the man Jesus Christ: and through Him were solved the doubts in which human nature had been held perplexed, the charter by which the fearful pride of our old enemy held us bound was torn up, the princes and potentates were despoiled by whose power we were forfeit to God's judgement, and God the Father was appeased by that one victim on the Cross: by the proofs of Holy Scripture our memory was restored, our understanding by the pact of the Faith, our love by the daily increase of His love. Now there could be a perfect reforming in man of God's image, if it were not for the memory's failure through forgetfulness, knowledge's darkening through error, love's impeding through cupidity. But when and where shall that perfect reforming be? This peace, this calm, this happiness is to be looked for in our Father's home: there, when we live in eternity, there will be no room for forgetting, when we rejoice in truth there will be no deception by error, when we are swallowed up in God's love there will be no impulse of cupidity. O eternal and true love, O true and lovely eternity, O eternal and true and lovely Trinity! Here will be rest, here peace, here happy tranquillity, here tranquil happiness, here happy and tranquil joy. What are you doing, human soul, what are you doing? Why are you turned aside by this and that? One thing only is necessary for you, so why should you seek many things? All that you seek for in these many things is to be found in that one alone. Do you want to rise on high, to have knowledge or delight or riches? Here you shall have it, all of it, nothing but it, and nowhere but here. How could you truly rise on high from this well of misery and these slimy dregs? How could you find perfect knowledge in this land of the shadow of death? How can there be true delight in this place of terror and desolation, true riches among such calamities? What man is there in this world who rises, whom fear does not cast down? who has knowledge, and knows himself? If you delight in flesh, so do the horse and the mule, who have no intellect. If you have pleasure in fame and wealth, what wealth will you take with you when you die, what glory will you have in the grave? But you will truly rise on high when you come to the highest heaven: you will truly have knowledge where nothing remains unknown: you will have true delight when it is never tainted with disgust, and true riches when they can never be exhausted. Alas for us, for we have strayed away from You, O Lord! *Alas for me, for my days on earth are drawn out. When shall I come and stand before Your face? Who will give me wings, as of a dove, that I may fly, and find rest?* Till then let my soul be fledged, Lord Jesus, let it grow wings, I pray You, in the nest of Your chastening: let it rest in the cleft of the rock, in the cavern of Your wounds.

Let it embrace You, the crucified one: let it take from You the draught of Your precious blood. While I wait, let this sweet meditation fill my memory, lest forgetfulness darken it for me: while I wait, let me look upon myself as knowing nothing, except my Lord, and Him crucified, lest empty error seduce my knowledge from the firm foundation of the Faith, let the delight of all my love be in You, lest I be taken up by any worldly desire. And what then, shall I have then all that I should ask for? Lord, I pray, let the prophecy be fulfilled to me: *All the ends of the earth shall be recalled and turned to the Lord.* "Shall be recalled", the prophet says: for by that he understood man's memory of God, hidden, not entombed, in the rational mind, and you should realise that this is nothing new added to you but something old restored to you. For if it were not somehow natural for the spark of human reason to illumine, however feebly, the soul's memory of God, I think such memory might not exist, and that the fool might then say in his heart: *There is no God.*

(CHAPTER 6: *That man's ignorance of God is an attribute of folly, to be dispelled by wisdom.*

CHAPTER 7: *That man, who should take the Cross and follow Christ, by self-will turns away from Him.*)

CHAPTER 8: *That man may be reformed to the image of God by divine love.*

I THINK that it is plain that the soul turns away from God not in any physical sense, but because the mind diverts its love away from the highest good, and, growing hardened in pride, deforms in the soul the image of God:

and so if in humility it directs its love back towards God, it is restored to the image of God Who created it. So the apostle says: *You must be renewed in the spirit of your minds, and put on a new man, made like to God.* And how could this renewing be made, except by the new law of love, of which our Saviour says: *I give a new commandment to you?* When then our minds have perfectly put on this love, it will at once reform those two powers, memory and knowledge, which two we called corrupted, and therefore this one law, brief though it is, shows us how souls can be healed, for in it are contained the stripping off of the old man, the renewing of the mind and the reforming of the soul to the divine image. Our earthly love has been poisoned with the venom of cupidity, wretchedly and helplessly ensnared in the lime of carnality, and this will go from worse to worse, it will be dragged down by its own weight from one vice into another: but divine love flowing into it from above will dissolve by its heat our inborn sloth and will rise on high, and we shall put off the old and put on the new, the soul will gain the silver wings of a dove and it will fly up towards that sublime and pure goodness of which our nature had its being. St. Paul declared this openly to the Athenians, when, skilfully teaching to them many truths concerning God and proving irresistibly from the works of philosophers that there is one God in Whom we live and move and have our being, he said, among other things: *And we are born of Him,* and he added *and so, if we are born of God*—in case anyone should think that by being "born of God" we share His nature in our substance. Beings liable to change and corruption, as we wretched mortals are, can never so share that nature, which is of God alone and of His only begotten Son, born of His substance and made like to Him in all things.

But St. Paul affirms that we are born of God, or rather, he does not deny it, because the rational soul is made in the likeness of God and sees that it can share in God's wisdom and blessedness. And it is divine love which lifts up our soul to that for which it was made, but from which our cupidity so easily makes it to fall away.

CHAPTER 9: *That man's love may be divided by the interior conflict between divine love and cupidity.*

AND BECAUSE there is only room in that part of our soul which is usually called our love[1] for divine love[2] or for cupidity, our love is divided against itself, as it were by conflicting desires, between the new inpouring of divine love and the remains of its old cupidity. Of this the apostle says: *I do not do what I wish to do,* and again: *The desires of the flesh are opposed to the spirit, the desires of the spirit to the flesh. These two are at war with one another, so that you do what you do not wish to do.* If this is rightly understood, it will be seen that the apostle by what he calls "spirit" and "flesh" is not describing two opposing natures in one man, as the Manichaeians in their error imagine; by "spirit" he means that new quality of the mind which comes through the inpouring of divine love, that same divine love which elsewhere he speaks of as *the love of God which is poured into our hearts by the Holy Spirit Who is given to us.* And by "flesh" St. Paul means the wretched slavery of the spirit, through the remains of our old nature, ingrown in Adam's seed, strange to our new man, constantly stirring up strife within the mind of every single human being.

[1] *amor.*
[2] *caritas.*

(CHAPTER 10: *That in this conflict man's free will, which can choose between good and evil, arbitrates.*

CHAPTER 11: *That we are not deprived by grace of free will.*

CHAPTER 12: *That free will is not withdrawn from the saved or from the damned, and that grace is given only in the freedom of the will.*

CHAPTER 13: *Why free will is not of equal avail to the good and to the evil.*

CHAPTER 14: *How the grace of the first humans in Paradise differs from that of men predestined in this world; and that man is justly accused of a will for evil, even though his free will is not alone sufficient for him to achieve a will for good.*

CHAPTER 15 *That the damnation of infants is also just.*

CHAPTER 16 *That nothing of perfection is lacking in divine love.*

CHAPTER 17: *The spiritual fulfilment of the Old Law of a "spiritual circumcision", an abandonment of sin in divine love.*)

CHAPTER 18: *The spiritual interpretation of the Old Law of a true and spiritual Sabbath, kept in divine love.*

THE OLD LAW may have told what the Sabbath then was; but I would tell you what it should be now, if so vile a wretch as I, groaning under the burden of his sins, bound in the toils of his passions, who has tasted nothing or little of such sweetness, could say anything of this. If only a little respite from Pharaoh's oppressors might be given to me, so that my soul might rest for one half hour in the silence of this Sabbath, that I might truly hold my peace and fall asleep in it, and in my sleep might take my rest with the kings and counsellors who build solitary places for themselves and fill their houses with silver! But how should I, wretched creature, hope for this? Yet I shall always seek that Sabbath, if You, Lord, will ever listen to a poor man's prayer, so that when I have been led out of the pool of misery and the mire of filth, You may grant me to learn, if only from tasting the merest drop, *How great is the store of Your sweetness, which You have kept secret for those who fear You,* for this You have not made known except to those who love You. For those who love You take their rest in You, and where there is true rest, there is also true tranquillity, true peace, the mind's true Sabbath. The Old Law taught us that the Sabbath was ordained because on the seventh day God rested from all His labours. But does this mean that on the first six days He had no rest? The Old Law would say that He had not, that in those six days He made heaven and earth, and that on the seventh day He rested, and that it is therefore ordained that the Synagogue should on that day cease from work and should not play. But if only the Synagogue knew how its work should cease, how it should see that Jesus is the very God, then the cloud of its unbelief would soon be rolled away, it would see God face to face, and in His love would see the perfect law of the Sabbath. The Synagogue would not longer strive after the earthly feast of its earthly Sabbath when it had once entered into the house of God and gone to the place where His wonderful tabernacle is, for it would then burst out with the song of joy, singing with exultation and acknowledging His riches: *We shall exult and take our joy in You, remembering Your*

breasts that are sweeter than wine. And the holy man
Habacuc, taken up into the cloud of his joy in You, said:
*Yet I will rejoice in the Lord, and I will exult in God my
Saviour.*

(CHAPTERS 19-20: *That the rest on this seventh
day is better than all the works of creation of the
other six.*

CHAPTER 21: *That some trace of divine love is
found in all God's creatures, so that they all seek
their Sabbath, which is rest.*

CHAPTER 22: *That a rational creature can find
no true rest until he finds blessedness and that
to choose true blessedness is to abandon false happiness.*)

CHAPTER 23: *Of the prerogative of every rational creature,
and that the rest which the creature by nature desires is not
to be sought in bodily well-being or in worldly riches.*

O WONDERFUL CREATED BEING, lower only than your
Creator, why do you abuse yourself? Do you love
the world? Your being is higher than the world. Does the
sun dazzle you? You are more dazzling than the sun. Do you
speculate about the motion of the heavens? You are exalted
above the heavens. Do you search for the mysteries of life's
beginnings? No life began more mysteriously than yours.
If your mind is perplexed when you reason about these
things, are you yourself not also perplexing? Reason if you
will, but still do not forget to love: and do not love
reasoning, love Him who has confronted you in all these
things with Himself, Who is not subject to your reason.

He places them before you, not so that in them you should be the more blessed but so that you may rise above them, making all created things inferior to you that your dignity may be the greater, and that you may so come to enjoy your blessedness. Why should you pursue the transient beauties of the world, when your soul has a beauty which age cannot wither, poverty cannot mar, sickness cannot dim, death itself cannot destroy? Seek what you are seeking, but do not seek it there. Seek so that all your desires may be fulfilled, and you may rest: seek for this. "Where shall I see this?" you ask. Not in bodily health: for if you were to lack the health which you love and seek your rest in, and labour to acquire, see how grievous is even the cure, very often, for grievous sickness. And even if you have health, with what care it must be tended, how often it is attacked by sicknesses, fevers, plagues and death itself. "Where else shall I seek? In riches?" But how you must toil to gain them, slave to keep them, fear to lose them, sorrow to lack them. As you pile up wealth, you pile up fear: fear of the great man, in case he despoils you, fear of the thief, in case he steals from you, fear of your apprentice, in case he cheats you. The Wise Man says: *Riches are stored up for the harm of their possessor:* and who can say how often this comes about? The poor man has better rest. It has been said by someone that the traveller with empty pockets and empty hands does not fear thieves. The poor man sleeps well at night, he does not fear to be robbed, even if his door be open. There is a verse which runs:

The footpad makes the penniless traveller laugh;[1]
and the Wise Man made a neat jest about the cruel cares of the wealthy, where he writes: *The rich man's riches will not*

[1] Juvenal, Satire X, 22.

suffer him to sleep. If we take this merely in its literal sense, we know how often it happens that some rich man, having stuffed himself with food to the point of nausea, lies down with overloaded stomach hoping for rest, but is kept awake belching and groaning: yet let us rather understand this saying as it applies to that sleep which the spouse makes her glory in the Canticles, saying: *I sleep, and my heart wakes.* It is of this sleep that the Psalmist also says: *In peace I shall sleep and take my rest.* This is the sleep in which the blessed soul has rest in God's sweetness, when the body's senses are drowsy and the cares of the world are shut out from the heart, when the soul tastes and sees how sweet the Lord is, how blessed is the man who trusts in Him. But this is not the sleep which you will have if you aim to sleep as the rich do, their mouths agape for profit, and ever longing, the more they amass, to cram still more into their insatiable maws. So Solomon says: *The rich man is never satisfied with riches: and the man who loves wealth has no enjoyment of it;* and such are the men foreseen by the prophet, who cursed them saying: *Woe to him who amasses what is not his own.* And the prophet goes on at once to mock the value of their hoards: *Why does he weigh himself down with all this dross?*

(CHAPTER 24: *The soul must despise earthly riches and long for spiritual riches.*

CHAPTERS 25-26: *That rest cannot be found in any earthly love, nor in the delights of the flesh or temporal power.*)

CHAPTER 27: *That divine love is the easy yoke beneath which we shall find true rest and our true Sabbath.*

Let us then listen to Him Who says: *If the Son sets you free, you will indeed be free;* and I tell you that it is He Whom we hear calling us, imploring us, bidding us who labour to the rest of His Sabbath. *Come,* He says, *to Me, all you who labour and are burdened down, and I shall refresh you.* "Refresh," He says, offering us as it were a preparation for the Sabbath; and now let us hear Him speak of the Sabbath itself. *Take upon you My yoke, and learn from Me, for I am meek and humble of heart, and you will find rest for your souls.* This is rest, this is tranquillity, this is the Sabbath. *You will find rest for your souls, for My yoke is easy, and My burden is light.* It is because this yoke is easy, this burden light, that you will find rest for your souls. This yoke does not bow you down to earth, but lifts you up to Him: this burden has wings, not weight. This yoke is divine love, this burden is brotherly love. Here may rest be found, here may the Sabbath be kept, here is freedom from servile works; for *divine love is not perverse, and thinks no evil,* and the love of one's neighbour cannot do evil. Here is the Sabbath, if the Synagogue could see it: and even if there should be found some imperfection coming not from divine love but from human weakness, still that will not break our Sabbath, *for divine love covers a multitude of sins.* And it is fitting that this rest should be allotted to the seventh day, *for the love of God is poured into our hearts by the Holy Spirit, Who is given to us,* since now the number "seven" signifies for us the gifts of the Holy Spirit. . . .

CHAPTER 28: *The writer tells of himself and of his conversion.*

S EE sweet Lord, how I have wandered through the world, how *I have tried all things of this world, yet whatever there is in the world is lust of the flesh or desire of the eyes or the pride of life.* So said he who knew Your secrets.[1] I have sought rest in these things for my unhappy soul, but everywhere there was toil and mourning, sorrow and affliction of the spirit. You called me, Lord, You called, You cried, You terrified me, You forced my deaf ears to hear You: You struck me down, beat me, conquered my hard heart: You sweetened and softened and dispelled my bitterness. And then I heard You—but, alas, how late!— calling *Come to Me, all you who labour and are burdened down;* and I replied: *You will stretch out Your right hand to protect the work of Your hands.* For I was prostrate, fouled and smeared, bound and captive, hopelessly snared in the trap of wickedness, weighed down with the burden of habitual sin. So I considered myself: who and where and what was I? Lord, what I saw filled me with horror and fear: the loathsome likeness of my wretched soul struck terror in me. Now that I loved You, I loathed myself, and I wanted to flee from myself and flee to You: but I was held back inside myself. Someone[2] has said: "Very toys of toys and vanities of vanities they were, these ancient favourites of mine which detained me"; and the chain of my evil habits bound me, the love of my kinsfolk conquered me, the shackles of worldly frivolity fettered me, and, more than all these, I was tied by the knot of one particular friendship,

[1] St. John, *First Epistle* ii 16.
[2] St. Augustine, *Confessions* VIII II: the translation quoted here is that by Tobie Matthew.

E

sweeter to me than all the sweets of my life. But though all these things were fine and pleasing to me, You were more, so that as I looked at them one by one I saw how sweetness is mixed with bitterness, sorrow with joy, calamity with good fortune. Friendship was pleasant to me, but I always feared a rift, and I knew that some day parting must come. I saw how my joys had begun, I watched how they progressed, I waited for their end: and I knew that such joys cannot begin blamelessly, progress peacefully, end harmlessly. Always I lived in fear of death, knowing that after death certain torment was prepared for such a soul as mine. And all the time men, who saw what I did but could not know what I was, kept on saying: "How good he is! How good he is!", for they did not know that there was evil in me in the place where only good should be. My sickness was a great and secret one, tormenting, terrifying, corrupting all my vitals with its intolerable stench, and had You not quickly stretched out Your hand, I might have sought the worst remedies of despair when I could no longer endure what I was. And so I began to perceive, Your grace conquering my ignorance, what joy there is in Your love, what peace in Your joy, what refuge in Your peace. Who chooses You cannot go astray, for there is nothing better than You: his hope cannot fail, for nothing is loved more blessedly than You: he need not fear excess, for no limit is set to loving You: he need not dread death, that severer of the bonds of earthly love, for You give eternal life which cannot die. He need not fear estrangement, for nothing estranges You from him except the cooling of his love: no suspicion will come between You, for You judge him by the witness of his own conscience. Here is the joy which shuts out fear: here the peace which stills anger: here the safety which despises the world. And so little by little You began to taste sweet upon my tongue, sick though I was, and I said: If only I might be cured, and might be taken to You! Yet still I was held back, the delights of the flesh which I knew held me fast as if with a tether, the power of my evil habits: but now other delights were more pleasing to me, those which my spirit saw by the power of reason. And often I would say to others: Where are all our pleasures gone, our delights, our joys which till today we knew? What is it that we feel now, in this moment of time? All that was joy to us has now departed: of it all, nothing is left except what pierces our conscience and teaches us to fear death and warns us of everlasting damnation. I said to them: Compare the much which we had, our riches, our delights, our honours, with the little which those children of Christ have who do not fear death. And as I spoke I often saw my own worthlessness, and sometimes I wept for this bitter conflict in my soul. Whatever I saw seemed of no worth to me; and still my old worldly habits drove me on. Yet You who hear the groans of the enslaved, You who set free the sons of the slain, You broke my bonds asunder: You Who promised Paradise to sinners and publicans, You turned me, the worst of sinners, to You. And now I breathe again beneath Your yoke, I rest under Your burden, for Your yoke is easy and Your burden is light.

ST. EDMUND RICH

The Mirror of Holy Church

Although mediaeval English and Latin translations of this work were made and survive, it was composed by St. Edmund in French, and this translation is made from the critical edition of the French by H. W. Robbins (see 33), published by the University Print Shop, Lewisburg, Pennsylvania. The original text was interpolated, perhaps by St. Edmund himself, with a number of devotional passages which have now been omitted in an attempt to restore the homily to the form in which it was first preached and recorded.

THE MIRROR OF HOLY CHURCH

Videte vocationem vestram. These words of the apostle apply to us who are in religion. 'See,' he says, 'to what you are called,' and he says this to urge us on towards perfection. And therefore whenever I think about myself, night or day, on the one hand I feel great joy and on the other great sorrow—joy because of our holy order, sorrow and confusion for my wretched way of life. You need not be surprised, for I have good reason. This is what St. Eusebius means when he says in a sermon: 'To enter religious life is the highest perfection, but then to live imperfectly is the deepest damnation.' And therefore only one course is open to you who live in this community, to follow the way of perfection. If you want salvation, forsake the things of this world and everything to do with it, and do all that you can to live perfectly.

To live perfectly, as St. Bernard teaches us, is to live humbly, lovingly and honorably. To live honorably towards God is to intend nothing except to do His will; and that means to do His will in everything, in the thoughts of your heart and the words of your mouth and the deeds of your hands, in each of your five senses. Seeing, hearing, tasting, smelling, touching, when you walk or stand, lie down or sit, always begin by asking yourself, is this His will or not? If it is His will, do it with all your might: if not, die rather than do it. But now someone may be asking, what is the will of God? His will is for nothing else than our holiness: for that is what the apostle tells us: *Haec est voluntas Dei, sanctificatio vestra*—'This is God's will, that you be holy'.

There are two things, only two, which make a man holy, knowledge and love: knowledge of truth and love of goodness. But the truth is the knowledge of God, and you can never come to that except through knowledge of yourselves: nor can you ever come to the love of God, which is goodness, except through the love of your neighbour. You can come to know yourselves as you practise the highest forms of meditation: you can come to know God through pure contemplation.

Here is a way to reach knowledge of yourselves. Think carefully and often what you are, what you were, what you will be. Think of your body first, then of your soul. There is no dunghill viler than what your body is now: and it would be shameful to say, abominable to think of the filth of which you were engendered. You will be given to toads to feed on and devour. As to your soul, you should think of what you have been and what you are now; for what is to become of your soul you can never think. Think, and think again, how much and how often you have sinned, how much and how many good deeds you have left undone. Think of the good life which you have been granted and of all the good things which you have received, and of how you have squandered them. For every hour in which you have not thought of God has been an hour lost. You must make account for every idle word, every idle thought, every idle deed. And just as there is not one hair of your head which shall not be glorified if you shall be saved, so there is not one hour of your life which must not be accounted for.

Ah, my great God, if all this world were filled with grains of dust, who could be wise enough to know each one grain by itself and tell it apart from the others? There is no such man, of course; but the soul is a thousand times bigger than this whole world, even if the world were a thousand times greater than it is, and still the soul is filled with different thoughts and wishes and longings. Who is there then who could search his heart to know and to ponder all that is in it? Now you can see, my dear brother, how much you need to know yourself.

Then next take good heed of the present state of your soul, how little good there is in you, how little intellect, how little ability. All the time you long for that which is no good to you, and never or seldom for that which could help you. How often you are led astray, now by excessive grief, now by vain joy, now oppressed with fear, now deceived by false hopes: and on the other hand, you are so fickle that what you want today you do not want tomorrow. You are often anxious, longing for so many things and in torment if you do not have them; and then when you have them, that itself is a grief to you. Then, again, think how easy you are to tempt, how frail in resisting, how prompt in surrendering. Your Spouse has saved you from all these harms, and saves you again every day of your life. For when you did not exist, still He created you, in soul resembling His very self; and out of vile and stinking slime, unfit even to think of, He formed your body, fairer and nobler in its senses and shape than any man can describe.

And now think carefully, all you who love your earthly parents so tenderly, why are they so dear to you? If you say that you love your father and mother because you were born of their flesh and blood—so now are the worms that feed on them every day. And yet it was not from your parents that you received either soul or body, but from God through them. For what would you have been if you had stayed as that which was begotten of them in filth and sin? And if

E*

you love a brother or a sister or some other relative because they are of your flesh and blood, you ought for the same reason to love a piece of flesh that might be cut from your father or your mother, which would be the worst folly. If you say that you love them because their flesh is formed in human shape and because they have souls just as you have, then your own blood brother is no nearer to you than another man, for you and he are one flesh, just so much rotting, stinking, dirt, and you both took that flesh from one Father.

Therefore love Him from Whom all beauty comes, and love every man spiritually, and cease from now on to love carnally. And undoubtedly you will do this if you will think of all the benefits which God has given you so often, and will give you still more if you love Him with your whole heart. For as I said at the beginning, when you did not exist He created you out of nothing: and when you were lost he searched for you, when you had gone astray He found you, when you were enslaved in sin He brought you freedom; and when you were condemned He saved you, and when you were born in sin He baptized you. Then, afterwards, when you sinned so vilely and so often, still He bore with you so generously and waited for you so long, and then received you so tenderly and welcomed you into so sweet a house. Every day when you do evil, still He takes you back again, and when you sin still He forgives you, and when you wander still He calls you back, and when you doubt still He teaches you, and when you are hungry still He feeds you, and when you are cold still He warms you, and when you are warm still He cools you, and when you wake still He guards you, and when you sleep still He protects you; when you rise, still He supports you, when you fall, still He sustains you, when you sit, still He holds you, when you stand, still He steadies you, when you walk, still He leads you, when you turn back, still He guides you, and when you return to Him, still He receives you, and when you go away, still He waits for you, when you lose the way, still He recalls you, and every day when you are in distress, still He comforts you.

All these benefits and many others He has done to you Who is your Spouse and the sweetness of your heart. Therefore every day you ought to speak of Him, every day to thank Him, every day to praise Him, every day and every night if you know anything of love[1].

There are three kinds of contemplation. The first is contemplation of created beings, the second of the Scriptures, the third of God Himself and His nature. Contemplation is nothing else than looking at God: and His creatures can look at Him in this way. There are three things in God, power, knowledge and goodness. Power is the attribute of God the Father, knowledge of God the Son, goodness of God the Holy Spirit. By His power all things are created, by His knowledge they are wonderfully ordered, by His goodness they are multiplied every day. You can see His power in their greatness and in their creation, His knowledge in their beauty and in their disposition, His goodness in their excellence and in their multiplication. Their greatness you can see in their four dimensions, that is, in their height and in their depth, in their breadth and in their length. You can see His knowledge if you observe carefully how He has endowed each creature, giving to some existence and no more, as to stones, to others existence and life, as to trees, to

---

[1] A section is omitted after this, with prayers and themes for meditation to be used at the beginning and end of the day.

others existence, life and sense, as to beasts, and to others existence, life, sense and reason, as to men and angels. For stones exist, but they do not live or feel or reason: trees exist and live, but they do not feel or reason: beasts exist and live and feel, but they do not reason: men exist and live and feel and reason. They exist, as I have said, along with the stones, they live along with the trees, they feel along with the beasts, and they reason along with the angels.

Then you should think of the dignity of human nature, and how it surpasses that of every other creature. That is why St. Augustine says 'I would not have the place of an angel if I might have the place which is provided for man'. Think also of the great trouble which any man deserves who is not willing to live as his degree and condition require. For all the creatures of this world have been made for man alone. These goods have been made for man for three reasons: to help us to work, as oxen, cows and horses: to clothe and shoe us, as flax and wool and leather: to feed and nourish us, as beasts, the grain of the earth and the fish of the sea. Harmful creatures, such as poisonous plants and venomous beasts, are created for three reasons: to chastise us, to improve us, to instruct us. We are punished and chastised when we are wounded or fear to be wounded; and this is a great mercy of God, Who is willing to chastise us in this world so that we may not be punished in eternity. We are improved when we think that these things all happen to us because of our sins, for when we see that such little creatures are able to harm us, then we think of our weakness and we are humbled. We are instructed when we see in these creatures the wonderful works of our Creator, for the works of the ant can teach us more than the strength of the bear or the lion. And what I have said of beasts applies as well to plants.

When in this way you have looked at God in His creatures, lift your heart up to your Creator, and think of the great power with which everything was made out of nothing and given its existence, of the great wisdom which ordered them in such great beauty, of the great goodness with which they are multiplied every day for our use. Ah, God, have mercy on us, who so undo our own nature. We destroy all these creatures which He has created, we confuse what He has governed, we lay waste what He has multiplied.

Therefore say to Him in your heart: 'Because Thou art, they exist, because Thou art beautiful they are beautiful, because Thou art good they are good. Well do all Your creatures praise You, adore You, glorify You, most blessed Trinity! Well do they praise You through their goodness, adore You through their beauty, glorify You through their usefulness, most blessed Trinity, Trinity through Whose power all things are created, through Whose knowledge all things are governed, through Whose goodness all things are multiplied, to Whom honour and glory, world without end. Amen'.

Now you have heard a way in which you can look at God in everything and in every creature. That is the first step in contemplation. The second step is in the Scriptures. But now you will ask me, you who are no scholars, 'How could I ever manage to contemplate in the Scriptures?' But listen quietly, and let me tell you this: everything which is written can be spoken[1]. If you do not know how to read, listen willingly to the good things which people tell you. When you hear parts of Holy Scripture, either in public sermons or when you are conversing privately, pay good attention if you hear something which may be for your improvement, teaching you to hate sin, to love virtue, to fear torment, to

---

[1] There is a play here on *escripture* and *escrit* which cannot be translated, but which would help in driving home the preacher's point, that 'Scripture' is nothing hidden or mysterious, but merely words written down.

long for joy, to despise this present world and hasten to the other world: teaching you what you should do and what you should avoid, and whatever illumines your understanding and your knowledge of the truth, and whatever kindles your affection into a burning love. For everything in the Scriptures deals, either in hidden form or openly, with these two good things. In addition to Holy Scripture, you ought to learn and know what are the seven mortal sins, the seven virtues, the ten commandments, the twelve articles of the faith, the seven sacraments, the seven gifts of the Holy Spirit, the six works of mercy, the seven evangelic virtues, the seven petitions of the Our Father, the pains of hell and the joys of heaven[1].

The third degree of contemplation is in God Himself, and this may be of two kinds: from without, contemplating His humanity, from within, contemplating His blessed Divinity. For St. Augustine says: 'God became man to make man God according to his nature'[2] Wherever he goes, within or without, always he may find sustenance, within, contemplating God's Divinity, without, considering His humanity. Concerning His humanity you must think of three things: how humbly He was born, how sweetly He spoke, how lovingly He suffered. But no-one can look at all these things at the same time: and so that you may think of them I have divided them up according to the seven offices of the day which you sing in church, so that there is no office when you have not sweet occupation for your heart, and to do this you must know that each office of the day has two topics for

---

[1] The synopsis provided in this last sentence was later expanded into added chapters dealing with all this catechetic material: these have been omitted.

[2] Many scribes were unwilling to copy this as it stood: one French manuscript has '. . so that God might make man according to His nature', another '. . to make every man blessed in body and soul', another '. . to make man see God in His (?his) nature'.

meditation, one of the Passion and the other of some different season[1].

Now you have subjects and a way for thinking about God in His humanity; but after this you ought to know how you should think of Him in His high Divinity. To do this you must understand that God in this world when human nature began permitted only a partial knowledge of Him, wishing neither to show nor to hide all of Himself. For had He shown Himself completely, faith would have been of no profit and doubt would not have been vanquished, because faith is in those things which cannot be seen, and the things which I can see are not of faith. Had He concealed Himself completely, there would have been no aid to faith, and doubt would have been forgiven. And that was why He wished to show part and to hide part of Himself.

He wished to show Himself in four ways, two of them inward and two outward: inwardly by revelation and by reason, outwardly by Scripture and by His creatures. God shows Himself by revelation when He appears to someone through inspiration or through miracles. He shows Himself through reason to man's understanding in this way: every man can well see the nature of his being, that is to say that he exists and that he has not always existed. And from that he knows well that there was a time when he began to be, and therefore that there was a time when he was not. But when he did not exist, then in no earthly fashion could he make himself. And man can see this in every creature, for each day he sees some of them departing, others coming. Because all things exist and do not exist of themselves, it follows that there must be one thing which gives existence

---

[1] Then follow seven sections, omitted here, giving short narratives as described here to serve as subjects for meditation at each office.

to all things, that is to say from which all things have their being. From this it follows that He from Whom all things have being must be without beginning, for if He had had beginning He must have had it from someone else: and if He had had beginning from someone else He would not have been prime author and first beginning of all things.

From this it follows that He from Whom all things are has being before all things and no thing before Him. Therefore He comes from no other one, and if He comes from no-one, then He had no beginning, for everything which has beginning has it from another, for a thing which does not exist cannot give being to itself. And therefore it follows by all earthly means that there must be one thing which had no beginning. And when man's reason sees that this cannot be otherwise, then he begins to believe steadfastly that there is one thing without beginning which is author and defender and ruler of all things that exist. And this thing he calls "God", because the word "Deus" comes from a Greek word "Theos"[1], which means "create" or "nourish". And therefore man calls Him "God" because He creates and nourishes all things, which is what "Deus" means. And so man comes first to the knowledge of God, Who is all good, and from Whom comes whatever is good.

After this man's reason comes to see that necessarily this God is one single God and not more, one single beginning and not more, because if God is God, from this it follows of necessity that two would at the same time be too much and too little. If God were two, the first would be too much because the second would be enough, for if He were not enough He would not be God: and by the same reason the

---

[1] Strictly, "this he calls 'God' (*deu*), because this word *deus* comes from a Greek work called *theu*—". He naturally regards the French word as merely a changed form of the Latin: but he seems to think that the Latin is a borrowing from the Greek, and that the Greek is a verb.

second would be too much because the first would be enough. On the other hand, each one would be too little, because each one would have need of the other, because neither of them could be the other. But each of them must be sovereign good: and therefore each one of them would need the other, and therefore in either of them there would be too little. And therefore if there were two Gods, according to Holy Scripture, there would be in both superfluity and lack at the same time. Thus it follows of necessity that there may not be more than one single God. On the other hand, there is no good which can be lacking in God; but because the consolation of companionship is a thing sweet and good, God[1] cannot lack the good of companionship. Therefore it follows necessarily that in God Who is sovereign good there is a plurality of persons. And because there can be no companionship between less than two, it necessarily follows that in God there are at least two persons. And because companionship is worth little without alliance or love, it follows that in God there is a third person Who is the alliance and the love between these two. And because unity and plurality are equally good, it follows necessarily that unity and plurality are both in God.

By this reasoning man comes to know this of God, that He is one God in being and three in persons. And man can observe the same thing in himself: because he sees well that at the beginning he was endowed with power, and after power he had knowledge, and then he began to love knowledge, and so to see clearly that in his soul he had might, and that out of this might knowledge came, and out of both of them came love. And when man sees well that this is his own nature, from that he perceives that in God there must be the

---

[1] Many manuscripts here have "two": the similarity of *deu, deus* and *dieus* is a constant source of confusion in Old French texts.

same nature which is in him, that is, that in God there is might, from which comes His knowledge, and from the one and the other comes love. And because from the first person the second comes and from Them both comes the third, therefore he calls the first person God the Father, the second God the Son, the third God the Holy Spirit.

And because it is usual among men that the father because of his age is not so strong as the son, and that the son because of his youth is not so wise as the father, so that one should not think this of God, power is attributed to God the Father, wisdom to God the Son; and because the word "Spirit" conveys some idea of austerity, to Him are attributed sweetness, love and goodness.

In this way man first comes to knowledge of his Creator, knowing how He is without beginning and why He is called God, one in substance and three in persons, and why the first person is called God the Father, the second the Son, the third the Holy Spirit. In this way you must recognize your God, and this way of recognition is the foundation of contemplation.

And since you have in this way established your heart in right faith and firm hope and perfect love, you ought now to lift it up in the high contemplation of your Creator. But often the soul would wish to see God in His own nature in contemplation; and it cannot do this. And so the soul returns to itself, and makes in itself steps by which it can climb to the contemplation of God: first it is able to look at its own nature and then at the nature which is beyond it. But if your way of thinking is distracted by corporeal images[1]

---

[1] "Par corporeles ymaginacyouns", a technical term familiar to all mediaeval students of psychology, meaning, roughly, attributing mortal, physical characteristics to spiritual beings or to abstract ideas, or, very often, interpreting metaphors literally.

you will never be able to enquire into the nature of God, because the soul will find that all such thoughts by which she is led become obstacles to her progress.

The first step in contemplation is for the soul to retreat within itself and there completely to recollect itself. The second step in contemplation is for the soul to see what it is when it is so recollected. The third step is for the soul to raise itself beyond itself and to strive to see two things: its Creator, and His own nature. But the soul can never attain to this until it has learned to subdue every image, corporeal, earthly and celestial, to reject whatever may come to it through sight or hearing or touch or taste or any other bodily sensation, and to tread it down, so that the soul may see what it itself is outside of its body. To do this, see what a wonderful thing the soul is in itself: how in its nature it is single, and none the less made of so many different things, for it is the soul itself which sees with the eyes, hears with the ears, tastes with the mouth, smells with the nose, touches with the hands and other members.

Then, next, think how great is the soul which in one single thought could comprehend heaven and earth and everything in them, even if they were a thousand times greater than they are. If man's soul is a thing so great and so noble that no created being can perfectly understand it, how great and how noble is He Who made something so noble out of nothing. For He is above all things and beneath all things and within all things and without all things. He is the highest and the deepest, the innermost and the widest: the highest, ruling all things, the deepest, supporting all things, the innermost, fulfilling all things, the widest, encompassing all things. This kind of contemplation engenders in men firm faith and great devotion.

After this you must understand how great He is; and this you can see in many ways. First, see how generous He is with temporal goods, how He gives His wealth to evil men as well as to good in all things which you can see upon earth: and then how generous He is in forgiving, for if there were a man who had committed as many sins as all the men on earth, still He would be a hundred times more ready to forgive than that wretch would be to ask for forgiveness. Then you should think how generous He is with spiritual goods, that is to say with the six[1] virtues, for whoever has one has all of them. Fourthly, you should think how generous He is with material goods to all those who are willing to ask for them as they should: for how can He deny you what He admonished you to pray for? Furthermore, He is willing, if we ask Him for something, to grant us even more. "Ask me", He says, "to give you the joy of heaven, and I will give you all temporal goods without your having asked'. This contemplation of His power and His generosity engenders in man true hope.

After this you ought to recognise and think of His goodness and His sweetness and His beauty. To do this you should well consider the great beauty and the great goodness and the great sweetness which there is in earthly creatures. How many things there are which delight our earthly eyes by their beauty and our taste by their sweetness and our touch by their smoothness and so all our other senses! See then how great goodness, sweetness and beauty there must be in a spiritual creature which is everlasting, when there is so much beauty and sweetness and goodness in a thing which exists today and tomorrow will have passed away. On the other hand, if there is so much beauty, sweetness and good-

[1] Some manuscripts read "seven".

ness in every created thing, how much beauty must there be in its Creator, Who made all this and every thing, and out of nothing! You know well how great, beyond measure, the difference must be. This kind of contemplation engenders in man love towards his Creator.

After this, when you have in this way looked at your Creator and His creatures, put every corporeal image outside your heart, and let your naked intention fly up above all human reasoning, and there you shall find such great sweetness and such great secrets that without special grace there is no-one who can think of it except only him who has experienced it. And if you wish to know by instruction, go to him who has experienced it. And even though I, wretch that I am, might have experienced it, still I cannot tell of it: for how could I tell with my lips what I cannot think of in my heart? This is a thing so great and so secret that it surpasses every thought, and therefore I keep silence. And it is right that I should do so, for the tongue cannot teach this, but only divine grace.

Now you have three kinds of contemplation: one in created things, one in Scripture, the third in God Himself in both His natures. If you live according to this instruction you will live honorably; and that was the first point in our sermon which we mentioned at the beginning.

After that you must study how to live lovingly towards your neighbour. To do this, you must strive your utmost to love and to be loved. You ought to love every man in God: that is to say, only because he is good, not because he is physically beautiful or a fine singer, nor for any quality such as strength or other bodily power. Because physical beauty and all such things as strength or riches or other bodily powers can be loved without God. And therefore to love man in God is nothing else than to love him for nothing which can be loved without God, to love him for such qualities as goodness or justness or truthfulness. For you cannot love men for such things if you do not love God. And therefore when you love a man for his goodness or his justness or his truthfulness, you love him in God, because God is justness, goodness and truth. If we are good, we have no friend who is not good, nor any enemy. And therefore we ought to love the good because they are good and the wicked because they can be good. In this way you love nothing but goodness, since you love because of goodness. And if you wish to be loved, show yourself to be loveable. If you wish to be loveable, take these three counsels and do not forget them: Do as you are told and asked, Take what you are given without grumbling, Suffer patiently what may be said to you. If you live in this way, then you will live loveably.

Then next you must study to love humbly; and for this you must understand that there are two kinds of humility. One comes from truth, the other from love. You can have the first through knowing yourselves, because there is no way at all of looking at yourselves, seeing what you really are, after which you shall not be humbled. You can have the second kind if you think often of the humility of our sweet Lord Jesus Christ, and of how He Who never sinned humbled Himself. And this humility comes only through love.

Now you know what it is to live honourably, loveably and humbly: and to do this is to live perfectly. May our sweet Lord Jesus Christ grant us here to honour God, to love our neighbour and to humble ourselves, so that we may be honoured for our honour, loved for our love, and for our humility be exalted to that joy in heaven which has been prepared for us. Amen, through His sweet pity.

RICHARD ROLLE

I Sleep and My Heart Wakes

This translation has been made from Rolle's original English, as edited from three manuscripts by Dr. Hope Emily Allen (see 81), by kind permission of the Delegates of the Clarendon Press.

EGO DORMIO

Ego dormio et cor meum vigilat. Those who long to love, listen and hear of love. In the Song of Songs it is written: I sleep and my heart wakes. He shows great love who never wearies of loving, but always, if he is standing, sitting, walking or working, is thinking of his love, and often too is dreaming of it. Because I love I woo you, so that I might have you as I would, not for myself, but for my Lord. I wish to be the go-between to bring you to the bed of Him who has created you and redeemed you, Christ, the Son of the King of Heaven. For it is His wish to dwell with you if you will love Him. He asks nothing more of you than your love. And, my dear sister in Christ, you do my will if you love Him. Christ asks nothing else than that you should do His will and should discipline yourself day and night, so that you abandon all earthly love and every pleasure which prevents you from truly loving Jesus Christ. For as long as your heart is inclined to the love of any fleshly thing, you cannot perfectly be united with God.

In heaven there are nine orders of angels, which are grouped into three hierarchies. The lowest hierarchy contains angels, archangels and virtues. The middle hierarchy contains principalities, powers and dominions. The highest hierarchy, which is closest to God, contains thrones, cherubin and seraphin. Angels are the lowest, seraphin the highest. And that order which is least bright is seven times brighter than the brightness of the sun compared with a candle, than the candle's beams compared with the moon, than the moon's beams compared with a star. So the orders in heaven are each one brighter than the next, from angels up to seraphin. I say this to kindle in your heart a longing for the fellowship of the angels, because all those who are good and holy when they depart from this world shall be admitted into these orders. Some, who have loved much, into the lowest; some, who have loved more, into the middle order; and others, who loved God most and are most ardent in His love, into the highest. The word seraphin means "burning", and into their order are those received who desire least the things of this world and feel the highest sweetness in God, and have hearts most ardent in His love.

I write especially to you because I believe that there is greater goodness in you than in many another, and that you intend to set your mind to fulfilling in your deeds that which you see to be most profitable for your soul, and to dedicate yourself to that life in which you may sanctify your heart to Jesus Christ and least be concerned with the affairs of this world. For if you will found your love firmly, and be ardent whilst you are living in this world, without doubt a place is prepared for you very high in heaven and joyful before the face of God among His holy angels. For in the very place from which the proud devils fell down, humble men and women, Christ's doves, are seated to have rest and joy eternally, in return for a little short penance and labour which they have endured for the love of God. Perhaps now it seems hard to you to turn your heart away from all earthly things, from all empty and frivolous speech and from all carnal love, and to be alone, to watch and pray and think of the joy of heaven and of the Passion of Jesus Christ, and to imagine the torments of hell which are ordained for sinful men. But without doubt, once you have become accustomed, this will seem easier and sweeter to you than any earthly matter or comfort. As soon as your heart is touched by the sweetness of heaven, you will find little pleasure in the joys of this world; and when you feel joy in the love of Christ, you will feel loathing towards the joys and the comforts of this world and towards earthly delights. For every melody, every rich thing, and every pleasure which all the men upon earth are able to devise or imagine seem but grief and anger to the heart of a man who is truly burning in the love of God. For his delight and joy and melody is in the song of angels, as you may well come to know. If you abandon everything which is pleasing to your love of this world, for the sake of the love of God, and if you have no thought for your kinsmen, but forsake everything for the love of God and give your heart only to desire God's love and to please Him, you shall have and shall find in Him greater joy than I can imagine. How might you then know of these things?[1] I can never know if any man loves in this fashion. For always, the higher the form of life, the fewer followers it has here on earth. As you can hear and see, there are many things which distract man from the love of God: and God comforts His lovers more than they believe who do not love Him. Therefore, though from the outside we seem to live in penance, we shall have great joy within ourselves if we wisely dispose ourselves in the service of God, and fix all our mind on Him, and forsake all the vanities of this world.

Do all that you can to understand what I write, and if all your desire is directed towards loving God, then understand these three degrees of love, so that you may rise from one to another until you have come to the highest. For I do not

---

[1] Another manuscript reads: "How might I then write of these things?"

wish to conceal anything from you which I believe may help you towards holiness.

The first degree of love is when a man observes the ten commandments and keeps himself from the seven deadly sins and is firm in the faith of Holy Church; and when he will not anger God for the sake of any earthly thing, but remains loyally in His service and persists in it to the end of his life. This degree of love is necessary for every man who wishes to be saved. For no man may come to heaven unless he love God and his neighbour without pride, anger, envy or malice and without all other deadly sins, gluttony, lechery and cowardice, because these vices kill the soul and make it separate itself from God, without Whom no creature can live. For just as a man who is poisoned by a tit-bit eats venom which kills his body, so does a sinful wretch through the pleasures and desires of his flesh. He kills his soul and brings it to everlasting death. Sin seems sweet to men, but the reward which is ordained for them is bitterer than gall, more deadly than poison, worse than all the woe which we can see or feel here on earth.

> All things perish and pass away on which we look:
> The wealth of this world dwindles into woe.
> Robes and rich things are rotting in the ditch,
> Proud painted ladies are cast down into care.
> Delicate delights shall soon die and be corrupted,
> And jewels and gold are chains dragging men to death.
> The wicked of this world are rushing pell-mell to the pit
> Where they shall rest and rue, where woe is everlasting.
> But he may sing of his solace who loves Jesus Christ,
> When wrongdoers out of bliss fall down into hell.

But when you have lived faithfully[1] according to God's ten commandments and have resolutely kept yourself from

---

[1] The manuscripts quoted have "when you have truly believed," which seems to be a mistake.

every mortal sin, and when you are pleasing to God in that degree of love, then reflect that it is your wish to please Him more and to do better with your soul and to become perfect. Then you enter into the second degree of love, which is to forsake all the world, your father and your mother and all your relatives, and to follow Christ in poverty. In this degree you must take thought to be utterly clean in heart, utterly chaste in body and dedicate yourself to humility, patience and obedience, and see how beautiful you can make your soul by loving virtues and hating vices, so that all your life may be spiritual and not carnal. Never speak evil again of your neighbour, nor give one angry word in reply to another, but suffer meekly in your heart everything which men say, evil or good, without letting it move you to anger. And then you shall be at rest within and without, and so you shall easily come to a spiritual life which you shall find sweeter than any earthly things.

It is a perfect spiritual life to despise the world and to desire the joy of heaven; to destroy through the grace of God all the wicked desires of the flesh; to forget the solace and the love of your family, and only to love in God. Whether those who are dear to you die or live, or whether they are poor or rich, in sickness or in sorrow or in health, always thank God and praise Him in all your deeds. For His judgments are so secret that no created being can understand them. Often those who have their pleasure and their will in this world have hell in the next; and some men live this life in torment and persecution and anguish, and have heaven for their reward. Therefore if your dear ones always enjoy ease and health and wealth in this world, you and they may both have more reason to fear lest they should lose the everlasting joy of heaven. If they live in penance and sickness or if they live righteously they may have faith that they shall come to joy. Therefore in this degree of love you shall be filled full of the grace of the Holy Ghost, so that you shall not suffer sorrow or remorse except for spiritual causes, such as your own sins and other men's sins, or in desiring the love of Jesus Christ and in meditating upon His Passion; and I wish you often to think upon the Passion, for that will kindle your heart to despise all the good things of this world and its joys, and to desire ardently to live with angels and saints in the light of heaven; and when your heart is completely disposed to the service of God, and when all worldly thoughts are expelled from it, then you will wish to steal away and be alone to think of Christ and to spend much time in prayer. For through devout meditations and holy prayers your heart shall be made ardent in the love of Jesus Christ, and then you shall feel sweetness and spiritual joy both in your prayers and in your meditations. And when you are alone often recite the psalms of the psalter and the Our Father and the Hail Mary. And do not count how many you say, but see how well you can say them, with all the devotion of which you are capable, lifting your mind up to heaven. It is better to say seven psalms longing for Christ's love and putting your heart into your prayer, than to say seven hundred thousand letting your mind wander upon earthly vanities. What good do you believe can come from letting your tongue babble the words in your book and your heart roam around from one part of the world to another? Therefore set your mind upon Christ, and He shall govern your mind and make it His; and keep yourself from the poison of worldly affairs.

And I pray you, as you long to be God's lover, love the name of Jesus and meditate upon it in your heart, so that you never forget it wherever you may be. And I tell you truly that you shall find great joy and comfort in it, and through the love with which you love Jesus so tenderly and so specially you shall be filled with grace on earth and you shall be Christ's dear servant in heaven. For there is nothing which pleases God so much as the true love of this name Jesus. If you love it truly and constantly and never weary of your love because of anything that men can do or say, you shall be received into a higher life than you know how to wish for. The goodness of God is so great that He will give us five for every one of our asking, so well is He pleased when we intend to devote all our heart to His love.

In this degree of love you shall overcome your enemies, who are the world, the devil, and your flesh. But none the less you must keep on fighting as long as you live. Until you die you must be careful to stand upright, so that you do not fall into vain pleasures, whether they be evil thoughts or evil words or evil deeds. Therefore your longing to love Christ truly ought to be very great. You shall conquer your flesh by preserving your virginity only for the love of God; or, if you are not a virgin, through living chastely and rationally in thought and deed and through discreet abstinence. You will overcome the world through desiring Christ's love and meditating upon the sweet name of Jesus and upon your longing for heaven. For as soon as you feel sweetness in Jesus, all the world will seem to you nothing but vanity and grief to the souls of men. You will not yearn then to be rich, to have many fine cloaks, many gowns and jewels, but you will regard all these things as nothing and despise them as useless, and you will accept nothing more than is necessary. Two cloaks or one will seem enough to you; if you have five or six, give some of them to Christ Who wanders naked in His wretched rags. Do not keep them all, because you do not know if they will be half worn out when you die. The devil is overcome when you shall stand firmly against all his temptations in true charity and humility.

I do not wish you ever to be idle, but always either talk of God or perform some good work, or fix your meditation upon Him, so that He is always in your mind. And often think of His Passion.

A MEDITATION ON CHRIST'S PASSION

It was my King who shed those bitter tears, who bled
Waiting in mortal dread till His betrayers led
Him to be tormented.
Pitilessly did they strike Him and at the pillar smite Him,
Spitting in His fair face so foully to despite Him.

My King's crown is of thorns, that cruelly pierce His brow.
Alas, my joy, my love is dragged to judgment now.
Nails pierced His feet and pierced those hands so dear,
And His unblemished body was wounded with a spear.

Naked is His white breast, red is His bleeding side,
Livid His lovely face, and His wounds deep and wide:
From those five wounds, as though a crimson tide,
The blood runs down: His pains no man can hide.

Who will not weep to see the Lord of life hang dead,
Nailed to a shameful tree, who was the angels' bread?
He was cast out who opened heaven's gate:
He who is heaven's joy was slain through mortal hate.

Here let men see, and let them wonder now,
That God's own majesty to death does bow.
Yet love can conquer all things, well we know:
It is not death but love has laid Him low.

Bring me to Thy love: O Jesu, take my heart,
Cleanse it from every sin, and let us never part.
Thou art my whole desire: I long to be with Thee:
Kindle within me fire, that I, of earth's dross free,
May climb where I aspire, at last Thy face to see.

Jesu, my soul amend, Thy love into me send,
That I may with Thee wend to joys that never end.
Wound with love's lance my mind: my heart now take to
Thee.
Thou didst with Thy precious blood my soul unbind: make
it Thine own true love to be.

I covet Thee: this world I hate, I flee, I fight:
Early I sought and I seek late for Thy sweet sight.
Make my soul bright: Thy love is all my light:
How long must I remain in night?
When may I come to Thee, and in Thy melody delight,
Hearing that psalmody
That lasts eternally?
When Love His love shall bring
Then I of Love may sing.

If you will begin today to meditate, you shall discover a
sweetness which will draw your heart up to heaven, and
which will make you weep and long greatly for Jesus. And
all your thoughts shall be of Jesus, and so they shall be received above all earthly things, above the firmament and the
stars, so that the eye of your heart may look into heaven.

And then you enter into the third degree of love, in which
you shall have great comfort and delight, if you may obtain
the grace to come to it. For I do not say that you or any one
else who reads this shall accomplish it all; for it is according
to the will of God whom He chooses to do what is said
here, whom He wishes to do other things in other ways, as
He gives grace to men to have their salvation. For different
men obtain different graces from our Lord Jesus Christ, and
all shall be placed in the joy of heaven who end their life
in love. Whoever is in this degree has wisdom and discretion
to love according to the will of God.

This degree is called contemplative life, the life which

F

loves to be solitary, not clamouring or making a noise, not singing or crying aloud. At the beginning, when you come to this degree, the eye of your spirit is taken up into the bliss of heaven, and there it is illumined with grace and kindled with the fire of Christ's love, so that you shall truly feel love burning in your heart more and more, raising your thoughts to God, and feeling such great love and joy and sweetness that no sickness or anguish or shame or penance may afflict you, but all your life shall be turned into joy; and then, because your heart is so exalted, your prayers shall turn into joyful song and your meditations into melody. Then Jesus shall be all your desire, all your delight, all your joy, all your solace, all your comfort; I know that all your song shall be about Him and all your rest shall be within Him. Then you may say:

> I sleep and my heart wakes:
> Who shall to my lover say
> I long for His love for aye?

All who love the vanities and the darlings of this earth, and who set their hearts on anything else than the things of God, shall never come to this degree, nor to the second degree of love which I named before. And therefore you must forsake all worldly solace, so that your heart is not inclined to the love of any created thing or to any earthly concerns, so that you may be in silence, so that your heart may always be steadfastly and valiantly fixed upon the love and the fear of God. Our Lord does not give beauty and riches and delights to men so that they should set their hearts on them and waste them in sin, but so that they shall know Him and love Him and thank Him for all His gifts. The greater shame it is to them if they anger Him who has given them gifts both for their bodies and their souls. Therefore, if we wish to flee from the torments of purgatory, we must perfectly keep ourselves from the desire and the pleasure and all the evil delights and the wrongful fears of this world, and there must be no worldly sorrow within us, but we must put all our hopes firmly in Jesus Christ, and we must stand up manfully against all temptations.

Now I write a song of love in which you will find delight when you are occupied in the love of Jesus Christ:

A SONG OF LOVE

My song is all sighing, for love I am repining,
For that sweet King's love dying, brightness' self outshining,
Beauty's own self outvying.
To Thy light lead me, with Thy love feed me,
As a lover speed me, with Thine own love meed me.

When wilt Thou come, Jesu my joy,
And rescue me from woe,
And give Thyself to me, and be
With me for ever so?
All my desires would be fulfilled if that were given to me:
All my desires are one desire and that for nought but Thee.

My saviour, Jesu, in danger's hour, my comfort, Jesus,
through Thy power,
Jesu, my beauty's flower, my harbour and my bower,
When may I see Thy tower?
When wilt Thou send the call to come into Thy hall,
To be with Thee, my all? Must I in battle fall
Who am Thy knight, and in the field wear my heart upon
my shield?

Now I grow pale and wan for love of one above.
For Jesu, God and man, who taught me first to love:
No other love His lessons from my mind can move.

I sit singing of the love-longing that grows with my breast.
Jesu, Jesu, Jesu, I yearn with Thee to rest.

Full well I know Thou seest how I live in constancy,
Until the day when first I may live perfectly in Thee.

Jesu, no other love seek I my heart to satisfy:
When will it break, when shall I die, and come to Thee, and
    rest for aye?
Jesu, Jesu, Jesu, for Thee and only Thee I long,
When shall I leave this life and come where I belong?

Jesu, my dear one, my delight, it is my joy of Thee to sing.
Jesu, my song, my soul's one light, when wilt Thou come,
    my King?
Jesu, my sweetness, my respite, my peace, my comforting,
Jesu, grant me death, that night me into day may bring.

I am Love's prisoner, since He did conspire to consume my
    heart with fire,
Robbing it of all desire, save only to climb ever higher,
To seek no other goal, to burn and never cool,
To serve no other rule, to learn but in love's school
Where every sorrow shall decrease, where all my wants shall
    cease,
In Jesu, prince of peace.

I am Love's prisoner, and for His delight He holds me, day
    and night,
Longing still for one sight of His face so fair and bright.
Jesu, my soul's one hold on health, and all my gold,
Be to me all I have been told, let not Thy love to me grow
    cold,
But bring me safe into Thy fold.

Jesu, in Thee I grow in grace: death were more dear to me
Than to be ruler of the race, and king of all I see.
Jesu, when wilt Thou pity me, that I might with Thee be,
To love and look on Thee?
Prepare a place for me and lead me thither
That nevermore we may be severed,
And in Thy light my soul shall soar; I shall Thy love adore
In heaven for evermore.

                             AMEN

The Author of
THE CLOUD OF UNKNOWING

The Book of Privy Counsel

This translation has been made from Professor Phyllis Hodgson's critical edition of the original English (see 27), by kind permission of the Council of the Early English Text Society.

Spiritual brother in God, I speak now particularly to you, about your disposition towards contemplation as I think it to be, and not to all those others who shall hear what I write. For if I were to address myself to everyone, then what I write should be applicable to everyone; but since now I write particularly to you, I therefore write nothing but what seems to me most profitable and suitable to your disposition. If some other man share your disposition, so that he may gain as much from what I write as you, so much the better, for I shall be well satisfied. None the less as I now write, it is your own inward disposition, so far as I am able to understand it, which is my only object of attention; and therefore I say to you, as representing all others who may resemble you, as follows:

When you shall have time for solitude, do not think in advance what presently you must do, but abandon good thoughts just as evil thoughts; and do not pray with your lips unless you have a special desire for this. And then if you do use any words, pay no attention to how many or how few, have no care for what they are or what they mean, whether you have used collect or psalm, hymn or anthem, or any other prayer, mental and inward and coming from the thoughts or vocal and outward by speaking words aloud. And see that nothing remains in your active mind but a naked intention reaching up into God, not into God as you in particular may think of Him as existing in Himself or in any of His works, but into Him knowing Him to be only as He is. Let God be so, I beg you, and do not seek to make Him anything else. Do not seek to come closer to Him by intellectual subtlety. Let faith be your foundation.[1] This naked intention, fastened and founded only in true faith, shall be nothing else in your thoughts and feelings than a naked thought and a blind feeling concerning your own being: as if you were to say to God, inwardly, in intention: "What I am, Lord, I offer to You, having regard to no quality of Your being, but only that You are as You are, without anything more."

Let this humble darkness be all your mirror and your recollection. Think no more about yourself than I command you to think about God, so that in this way you may be one with Him in spirit, without any division or distraction of your recollection. For He is your being, and you are what you are in Him, not only by cause and by being but also since He is in you both your cause and your being. And therefore when you are so occupied, think of God as you think of yourself, and think of yourself as you think of God, that He is as He is and that you are as you are, so that your thoughts be not distracted or divided, but united in Him Who is everything —preserving always this difference between you and Him, that He is your being and that you are not His. For though it may be so that all things are in Him through cause and through being, and that He is in all things their cause and their being, yet in Himself He alone is His own cause and His own being. For just as nothing may be without Him, so He may not be without Himself: He is being both to Himself and to everything. And that distinguishes Him alone from everything else: that He is the being both of Himself and of everything; and so He alone is in all things, and all things

---

[1] Professor Hodgson notes several textual variants here, and suggests several possible alternatives to this interpretation, none of which, however, has here been adopted.

are in Him, since all things have their being in Him, and
He is the being of all things. In this way your thoughts and
your feelings shall be united with Him in grace without any
division, and with all subtle enquiries into the peculiar
qualities of your own blind being or of His being banished
far off: and therefore let your thought be naked and your
feelings in no way defouled, and be you, nakedly as you are,
secretly fed in your feelings only by Him as He is; though
this shall only be as it can be here in this life, blindly and
partially, so that your longing desire may always remain
active.

Look up then easily and say to your Lord, either with your
lips or in your heart: "What I am, Lord, I offer to You, for
You are that which I am"; and think, nakedly and simply
and crudely, that you are as you are, without any kind of
subtlety.

It seems to me that this is not difficult to think, even if it
were commanded to the most ignorant man or woman
alive, endowed with the minimum of natural intelligence.
And therefore I am sometimes secretly amazed, not knowing whether to laugh or weep, when I hear some men—I
do not mean simple, ignorant men and women, but scholars
and very erudite men—say that what I write to you and to
others is so difficult and so advanced, so subtle and so strange
that the most subtle scholar or the most intelligent man or
woman alive can hardly grasp it. This is what they say:
but I am obliged to answer these men, and to say that it is
a great merit to be afflicted, and in mercy to be despised and
bitterly reproached by God and those who love Him,[1] so

---

[1] So all the manuscripts. It is tempting to presuppose some scribal corruption
here, but they provide no evidence; and as it stands the passage is explicable: that
in such contempt which they suffer, God's chosen children may share in His
earthly sufferings.

F*

that nowadays not merely a few, but almost everyone (except perhaps one or two of those specially chosen by God in some place) is so blinded by subtlety, both intellectually acquired and natural, that the proper understanding of this easy work, through which the soul of the simplest living man or woman is truly united in loving humility with God in perfect charity, can no more be grasped in spiritual truth by such a one, because of pride and subtlety, than the knowledge of a great scholar in the university can be grasped by a little child still on its alphabet. And because of their blindness they wrongly call such simple teaching intellectual subtlety, whereas, if it be rightly regarded, it shall be seen to be a simple and an easy lesson taught by an ignorant man.

For I consider that man to be altogether too ignorant and too crude who is unable to think and to feel, concerning himself, not what he is, but merely that he is. For plainly it is characteristic of the most ignorant cow or the least reasonable animal (if it could be said, as it cannot, that one were more ignorant or less reasonable than another) to feel its own characteristic being. How much more, then, is it characteristic of man, who is singularly endowed with reason above all other animals, to think and to feel his own characteristic being.

Therefore come down to the lowest level of your intelligence, which some believe that they can prove to be the highest, and think in the fashion appropriate to the most ignorant, which some hold to be the wisest, not what you are, but that you are. This is because much scholarship and learning and much subtle investigation of your natural intelligence is needed for you to think what you are, in all your characteristics, and you have thought of this, by the help of grace, for a long time now, so that you partially

know what you are, and, I suppose, such knowledge has been
of use to you: you know that you are by nature a man, and by
sin a filthy, stinking wretch. You know well that this is so:
and perhaps sometimes it seems to you that you acquiesce[1] in
all the filths which pursue a man and are his lot. Fie on them:
let them alone, I beg you. Have nothing more to do with
them[2] for fear of their stench. But you may easily in your own
ignorance and simplicity attain to thinking that you are,
without any great knowledge, acquired or natural.

Therefore in this case I beg you not to do more than to
think simply that you are as you are, however filthy or out-
cast you may be, provided only that you have already (as
I assume) been lawfully shriven of all your sins, particular and general, according to the true counsel of Holy
Church; for unless you have done this, neither you nor any
other man shall be so presumptuous as to take on this exercise, by my consent. But if you feel that you have done the
best that is in you, then you may apply yourself to this exercise, and then, even if you feel yourself to be so vile and so
wretched that you, weighed down by yourself, do not know
what best to do with yourself, still you shall do this, as I tell
you:

Take our good and gracious God as He is, as quickly and
simply as you would take a plaster, and apply it to your
sick self as you are. Or, if I must use other words, lift up
your sick self as you are, and try to touch by desire our good
gracious God as He is, to touch Whom is endless health, as
the woman in the Gospel witnesses: *Si tetigero vel fimbriam
vestimenti eius, salua ero:* "If I touch only the hem of His
clothing, I shall be saved." Much more then shall you be

---

[1] *That you acquiesce:* "to wele", which is capable of several interpretations, of
which this seems the most probable.
[2] That is, think no more about them.

healed of your sickness because of this high heavenly touching of His own being, of His own dear self. Step up then
resolutely and take this remedy: lift up your sick self as you
are to our gracious God as He is, without any subtle or
special regard for any of the qualities which belong to your
being or to God's, whether such properties be pure or foul,
of grace or of nature, divine or human. Nothing is now required of you except that your blind beholding of your
naked being be lifted up joyfully in loving desire to be fastened and united in grace and in spirit to God's precious
being, in Him only as He is, and nothing else.

And even though your wayward and curious intelligence
can find no food for itself in this sort of exercise, and will
therefore grumble and prompt you to give it up, and to perform some good action in which intelligence may be put to
work (for it will seem to your intelligence that what you
do is useless, and this is merely because intelligence cannot
judge it), this would make me love this exercise even more,
because this shows that it is more estimable than is the intelligence. Why indeed should I not love it more, especially
since there is no work which I can do, nothing which can
be achieved by any labour of my intelligence or faculties
which could bring me so close to God and so far from the
world as this little naked feeling and offering up of my blind
being would?

And so, even though your intelligence can find no food
for itself in this exercise, and would therefore like to distract you from it, still take care that you do not give it
up on this account, but be the master of your intelligence.
Do no turn back merely to appease it, however violent it
may be. It is turning back to appease the intelligence when
you allow it to speculate upon the qualities of your being in

various laborious ways. Such speculation may be very good and very profitable, yet even so, in comparison with this blind feeling and offering up of your being, it can only withdraw and distract you from the perfection of unity, that unity which should properly be between God and your soul. Therefore press on in your being, the first characteristic of your spirit, and do not turn back on any account, however good or holy the thing may be which your intelligence would direct you to.

And obey the counsel and teaching of Solomon, when he said to his son: *Honora Dominum de tua substantia et de primitiis frugum tuarum da pauperibus: et implebuntur horrea tua saturitate et vino torcularia redundabunt:* "Honour your Lord with your substance, and feed the poor with your first fruits: and your barns shall be full of plenty and your presses shall abound with wine." These are the earthly words which Solomon spoke to his son, but it as if he said for your comprehending as I in his person say spiritually to you: "My spiritual son in God, see to it that when you have abandoned all subtle speculations of your natural intelligence, you offer your substance wholly to the honour of your Lord God, offering up simply and entirely to Him your own self, all that you are and such as you are, but generally and not particularly—that is, without any particular regard to what you are—so that your vision is not distracted and your feelings are not debased, for this would diminish your unity with God in purity of spirit. And with your first fruits feed the poor: that is, with the first of your spiritual or bodily qualities which have grown up within you from the beginnings when you were first made until this present day."

I call all the gifts of nature and of grace which God ever gave to you your fruits, with which you are bound in this life to nourish and feed, both physically and spiritually, all your brothers and sisters by nature and by grace as well as your own self. I call the first of these gifts your first fruits. The first gift in every living thing created by God is nothing else than that creature's being. For though it may be true that the qualities of your being are so closely united to your being itself and are inseparable from it, still, because all those qualities depend upon that being, it may in truth be called what it is, the first of your gifts: and so it is nothing else than your being which is your first fruits. For if you extend your subtle regard to any or all the nice qualities and the honorable conditions which belong to man's being, which is the most noble being among all created things, always you shall find that the only object of your attention, whatever it may be, is your naked being. It is as if you were to say within yourself, every time you so regard yourself, rousing yourself by means of this regard to the love and praise of your Lord God, Whose gift to you it is not merely that you have being, but that that being has such nobility as its qualities witness, when you regard them: "I am, and I see and feel that I am, and not only that I am, but that I am such, and such, and such, and such," adding up as you regard them all the particular qualities of your being. Then, far greater than all this, add it all up together and say: "What I am and how I am, both in nature and in grace, I have it all of You, Lord, and You are what it is: and I offer it all to You, first to Your glory and then for the help of my fellow Christians and myself." And in this way you may see that the first and the only object of your regard is most substantially fixed in the naked seeing and the blind feeling of your own being. And so it is only your being which is the first of your fruits.

But even though it may be the first of every one of your

fruits, and though all the other fruits may depend on it, still it is not profitable for you in your present state to fashion or fix your regard upon it in any one or in all of its special qualities. I call them your fruits, and in the past you have been exercised about them. But now it is enough for you to pay full honour to God with your most fundamental existence,[1] and to offer up your naked being, which is the first of your fruits, in a continual sacrifice of praise to God, both for yourself and for all others as holy love may demand, a praise not clothed by thought of any quality or particular regard, however it may come, for your own being or that of anything else, even though you may wish, by such a regard, to help the needs, to promote the prosperity or to increase the progress towards perfection of yourself or of someone else. Leave this alone: in such a case as yours it truly cannot be. Far more profitable to the needs, the progress and the perfection in purity of spirit of yourself and of all others is such a blind and general regard than any special regard which any man may have, however holy it may seem.

The Scriptures bear witness that this is true, through Christ's example and by the use of reason. For just as all men were lost in Adam, for he fell from this uniting affection, and just as all who by that work to which they are called are willing to bear witness to their desire for salvation, are saved, and shall be saved by the power of the Passion of Christ alone, offering Himself up in the truest sacrifice, all that He was in general, not in any one particular, and He not regarding any one man in this life, but offering Himself generally and commonly for all: just in the same way, a man who truly and perfectly sacrifices himself in this way by a common intention for all does everything which is in him

---

[1] "With thy substance".

to join all men to God as effectually as he himself is joined.

And no man can exercise a greater love than thus to sacrifice himself for all his brothers and sisters in grace and in nature. For just as the soul is more honourable than the body, so the joining of the soul to God (the soul's life) by the heavenly food of love is better than the joining of the body to the soul (the body's life)[1] by any earthly food in this life. To join the body to the soul is good in itself, but without joining the soul to God it is never well done. Both are better than merely feeding the body; but joining the soul to God is best. To join the body to the soul never alone merits salvation; but to join the soul to God, where the riches of the union of the body with the soul are lost, merits not only salvation but leads to the greatest perfection.[2]

Because now, to increase your perfection, you do not need to go backwards and to stimulate your intellect, as you might by regarding the qualities of your being, so that with such a regard you could feed and fill your affection with loving and delectable feelings about God and spiritual things, and feed and fill your comprehension with spiritual wisdom drawn from holy meditations as you seek to know God. For if you will exert yourself to remain, as by grace you may, constantly trained upon your spirit's first object, offering up to God that naked, blind feeling of your own being which I call the first of your fruits, you may be sure that the second and secondary clause of Solomon's lesson shall be most truly fulfilled as he promises, without your occupying yourself in laborious seeking and searching with your spiritual understanding amongst any of the qualities which are the properties not only of your being but also of God's being.

---

[1] These apparently interpolatory glosses are in the manuscript.
[2] In these three sentences, the author's "the one—the other" have been expanded.

For you must know very well that in this exercise you must have no more regard for the qualities of God's being than for the qualities of your own being. For there is no name nor feeling nor regard which agrees better, nor even so well, with eternity, which God is, as does that which may be had and seen and felt in the blind and loving regarding of this word "Is." For if you say "Good," or "Fair Lord," or "Sweet," "Merciful," or "Just," "Wise" or "Omniscient," "Mighty" or "Almighty," "Knowledge" or "Wisdom," "Power" or "Strength," "Love" or "Divine Love," or whatever else you say about God, all of it is hidden and preserved in this little word "Is." For it is proper to Him only to be all that all these are. And if you were to accumulate a hundred thousand such sweet words as these, "Good," "Fair" and all the rest, still you would not depart from this word "Is"; and if you were to recite them all, you would add nothing to it, and if you were to name none of them, you would take nothing from it. Therefore be as blind in your loving regard of the being of your God as you are in your naked regard of your own being, without any laborious intellectual investigations for some quality proper to His being or to yours. Abandon all such subtlety and leave it far behind, pay honour to God with your fundamental existence, with all which you are, so that you are towards the whole of Him that which is as He is, He Who alone is by Himself and without any addition His own and your own blessed being.

And so, unitively and in a wonderful way, you shall pay honour to God with Himself: for that which you are you have of Him, and what it is He is. And although when you were created in substance you had a beginning, you who are that substance which once did not exist, yet still your being was eternally in Him without beginning, and it shall always be without ending, as He Himself is. And this is why I often cry, always the same cry:

"Pay honour to God with your fundamental being, and yield a common profit to all who are men with your first fruits; and then your barns shall be filled with plenty." That is, then shall your spiritual affection be filled with the plenty of love and of virtuous living[1] in God, your foundation and your purity of spirit. "And your wine presses shall abound with wine": that is, your inward, spiritual powers, which you are accustomed to strain and press together by various careful meditations and rational investigations into the spiritual cognition of God and of yourself, regarding His qualities and your own, shall then abound with wine, by which wine in Holy Scripture is truly and mystically understood spiritual wisdom in true contemplation and high fruition of the Godhead.

And all this shall be done suddenly, pleasurably and graciously, without any effort or labour on your part, only by the ministration of angels through the power of this blind work of love. For all angels know this work and render special service to it, as the maidservant ministers to her mistress.

It is in great commendation of this pleasurable and easy work, which in itself is the high wisdom of the Godhead graciously descending into man's soul, joining and uniting the soul to Him in spiritual ease and prudence of spirit, that the Wise Man, Solomon, cries out and says: *Beatus homo qui inuenit sapientiam et qui affluit prudentia—*[2] All this, as you should understand it, means: He is a blessed man who may find this unitive wisdom, and who may abound in his

---

[1] Or perhaps "of strong belief" ("leuying" is ambiguous); and some manuscripts have, instead of "leuying", "lykyng", that is, "joy" or "desire".

[2] The manuscripts quote the whole of the Latin of Proverbs iii 13-4, 21-6.

spiritual exercises with this loving ease and prudence of spirit, offering up his own blind feeling of his own being, and putting behind him all laborious academic and natural knowledge. To obtain this spiritual wisdom and this easy exercise is better than to gain gold or silver. The moral sense of this "gold and silver" is understood to mean every other kind of natural and spiritual knowledge, which is obtained by careful investigation and labour in our natural powers, below us, within us or on a level with us, regarding any of the qualities proper to the being of God or of any created thing. And Solomon shows why it is better when he says that it is because *primi et purissimi fructus eius*. That is, "because its fruits are the first and the purest"; and this is no wonder, for the fruit of this exercise is a high spiritual wisdom, suddenly and freely eructated[1] by the spirit, inwardly and within, formless, far removed from every fantasy, impossible to obtain by effort or to govern by the operation of natural intelligence. This natural intelligence, however subtle or holy it may be, may in comparison with this be called a mere feigned folly formed in fantasy, as far removed from the very truth which appears when the spiritual sun shines as is the dim moonlight on a foggy night in the depth of winter, compared with the brightness of the sunbeam in the middle of Midsummer Day.

"My son," says Solomon, "keep this law and follow this advice," in which all the commandments and the advice of the Old Testament as well as the New are truly and perfectly fufilled, without any special regard to any particular one by itself. And this kind of exercise is only called a law because it contains completely within it all the branches and the fruits of the Law. For if we look at it wisely, the founda-

[1] Or "lifted up" in other manuscripts.

tion and the strength of this exercise shall be seen to be nothing else than the glorious gift of love, in which, according to the teaching of the apostle, all the Law is fulfilled. *Plenitudo legis est dilectio:* "the fullness of the Law is love." And this law of loving and this advice for living, if you follow it, "shall be life for your soul," as Solomon says, inwardly in a yielding love towards your God, "and fairness for your face," outwardly in the truest teaching and the seemliest ruling of your bodily deportment towards your fellow Christians who can see your outward form of living. And on these two, the one inward and the other outward, according to Christ's teaching, "all the Law and the prophecies depend."

And therefore, when you are so made perfect inwardly and outwardly in your exercise, you shall then advance upon a firm foundation of grace, which shall be your guide upon your spiritual way, lifting up in love your naked, blind being towards God's blessed being; and your being and His are one in grace, even though you are separate in nature. "And the foot of your love shall not falter": that is to say, from the time when you have in steadfastness of spirit the proof of your spiritual exercise, you shall not be so easily hindered and retarded by the careful questions of your subtle intellect, as you are now in your beginning. Or you may otherwise understand this: then the foot of your love shall neither falter nor trip over any kind of fantasy coming from your careful intellectual investigations. The reason is that in this exercise, as has been said before, every careful investigation of any part of your natural intellect is utterly banished, far off, and totally forgotten, for fear of fantasy or any feigned falsehood that may come in this life, which in this exercise might sully the naked feeling of your blind being and draw you away from the excellence of this exercise.

For if any kind of special thought concerning anything, except only concerning your naked, blind being, which is your God and your intention, should come into your mind, then you are turned and drawn back to be active in exercising intellectual skill and subtlety, distracting and dividing yourself and your mind both from yourself and your God. And therefore preserve yourself whole and undistracted so far as you may by grace and by the skill of spiritual steadfastness. For in this blind regard of your naked being, so joined to God as I tell you, you must do all that you have to do: eat and drink, sleep and wake, walk and sit, speak and keep silence, lie down and get up, stand and kneel, run and ride, labour and rest. Every day, you shall offer this up to God as the most precious offering that you can make; and it shall be the chief of everything you do, in everything you do, whether it be of active or contemplative life. For as Solomon goes on to say, "whether you sleep," sleep, that is, in your blind regard, safe from the din and the incitement of the fierce fiend, the false world and the frail flesh, "you shall not fear any danger" nor any deceit of the devil. For by this exercise he is totally confused and blinded in sorrowful ignorance and mad surmise as to what it is which you are doing. But pay no heed to this, for "you shall graciously rest" in this loving unity between God and your soul, "and your sleep shall be very easy," for it shall be spiritual food and inward strength to your body as well as to your soul. Soon after this the same Solomon says: *Universae carni sanitas est:* "It is health to all the frailty and sickness of the flesh." And it is fittingly said: for since all sickness and corruption entered the flesh when the soul fell away from this exercise, all health shall come to the flesh when the soul by the grace of Jesus, Who is the first worker, rises again to this same exercise. And you shall hope to achieve this only by the mercy of Jesus and by your loving consent. And therefore I pray you, as Solomon goes on to say, that you persist valiantly in this exercise, always raising up to Him your loving consent in the joyfulness of love. *Et ne paueas repentino terrore et irruentes tibi potentias impiorum:* "And do not be dismayed" by any troubling fear, though the devil should come, as he will, "with a sudden terror," banging and beating on the walls of your house where you are sitting, or though he should raise one of his great limbs "to rush in upon you" suddenly, giving you no warning. You may be very certain that it shall be so, whoever you may be who set yourself to labour faithfully in this exercise, that you shall indeed see and feel, or else smell, taste or hear some astonishing thing conjured up outwardly by the devil before some of your five senses. And all this is done to pull you down from the heights of this precious exercise: and therefore guard your heart well in the time of this torment, and lean easily and trustingly upon the love of our Lord.

Quia dominus erit in latere tuo, et custodiet pedem tuum ne capiaris: "For our Lord shall be at your side," ready and near to help you, "and He shall guard your foot," that is, the ascent of your love, by which you go to God, "so that you shall not be taken prisoner" by any trick or deceit of your enemies, the devil and his minions, the world and your flesh. Brother, you may see that in this way our Lord and our love shall powerfully, wisely and generously succour, help and defend all those who will, for the loving trust which they feel in Him, utterly abandon their own safe-keeping. But where shall such a soul be found, so entirely made secure and stable in the faith, so fully humbled in self-abnegation, so lovingly led and fed in the love of our Lord, knowing altogether and feeling His omnipotence, His un-known wisdom and His glorious goodness: how He is one in all things, and all things in Him, so much so that without yielding up to Him everything, which is of Him, by Him and in Him, a loving soul is never truly humbled in total self-abnegation? Thus, by this noble denial[1] of itself in true meek-ness and by this exalted affirmation that all is in God[1] in per-fect charity, the soul deserves to have God, in Whose love it is deeply drowned in full and final forsaking of itself as some-thing which is nothing or less than nothing, if less than nothing could exist: to have God, Who powerfully, wisely and generously succours it and guards it and defends it from all adversities, bodily and spiritual, without any labour or effort, watch or scrutiny from the soul itself.

Put away your human objections, you half-humbled souls, and do not say in your logic-chopping way that such a humble and total abandonment by a man of his own safe-keeping, when he feels himself thus touched by grace, is in any way to tempt God: this is because reason tells you that you dare not so abandon yourselves. No, be satisfied with what you do, for that is enough in your active vocation to save your souls: and leave them in peace, those other con-templative souls who dare so abandon themselves. Nor should you ponder over their words and deeds and be sur-prised at them, even though they seem to you to exceed the way and the common judgement of your reason.

Ah, for shame! How often shall you read and hear, and yet give neither faith nor credence? I mean what all the Fathers of old before us have written and taught, that which is the fruit and the flour of all Holy Scripture. You seem

---

[1] "Denial—affirmation that all is—": the "noughtnyng—allyng" of the author are untranslatable.

either to be blind, so that you cannot in faith see what you read or hear, or else you are touched by some secret type of envy, so that you cannot think that so great a good, which you lack yourselves, can be the portion of your brethren. You should take good care, for your enemy is subtle, and he intends to make you have greater faith in your own intellect than in the ancient teachings of the truthful Fathers or the operation of grace and of our Lord's will.

How often have you read and heard from so many authorities, holy and wise and trustworthy, that as soon as Benjamin was born his mother Rachel died? By Benjamin we understand contemplation, by Rachel reason; and as soon as a soul is touched by true contemplation, as it is in this noble abnegation of itself and in this exalted affirmation that God is all, certainly and truly then every man's reason dies. And since you read this so often, not only in one or two men's works but in those of many most holy and most honorable, why do you not believe it? And if you do believe it, how dare you then probe and search with your reason among Benjamin's words and deeds? By this name Benjamin are understood all those who in the superabundance of love are carried away above the intellect, as when the prophet says: *Ibi Beniamin adolescentulus in mentis excessu,* which is to say: "There is Benjamin, a young child, in superabundance of the intellect." Take care, therefore, that your thoughts are not like the deeds of those miserable women who destroy their own children when they are newly born. It is good that you should beware, and that you should not aim the point of your presumptuous spear at the power, the knowledge and the will of God, obstinately trusting in your powers, blindly and ignorantly, dragging Him down when you most think that you exalt Him.

In the first beginnings of the Church, in the times of persecution, many and different souls were so wonderfully touched by a swift access of grace so that suddenly, with no other acts having previously served as means, craftsmen threw down their tools and schoolchildren their writing implements, and they ran, without pausing to probe with their intellect, to martyrdom with the saints. Since this was so, why should men now in our peaceful days not believe that God may and can and will and does, yes, indeed, touch different souls as suddenly with the grace of contemplation? And I believe that it is His will to do this with the fullness of grace in chosen souls. For it is His will to be recognized in the end, to the amazement of all the world. For such a soul, so in love denying himself and so highly affirming his God to be all, shall in the fullness of grace be preserved from all the attempts of his spiritual or earthly enemies to cast him down, without effort or labour from the soul, but only by the goodness of God: for divine reason requires that He should truly preserve all those who, labouring for His love, forsake and do not trouble to preserve themselves. Nor is it any wonder though they be marvellously preserved, since they have become so utterly humble in the valiance and the might of God's love.

And if any man fears to do this, or says it should not be done, either the devil is in his heart, robbing him of the loving trust in his God and the benevolence towards his fellow Christians which he ought to have, or else he is not yet so perfectly humbled as he needs to be, if, that is, he is intent upon the truly contemplative life. Therefore do not be afraid to be so humbled before your Lord, nor so to sleep in this blind regard of God as He is, away from all the noise of this wicked world, the false fiend and your frail flesh;

for our Lord shall be ready to help you and to guard your feet so that you are not taken captive.

And this exercise is properly compared with sleeping, for just as in sleep the use of the bodily intellect is suspended, so that the body may have complete rest, so that man's bodily nature may be nourished and restored, just so in this spiritual sleep the vagrant questionings of man's ungovernable spiritual intellect, its imaginative powers, are tied fast and completely emptied, so that the simple soul may softly sleep and rest in its loving regard of God as He is, so that man's spiritual nature may be fully nourished and restored.

And therefore tie your intellect fast, offering up your naked, blind feeling of your own being. And, as I often say, always take care that it is naked, and not clothed by any quality of your being. For if you were to clothe it with any quality, such as the honourable nature of your being or with any other special condition proper to man's being rather than to the being of other created things, at once you would give food to your intellect, and give it opportunity and power to attract you towards many things, and to distract you beyond your understanding. Take care that you are not trapped into this, I beg you.

But it may be that now your subtle intellect, which knows nothing about this exercise, suggests to you that the method is surprising and suspect. No wonder if it should be so: for up to now, you have relied too much on intellectual wisdom to be able to understand such a matter as this. And it may be that in your heart you are asking how you could know whether this exercise is pleasing to God or not; or, if it be pleasing to Him, how it can be so pleasing as I say that it is. My answer to this is that this question is prompted by a subtle intellect, which will under no circumstances suffer you to agree to perform this exercise, until the intellect's subtlety be satisfied by some good piece of reasoning.

And therefore I shall not desist, but I shall partly do as you do, pampering your haughty intellect, so that presently you may do as I do, following my advice without putting limits to your humility. For St. Bernard testifies that perfect humility knows no limits. You put limits to your humility when you will not follow the advice of your spiritual superior, unless your intellect can grasp what it is that you must do. By this you can see that I want to be your superior, and so I do indeed, and I mean to be it. It is love, I believe, that prompts me in this, far more than any ability which I feel in myself, more than any wisdom or capacity or degree of spiritual advancement which I may have. May God amend anything which is wrong here, for He knows all, and I know only a part!

But now, to satisfy your arrogant intellect, let me tell you truly, in praise of this exercise, that if a soul which is so occupied had tongue and words to say what it feels, all the scholars in Christendom would be amazed at the wisdom it would speak. And indeed, all their great scholarship would seem by comparison the merest folly. And it is therefore no wonder though I am unable to tell you of the excellence of this exercise, I who can only bark or gabble like a brute beast. And God forbid that this exercise should be sullied by being forced into any form which an earthly tongue can tell of. No, this cannot be, and indeed it will not be, and God forbid that I should desire that it should be. For everything which is said about it is not it, but about it. But now, since we cannot say it, let us talk about it, to the reproof of proud intellects, and particularly of your intellect, which is the cause, or at least the occasion, of my now writing this.

First of all I ask you: what is the perfection of the human soul, and what are the properties of that perfection? And I answer for you, saying that the human soul's perfection is nothing else than a unity made between God and it in perfect love. This perfection is in itself so high and so pure, beyond human understanding, that it cannot itself be recognised or perceived. But where the properties of that perfection are truly seen and perceived, one may guess that the perfection is present, substantially and in plenty. And therefore you must now know what are the properties of that perfection, so that the pre-excellence of this spiritual exercise may be made known.

The properties of perfection, which it is proper for every perfect soul to possess, are virtues. And if you will truly regard in your own soul this exercise and the property and the condition of each separate virtue, you will find that all virtues are clearly and perfectly contained in the exercise, without any deflection or corruption of the intention.

I am not going to deal with any one particular virtue here, because that is unnecessary: you can find them all set out in several places in my other books. For this same exercise, if it be truly conceived, is that reverent affection, and that fruit taken from the tree, which I speak of in your[1] little *Epistle of Prayer*. This exercise is the Cloud of Unknowing, this is that secret love established in purity of spirit, this is the Ark of the Testament, this is the Mystical Theology of Dionysius, his wisdom and his treasure, his shining darkness and his unknown knowledge. This exercise is that which puts you to silence, silence of thought as well as of word. This makes your prayer very brief. In this you are taught to forsake the world and to despise it. And what is more, in this you are

---

[1] Most manuscripts have "thy": one however has "the", another "this".

taught to forsake and despise your own self, according to Christ's teaching in the gospel, where He says: *Si quis vult venire post me, abneget semet ipsum; tollat crucem suam et sequatur me.* That is, "Whoever wishes to come after Me, let him forsake himself, let him carry his cross and follow Me." This is as if, in the sense in which we now are speaking, He were to say to your understanding: "Whoever wishes to come humbly, not with Me but after Me, to the joy of heaven or to the mount of perfection." For Christ in His humanity went before, and we by grace come after Him. His humanity is more precious than grace, and grace is more precious than our humanity; and so He teaches us plainly that we can in no way follow Him to the mount of perfection, as we must if we undertake this exercise, unless it be by the prompting and leading of grace.

And this is very true: and you must indeed know, you and all others like you who may read or hear this work, that even though I exhort you so simply and boldly to apply yourselves to this exercise, none the less I feel truly, beyond error or doubt, that Almighty God with His grace must at all times be the chief prompter and worker, either by some means or immediately. You, or anyone like you, can only consent to it and experience it, except that during the time of this exercise your consenting and your experiencing must be actively disposed towards and prepared for this exercise in purity of spirit, and fittingly offered up to the Almighty, as your spirit can see and teach you by proof.

And since God in His goodness prompts and touches different souls differently, in some by means, in others immediately, who then dare say that God does not prompt you through what I write, or anyone else like you who may either read or hear this, I, all unworthy as I am, being His only means, save for His honorable will which works as He pleases? It seems to me to be like this: the exercise shall bear witness when the proof is operative. And therefore I beg you to dispose yourself to receive your Lord's grace in this way, and to hear what He says. "Whoever wishes to come after Me"—in the sense now explained—"let him forsake himself." How, I ask you, can a man forsake himself and the world more completely, despise himself and the world more utterly, than in scorning to think of any quality of being which he or the world may have?

For know indeed that though I command you to forget everything except the blind, naked feeling of your own being, nevertheless it is my wish, and it was at the beginning my intention, that you should forget to feel your own being as you feel the being of God. This was the reason why I proved to you at the beginning that God is your being. But because it seemed to me that you were not yet prepared to be exalted all at once to a spiritual feeling of God's being, because your spiritual feeling is inept, I therefore first commanded you to chew on the naked, blind feeling of your own being, so that you could climb step by step to the point where you could be prepared, through spiritual perseverance in this secret exercise, for this exalted feeling of God.

For it must always be your intention and your wish in this exercise to feel God; and even though at the beginning, because of your crudity and your spiritual ineptitude, I told you to enfold and clothe the feeling of your God inside the feeling of yourself, still you must, later, when through perseverance you have become more apt in purity of spirit, denude, despoil and utterly divest yourself of every sort of feeling of yourself, so that you are prepared to be clothed with the gracious feeling of God's own self.

And this truly is what a perfect lover must always do, utterly and entirely despoiling himself of himself for the sake of the thing that he loves, never allowing or suffering himself to be clothed except only in that thing which he loves; and that not only for a time, but to be everlastingly enfolded in it, in a full and final forgetting of himself. This is the exercise of love, which no-one can know but he who feels it. This is what our Lord teaches when He says: "Whoever wishes to love Me, let him forsake himself," as if to say: "Let him despoil himself of himself if he will be truly clothed in Me, Who am the ample garment of love, a lasting love that never shall have an end."

And therefore always when you regard your exercise, and you see and feel that it is yourself whom you feel and not God, you must mourn earnestly and long with all your heart to feel God, evermore desiring without ceasing to lose the wretched knowing and the foul feeling of your blind being; and you must yearn to flee from yourself as you would from poison. When you do this, you forsake yourself and bitterly despise yourself as your Lord commands you to do. And when you yearn so greatly, not to cease to be, for that would be madness and contempt of God, but to lose the knowing and the feeling of your being, as you must indeed, if God's love is to be felt as perfectly as it may in this life; and when you will see and feel that you cannot in any way attain your end, for a naked feeling of your blind being will constantly follow and accompany what you do, however much you seek to avoid this, unless, rarely and for a moment of time, God will allow you to feel Him in an abundance of love (but this naked feeling of your blind being will always thrust itself above you and between you and your God, just as when you were a beginner the qualities of your being would thrust themselves between you and your self): when this happens, your self will seem to you a heavy and painful load. Yes, may Jesus then help you, for then you will need Him; for all the sorrow which can exist outside yourself is nothing in comparison with this sorrow inside you. For then you yourself are your own cross. And yet this is a true exercise and the true way to our Lord, as He says Himself: "Let him carry his cross," first, in this pain caused by his self, and then "let him follow Me" into joy or into the mount of perfection, tasting the sweetness of My love when, divinely, he feels My self. Here you can see how much you need this sorrowful longing to lose yourself, and this painful carrying of yourself as a cross, before you can be united with God in a spiritual feeling of His self, which is perfect love. And now, if you have been touched and spiritually imprinted with this grace, you can see a little and feel a part of how this exercise excels all others.

Next I ask you, how would you attain to this exercise by the use of your reason? Indeed, you never could; nor yet by your clever approach, your subtle and strange imaginings and meditations, whatever their subject may be, your own miserable life, the Passion of Christ, our Lady's joys, or all the saints and angels of heaven, or any quality or subtlety or condition pertaining to your own being or to God's. Indeed, I had rather have such a naked, blind feeling of myself as I described before—a feeling not of what I do, but of myself, for, although many men say that what they do is themselves, this is not true, for I who do am one thing, and the deeds which I do are another, and this is also true of God, for He Who is is one, and His works are another—and I could weep and it might break my heart if I were to lack this feeling of God, this feeling that my self is a painful burden which I must bear, and it would inflame my desire to love and to desire this feeling of God, more than would all the subtle and strange imaginings and meditations that men can describe or discover written in books, however holy they may be, however fine they may appear to the subtle sight of your enquiring reason.

Nevertheless, these excellent meditations are the surest way which a sinner in his beginnings may take towards the spiritual feeling of himself and of God. It seems to me that it would be impossible to human understanding—even though God can do what He wishes—for a sinner to attain to rest in the spiritual feeling of himself and of God, unless he were first to see and to feel by imagining and meditating the earthly deeds of himself and of God, by sorrowing over those which are sorrowful, rejoicing over the joyful. Whoever does not come by this way does not come by the true way. Therefore he must stand outside, and he is furthest outside when he believes that he is most inside. For there are many who think that they are inside the spiritual door, when still they stand outside, and they shall still stand there until the time when in humility they search for the door. And there are some who find the door soon, and come inside it before others: and clearly this depends on the doorkeeper, not on their efforts or deserts.

How wonderful a house is the spiritual life, in which the Lord is not only Himself the doorkeeper but also the door! By His divinity He is the doorkeeper, by His humanity He is the door. He says this Himself in the Gospel: *Ego sum ostium. Per me si quis introierit, salvabitur: et siue egredietur siue ingredietur, pascua inveniet. Qui vero non intrat per ostium sed ascendit aliunde, ipse fur est et latro.* To your understanding this is as if He, agreeing with our sense, were

G

to say: "I Who by My divinity am omnipotent, and Who may as doorkeeper admit lawfully whom I wish, by what way I wish, still, because I wish there to be one straight way for all and one door open to all who wish to come, so that no-one may be excused for not knowing the way, I have clothed Myself in the nature of all men, and have made Myself so open that I am through My humanity the door, and whoever enters by Me shall be saved."

They enter by the door who, beholding Christ's Passion, sorrow for their wicked deeds, which are the cause of that Passion, bitterly blaming themselves, who have deserved such pain and do not suffer it, and with pity and compassion for our dear Lord, Who suffered so vilely what He did not deserve. And then they lift up their hearts to the love and the goodness of His divinity, in which He condescends to humble Himself to our mortal humanity. All these men enter by the door, and they shall be saved. And whether they go in, beholding the love and the goodness of His divinity, or out, beholding the suffering of His humanity, they shall find spiritual food of devotion in plenty, enough and to spare for the health and salvation of their souls, even though in this life they never advance further inside.

And whoever does not enter by this door, but in some other way scrambles up towards perfection by the subtle investigations and the laborious and fantastic exercise of his ungovernable, vagrant intellect, forsaking this common straight way which I have described and the true counsel of our spiritual fathers, such a man, whoever he may be, is not only a thief by night but a prowler by day. He is a thief by night, for he goes in the darkness of sin, relying more on his presumptuous trust in his own intellectual distinction and his own will than on any true counsel or on this common way just described. He is a prowler by day, for under the guise of a candid spiritual life he goes about secretly, stealing the outward signs and the language of contemplation, but he has not its fruits. And because sometimes he feels within himself a loving longing, little as it may be, to draw closer to God, he therefore, dazzled by such a token, believes that everything which he does is good, when in fact there is no more dangerous enterprise for a young man than to follow his own ardent desires, ungoverned by advice, especially when what he desires is to scramble up among high places, not only above himself but above the common straight way of Christians, which I have just described, and which by Christ's teaching I call the door of devotion and the surest entrance into contemplation which there can be in this life.

But let us now go on with those topics which are of particular concern to you in this work, and to all others who like you may be especially disposed to this exercise. If, as I say, this be the door to contemplation, must a man always stand outside it or on the threshold, shall no-one ever come inside? I can answer for you and say that it is good for him to stand outside, until his counsellors and his conscience tell him that most of the rust of his crude carnal nature has been rubbed away: and, most important, until he has been called inside by the secret monition of the Spirit of God, which monition is the readiest and surest witness which a man may have in this life that his soul is called and drawn inside to a more special exercise of grace.

This is how a man may have evidence that he is so touched: if, as he continues in his exercise, he feels as it were a tender and growing desire to come closer to God in this life, a desire intimated, it may be, by some special spiritual sensation, such as he hears men speak of or else finds described in books. But if a man does not feel himself moved by hearing and reading about spiritual exercises, especially in his own daily exercise, to a growing desire to come closer to God, let him go on standing still at the door, as a man called to be saved but not yet to be perfect.

And I warn you of one thing, whoever you may be who may read or hear what I write, especially when you come to this place where I make a difference between those called to be saved and those called to be perfect, in whichever direction you feel yourself called, see to it that you do not judge or discuss the deeds of God or of men. Regard only yourself, pay no attention to the others, whom He moves and calls to perfection and whom not, or why one is called sooner than another. If you do not wish to err, see to it that you do not judge. If you are called, give the glory to God, and pray that you do not fall. If you have not yet been called, pray humbly to God that He call you when it is His will. But do not teach Him what He ought to do. Leave Him alone. He has the power, the knowledge and the will to do what is best for you and everyone who loves Him. Find peace in your lot. Whichever it may be, you have no need to complain, for either is precious. The first is good, and necessary to every man. The second is better, let them obtain it who may, or rather, to speak more truly, let them have it who are given it and called to it by our Lord's grace. We in our vanity may struggle and strain towards this end, but truly without Him what we do is nothing, as He says Himself: *Sine me nihil potestis facere*. This, as you should understand it, is: "Without Me first stirring and principally moving, whilst you only consent and experience, you can do nothing which is perfectly pleasing to Me"; and the method of the exercise about which I write should be so.

I say all this to confuse the false presumption of those who, trusting in their fine scholarship or in their natural intelligence, wish always to be themselves the principal agents and God merely to allow or consent, when indeed in the contemplative life the contrary is the truth. For in contemplation alone all the subtle devices of scholarship and of natural intelligence must be dismissed far off, so that God may be the principal. None the less, at the proper times, in the active life, human scholarship and natural intelligence should co-operate with God in all lawful deeds in which His consent is assured by these three witnesses: Holy Scripture, counsel, and the custom of man's nature, rank, age and constitution. This is so far true that a man should not follow the moving of the spirit, however pleasing or holy that may seem, unless it come within the bounds of his acquired or natural knowledge, however much it may seem to be supported by all or any of these three witnesses which I have mentioned. Indeed, it is a great truth that a man should be greater than his works, and this is why the law of Holy Church provides that no man shall be consecrated bishop, the highest rank in the active life, unless it can be truly shown that the duties of a bishop are within his competence. So it is that in the active life a man's knowledge and natural intelligence must be employed to the full in his acts, God by His grace consenting and these three witnesses approving. There is every reason why this should be so, for all things in the active life are subject to human wisdom. But in the contemplative life the highest wisdom, human wisdom, that is, is utterly subjected, so that God may be the principal in the exercise, and man only he who consents and experiences.

This is how I understand those words of the Gospel: *Sine me nihil potestis facere,* "Without Me, you can do nothing";

they apply in one sense to men living the active life, in another to contemplatives. God must be present in active men,
either by His sufferance or consent or both, in anything
which they do, whether it be lawful and pleasing to Him
or not: but He must be present as principal in contemplatives, asking of them only that they experience and consent.
So that the general application is this: in all our deeds, lawful
and unlawful, active or contemplative, we can do nothing
without Him. In sin He is with us only by sufferance and
not by consent, and unless we humbly make amends that
shall lead to our final damnation. In our deeds which are
active and lawful He is with us both by sufferance and consent, to our shame if we lapse, to our great reward if we
progress. In our contemplative deeds He is with us as the
principal mover and agent, and we are only consenting and
experiencing, to our great perfection and to the spiritual
union of our souls with Him in perfect love. And since all
the men on earth can be divided into three categories,
sinners, actives and contemplatives, these words of our Lord
can therefore be said with a general application to the whole
world: "Without Me", by sufferance only and not by consent
in sinners, or both by sufferance and consent in actives, or,
greater than either, as the principal mover and agent in
contemplatives, "you can do nothing".

 I have used many words to convey a little meaning, but
still I have said all this to show you which are the things
in which you must employ your reason, and when you
should not, and in what manner God is with you in one
work, in what manner in another. Perhaps it may be that
now you know this you may avoid errors into which you
might have fallen, had I not said all this. So now that I
have said it, let it stay, though it may have little relevance
to our subject. But now let us continue with that.

You may ask me this question: If you will tell me, by what special sign or signs may I soonest know for certain that this growing desire which I feel in my daily exercise, and the pleasure with which I am moved when I read and hear about this subject, are truly God's calling me to a more special exercise of grace, as you describe in this work? And how may I know which it is; is my spirit being nourished and fed for me to remain where I am, and to persevere, by a grace given to all men, which you call the door and the common entrance of every Christian?

I shall give you the best answer I can, though that is only a feeble one. You have seen that in what I have written I have put before you two kinds of evidence, by which you must test whether God has called you in spirit to this exercise: one kind of evidence is internal, the other external. Of these two, neither can be entirely satisfying in this case, it seems to me, without the other. But when you have both and they agree, then you have sufficient and indubitable evidence.

The first of these two, the internal evidence, is this growing desire which you feel every day in your exercise. You must know this about your desire: that even though the desire be an act, in itself blind, of the soul—for the desire of the soul is just like such acts of the body as touching or walking, and such acts, you know yourself, are acts which can be performed without seeing—however blind an act this desire may be, still it is accompanied and followed by a kind of spiritual sight, which is in part a cause and a means to promote this desire. Have then constant regard every day for your exercise, what it is in itself: and then, if it be the recollection of your own miserable condition, the Passion of Christ, or any such other matter belonging to the common entrance of Christians of which I spoke before, and if it be that this spiritual sight, which so accompanies and follows your blind desire, springs from these common considerations, that is to me without doubt a sign that your desire is growing only to nourish and feed your spirit to remain where it is, and to go on acting in the grace given to you in common with all Christians, a sign that you are not called or moved by God to any more special grace.

Then, next, the second evidence, the external evidence, which is when you feel yourself pleasurably moved when you read or hear about this matter. I call this evidence external, because it comes from outside, through the windows of your physical senses, when you hear or see at the time for reading. Concerning this second evidence, if it be that this pleasurable moving which you feel when you hear and read of this matter does not last or persist in you except whilst you are reading or listening, or if it ceases soon afterwards, so that you neither wake nor sleep in it nor with it, and, particularly, so that it does not accompany your daily exercise, as it were going ahead and thrusting itself between you and the exercise, moving and leading your desire: then this is a true sign, as I see it, that this pleasurable moving which you feel when you hear and read about this matter is only the natural joy which every Christian soul has when hearing or reading about the truth. And the soul feels this joy particularly when it sometimes hears, skilfully described and truly explained to it, those properties of perfection which are the purest characteristics of the soul, and, most of all, God. This is a sign that you are not spiritually touched by grace nor called by God to any exercise of grace more special than that which is the door and the common entry for all Christian men.

But if it be[1] that this pleasurable moving which you feel

---

[1] The whole of this following long paragraph consists of a series of subordinate clauses, describing the nature of the evidence which will lead to the conclusion stated in the final, principal clause: "still do not be too sad—"

when you read and hear about this matter is in itself so plentiful that it goes to bed with you, gets up with you the next day, follows you round all day long, whatever you may be doing, pulls you away from your usual daily exercise and comes between it and you, accompanies and follows your desire so that it seems to you either that it is all the same desire or that you do not know what it is which has altered your demeanour and made your face cheerful: if while it lasts everything brings you comfort and nothing can distress you: if you are willing to run a thousand miles to talk to someone else who, you know, has truly felt all this, and yet when you find him you cannot say anything about it, try as you may, you who wish to speak of nothing else but it: if your words are few but full of fruit and fire, so that one little word from your mouth contains a whole world of wisdom, which still seems only folly to them who live in their intellects: if your silence is gentle, your speech pithy, your prayer secret, your pride a purified one, your manners humble, your joy gentle, your mood mild enough to play with little children[1]: if you love to be in solitude and sit alone, for it seems to you that people would only hinder you, unless they are willing to do as you do: if you neither want to read books nor hear them read, unless they are concerned with it, so that your internal evidence and your external evidence may agree and be united: yes, and if both internal and external evidence, with every work which has been written in their support, after you have once learned everything or something of these works, ceases for a while, so that you are left as it were barren, deprived not only of your old accustomed evidence but of the feeling of this new fervour, so that you seem to have fallen between two stools,

---

[1] So the present translator guesses at the meaning of this obscure phrase, which the scribes of the several manuscripts found difficult and altered variously: one has made it read "to play with the little child Jesus".

G*

not having either and wanting them both, still do not be too sad because of this, but endure it meekly and patiently wait for our Lord's pleasure; for now, it seems to me, you are launched upon the spirit's sea, and you are being ferried over from the earthly life to the life of the spirit.

It may happen that now many great storms and temptations will arise, and you will not know where to run for safety. You will feel that you lack everything, common grace and special grace. But do not be too afraid, though it may seem that you have good cause: but instead have a lover's faith in our Lord, for He is not far off, however little of His love you may then feel. He shall look upon you, it may be very soon, and touch you again, with a more burning moving of that same grace than any other that you ever felt before. And then it will seem to you that you are healed again and all restored, but this is only for a while; for suddenly it will all go again, and you are there, barren, in your boat, battered about by the storm, now here, now there, never knowing where you are or where you are going. Still do not despair, for He shall come, and very soon, I promise you, when it shall please Him to relieve you, and mightily to deliver you of all your misery, more gloriously by far than ever He did before. And truly, if again He were to leave you, still He will come again, and every time, if you will endure His absence with patient humility, He will return more gloriously and joyfully than before; and all this He does because He wants to fit you to His will as a leather glove fits your hand.

And since sometimes He goes away and sometimes comes again, therefore in this double action He wishes doubly to test you in secret and to work you into his His own work. When your fervour is withdrawn, which seems to you as if

He goes away, though this is not so, He is in fact testing your patience. For you should truly know that though God may sometimes withdraw from you these sensible sweetnesses, these fervent feelings and these flaming desires, still for all this He never withdraws His grace from His chosen children; for indeed I cannot believe that His special grace can ever be withdrawn from His chosen children who have once been touched by it, unless this were caused by mortal sin. But all these sensible sweetnesses, these fervent feelings and these flaming desires, which are not in themselves grace but only the signs of grace, are often withdrawn from us to test our patience, and often for many other spiritual benefits to us, more than we think. For grace is in itself so exalted, so pure and so spiritual that it cannot be felt by our senses. The signs can be felt, but not it. And so sometimes our Lord will withdraw your sensible fervours, both to increase your patience and to test it, and not for this reason only, but for many others which I shall not deal with now. Let us go on with our subject.

By the excellence, the frequency and the increasing of these sensible feelings which I have described, and which might seem to you to be His coming, though this may not be true, He wishes to nourish and feed your spirit so that it may endure and live in loving and glorifying Him. So that in this way, through patience in the absence of these sensible feelings, which are the signs of grace, and through that living nourishing and that loving feeding of your spirit when they are present, it is His will to make you by both together so joyfully obedient and so happily pliant to perfection and to spiritual unity, that is, to His own will, where unity is perfect love, that you will be as glad and happy to forgo such sensible feelings when that is His will as you would be to have them and feel them constantly through all your life.

And now your love is both chaste and perfect, and it is now that you see both God and your love, and that you also feel Him nakedly through spiritual unity with His love in the highest part of your spirit, as He is in Himself; but you feel this blindly, as you must here on earth, utterly despoiled of yourself and nakedly clothed in Him as He is, neither clothed nor enfolded in any of these sensible feelings, however sweet or holy they may be, which may come to you in this life. But He is properly and perfectly perceived in purity of spirit, and felt in Himself as He is, removed far off from any fantasy or false opinion which may happen in this life.

This seeing and feeling of God as He is in Himself can no more be separated from God in Himself, as you understand Him who see and feel in this way, than God Himself can be separated from His own being, for They are only one, both in substance and in nature. So that just as God cannot be apart from His being, because of Their natural unity, so that soul who sees and feels in this way cannot be apart from that which he sees and feels in this way, because of their unity in grace.

So you see that in this way and by these signs you can to some extent feel and partly test how you are called and moved, and how well, in grace, in your inward spiritual exercise and in your outward reading and hearing about this subject. And then, when it may happen that you, or anyone else like you in his spiritual life, have had true experience of all of these signs—or of some of them, for in the beginning there are very few who are so especially touched and marked by this grace that they are able all at once to experience through true feeling all of these signs, though still it is enough to experience one or two, though one may not in the beginning experience them all—if you feel that you have truly had experience of one or two, and this is proved by honest examination of the Scriptures and of the counsel given to you and of your conscience, then it will be profitable for you presently to desist from elaborate meditations and subtle imaginings about the qualities of your being and of God's, and about your deeds and God's, with which meditations and imaginings your intellect has been fed and by which you have been led from the life of the physical world into that competence of grace in which you are now placed, and it will be profitable for you to learn how you ought to be occupied in the spirit, feeling about yourself and God, about Whom previously you have understood so much through thinking and imagining about your deeds.

Christ upon this earth gave us an example of this, for if it were true that there could be no greater perfection in this life than in regarding and loving His humanity, I do not believe that He would then have ascended into heaven whilst this world lasted, nor have withdrawn His bodily presence from His special lovers here on earth. But because there was a greater perfection which one can attain in this life, that is, a pure spiritual feeling in the love of His divinity, He therefore said to His disciples, who were grieved that they must lose His bodily presence, rather as you grieve when you must lose your careful meditations and your elaborate and subtle intellectual processes, that it was for their profit that in His body He should leave them: *Expedit vobis ut ego vadam*: "It is profitable for you that in the body I leave you". A commentator[1] has said about this text: "Un-

---

[1] St. Augustine in his *Sermons,* as Professor Hodgson points out.

less the form of His humanity be taken from before our bodily eyes, the love of His divinity cannot be fixed in our spiritual eyes". And so I say to you that it is sometimes profitable to abandon the laborious exercise of your intellect and to learn to taste a little, spiritually and by feeling, the love of your God.

And you shall come to this feeling by the way which I tell you, and by the help of preventive grace: and this way is that you constantly and incessantly lean upon the naked feeling of yourself, always offering up your being to God as the most precious offering which you can make. But take care, as I have often said, that this feeling be naked, for fear of being deceived. If it is naked it will be very hard for you at the beginning to persist in it for any length of time, and, as I said before, that is because your intellect finds nothing in this to feed it. But pay no attention: indeed, so much the better. Let your intellect starve for a while, I beg you, let it do without its natural pleasure in its own knowledge, for it has been truly said that a man by nature desires knowledge; but indeed man cannot taste of the spiritual feeling of God except by grace, however much natural or acquired knowledge he may have. And therefore I beg you to seek for feeling rather than for knowledge; because often knowledge deceives through pride, but humble, loving feeling cannot beguile. *Scientia inflat, caritas aedificat:* In knowledge there is travail, in feeling there is rest.

But now you may say: "What is this rest of which you speak? It seems to me that it is travail, and torment, and not rest at all. If I set about doing as you say, on every side I find affliction and strife. My intellect tries to pull me in one direction, and on the other side I want to feel God and to be without any feeling of myself, and that I cannot do, so that on every side there is strife and affliction; and it seems to me a strange sort of rest that you talk about".

To this I reply: You are not practised in this exercise, and that is why it is more of an affliction to you; but if you were practised in it, you would not voluntarily come out of it, not to have all the bodily delight and rest in the world. And yet it is an affliction, and a labour too. But still I call it rest, for the soul has no doubt what it must do, and also because the soul is made certain, when it does this, that it will not greatly go astray.

WALTER HILTON

The Scale of Perfection

EXCERPTS FROM BOOKS I AND II

THE SCALE OF PERFECTION *presents greater problems to its editors than perhaps any other mediaeval English mystical text. This is partly because of the great number of surviving manuscripts, English and Latin, and early printed editions, and their very complex inter-relations, which some scholars have thought to reflect Hilton's own after-thoughts in reediting his work. We now can hope for critical editions of* THE SCALE, *based on work begun by Miss Helen Gardner, continued by Mrs. Rosemary Dorward, and now being completed, Book I by Professor T. Dunning, C. M., assisted by Miss Clare Kirchberger, Book II by Mr. S. S. Hussey. These five scholars have all helped the present editor by advising him on the choice of manuscripts and lending to him photostats and other unpublished material; and he has used what they consider the best single manuscript for either book, Cambridge University Library Add. 6686 for Book I, British Museum Harley 6579 for Book II. The authorities of the Cambridge University Library and of the British Museum have permitted this, and Dom Gerard Sitwell and Burns & Oates of London have allowed him occasionally to cite readings from Dom Sitwell's modernised edition (see* 45).

THE SCALE OF PERFECTION

CHAPTER 4: *Of the first degree of contemplation.*

CONTEMPLATIVE LIFE has three degrees. The first part is a knowledge of God and spiritual things, acquired by reason through men's teaching and the study of Holy Writ, a knowledge without spiritual affection and that interior savour which is experienced by a special gift of the Holy Spirit. This degree of contemplative life is particularly known to certain learned men and great scholars, who through long study and work on Holy Writ attain this knowledge, more or less according to the ingenuity of their natural intelligence and their perseverance in study, through use of the common gift which God gives to every man who has the use of reason. This knowledge is good, and it may be called a degree of contemplation, in as much as it is a vision of truth and a knowledge of spiritual things. Nevertheless, it is the mere similitude and shadow of true contemplation, for it does not bring a spiritual savour in God, nor the interior sweetness of love which no man may feel unless he be in great love: for His love is our Lord's true well, to which no stranger to Him comes. Yet this kind of knowledge is common to good men and to bad, for it can be obtained without God's love, and it is therefore not true contemplation: and very often heretics and hypocrites and men devoted to carnality have more of such knowledge than many true Christians, and yet these men have not the love of God. . . . Such knowledge by itself is mere water, tasteless and cold, and therefore let them who possess it and who would transform it[1] offer it up humbly to our Lord and beg Him in His grace to give it His blessing and turn the water into wine, as He answered His Mother's prayer at the marriage feast: that is, ask Him to turn this tasteless knowledge into wisdom and this cold and naked reason into spiritual light and burning love, by the gift of the Holy Spirit.

CHAPTER 5: *Of the second degree of contemplation.*

THE SECOND degree of contemplation consists chiefly in affection without understanding of spiritual things: and this is often found in simple and uneducated people who give themselves up entirely to devotion; and it is felt in this way. A man—or a woman—will be meditating upon God, and will feel the fervour of love and a spiritual sweetness in recollecting His Passion or any of His deeds as man, or will feel great confidence in God's goodness and mercy, in the forgiveness of his sins and God's great gifts of grace. In his affection, it may be, he will feel the fear of God, with great awe for His secret judgments which he cannot see and for His righteousness. In prayer, perhaps, he will feel his heart's intention drawn upward, away from all earthly things, and mounting with the full concentration of all its powers into our Lord by fervent desire and with spiritual delight. Even so, at such times he will not receive a clear vision of comprehension of particular spiritual mat-

---

[1] This phrase is the present editor's conjecture: some words seem to be missing in the manuscript.

ters, of mysteries of the Faith or of Holy Writ; what he
will feel is that at these times nothing pleases him so much
as to pray or think of God, and he does this for the savour
and delight and consolation which he finds in it. But still
he cannot explain properly what it is, though he knows very
well that he feels it, for out of it rise many sweet tears, many
burning aspirations and many silent lamentations, which
scour and cleanse the heart of all its filth of sin, and make
it melt in a marvellous sweetness of Jesus Christ. The heart
is obedient and pliant and prompt to do all the will of God,
to the point where it seems to him that he does not care what
will become of him, if only God's will be done. And there
will be many other such aspirations, more than I know how
to describe. Such a feeling is not to be obtained without
great grace, and I believe the man who obtains it to have
the love of God at that time, and this love cannot be lost
or diminished, even though the fervour may die away, unless love be lost through mortal sin: and to know this is a
great consolation. This may be called the second degree of
contemplation.

CHAPTER 6: *Of the lower stage of the second degree of contemplation.*

E VEN so, this second degree has two stages. Men who
live the active life may by grace have the lower
stage of this feeling, when they are visited by our Lord
as powerfully and as fervently as those who devote themselves entirely to the contemplative life and who obtain
this gift: but in active men it does not last so long. Also, in
active men this feeling of fervour does not always come
when they wish, nor does it last for long. It comes and

goes, according to the will of Him Who gives it, and therefore let him who obtains it humble himself, and thank God, and keep it hidden, except perhaps to his confessor; and let him use discretion to keep it as long as he can, and when it is taken away let him not be too dismayed, but let him stand firm in faith and in great hope, patiently waiting till it shall come again. This is a little foretaste of the sweetness of the love of God, of which David in the Psalms said this: *Gustate et videte, quoniam suavis est Dominus:* "Taste and see the sweetness of our Lord".

CHAPTER 7: *Of the higher stage of the second degree of contemplation.*

B UT THE HIGHER STAGE of this degree of contemplation cannot be obtained or kept, except by those who are in great peace of body and of soul. Such men by the grace of Jesus Christ and by long physical and spiritual effort feel peace of heart and purity of conscience, so that nothing pleases them so much as to sit still, their bodies at rest, and continually to pray to God and to think of our Lord, and sometimes to think of the Holy Name of Jesus, which has become for them such a consolation and delight that they, recollecting it, feel their love fed, not only by the Holy Name, but by all other prayers, the "Our Father", the "Hail Mary", hymns, psalms, and the other pious prayers of Holy Church—all are as it were transformed into spiritual rejoicing and sweet singing, by which they are comforted and strengthened against every sin, and greatly relieved of bodily distress. Of this degree St. Paul says this: *Nolite inebriari vino, sed implemini Spiritu Sancto, loquentes vobismetipsis in hymnis et psalmis et canticis spiritualibus;*

cantantes et psallentes in cordibus vestris Domino: "Do not be drunk with wine, but be filled by the Holy Spirit, speaking to yourselves in hymns and psalms and spiritual songs, chanting and singing psalms in your hearts to our Lord". Whoever has this grace, let him keep himself in humility, always wanting to achieve a greater knowledge and feeling of God in the third degree of contemplation.

CHAPTER 8: *Of the third degree of contemplation.*

THE THIRD DEGREE of contemplation, which is as perfect as it can be in this life, consists in both cognition and affection. That is, it consists in knowing God and loving Him perfectly; and this comes when a man's soul is first cleansed from all sins, and formed again, through the fullness of virtues, into the image of Jesus. Then, next, when that man is visited by grace, he is taken up, away from all earthly and carnal affections, from empty thoughts and idle speculations about all physical matters, and he is as it were ravished out of his bodily senses, and then by the grace of the Holy Spirit he is illumined, to see through understanding that truth which is God, and also to see spiritual things, with a soft, sweet, burning love which is so perfect in him that by the power of this love to ravish him the soul is united and made conformable to the image of the Trinity. The beginnings of this contemplation may be felt in this life, but its perfection is reserved for the joy of Heaven. About this union and conformity of the soul with God, St. Paul says this: *Qui adhaeret Deo, unus spiritus est cum illo:* "Whoever" by the ravishing of love "is united with God, then God and his soul" are not two, but they "both are one", not one in flesh but in one spirit. And truly in this union a marriage is made between God and the soul which shall never be dissolved.

CHAPTER 9: *Of the distinction of the third from the second degree of contemplation: and in praise of the third degree.*

THAT SECOND DEGREE may be called burning love in devotion, but this is burning love in contemplation. That is the lower degree, this is the higher: that is sweeter to our bodily senses, this is sweeter to our spiritual senses, for it is more inward, more spiritual, more precious and more wonderful; for it is truly a foretaste and as it were a sight of heavenly joy, not a clear sight but half in darkness, yet this vision will be completed and fully illumined in the joy of heaven, as St. Paul says: *Videmus nunc per speculum in aenigmate, tunc autem facie ad faciem:* "Now we see God by means of a mirror and as it were in darkness, but in heaven we shall see plainly, face to face". This is the illumining of the understanding in the delights of love, as David says in the Psalter: *Et nox mea illuminatio mea in deliciis meis:* "My night is my light in my delights". That second degree is milk for children, this is solid food for grown men, with knowledge gained by experience of telling good from evil, as St. Paul says: *Perfectorum est solidus cibus qui habent sensus ad discretionem boni et mali.* No-one can have the exercise and the full use of this gift, unless he be first reformed into the likeness of Jesus by the fullness of virtues; and I do not believe that any man still living in the mortal flesh can have it habitually and in its fullness, but only from time to time when he is visited by grace; and as I understand from the writings of holy men, such times are very brief, for a man will quickly relapse into sobriety of his physical nature, and yet it is love which is the cause of all this exercise. . . . and all this, as St. Paul says, is worked by the Holy Spirit in man's soul. God bestows this degree of contemplation where He pleases, to the learned or the simple, to men and women, to those whose lives are busy with government of the Church or to solitaries: but it is a special gift and not a common one. And, furthermore, though a man of active life may have this gift by a special grace, still, as I believe, no man may have the full use of the gift unless he be a solitary, vowed to the contemplative life.

(CHAPTER 10: *that the physical phenomena of mysticism may be good or evil.*
CHAPTER 11: *How to distinguish between such good and evil phenomena.*)

CHAPTER 12: *What fastens Jesus to man's soul, and what loosens Him from it.*

A GOOD WILL and a great desire for Jesus and for Him alone, to have Him and to see Him spiritually in His bliss: this is what fastens and ties Him to a man's soul. The greater this desire is, the tighter Jesus is fastened to the soul: the less this desire is, the looser He is tied. Therefore, whatever spirit or whatever feeling it may be which diminishes this desire and would draw it down, away from the soul's natural ascent towards Jesus, and would attract desire towards itself, such a spirit wants to loosen and untie Jesus from the soul, and therefore it cannot come from God but is of the old enemy's operation. Yet if a spirit or a feeling or an angel's revelation increases this desire, if it ties the knot of love or of devotion for Jesus tighter, if it opens your soul's eyes wider to spiritual knowledge, if it makes your soul humbler within itself, then this spirit is from God. This will show you partly why you ought not to allow your heart deliberately to rest or completely to delight in any physical sensation deriving from spiritual consolations or sweetnesses, however good they may in themselves be: in your own estimation you should consider them as nothing or little in comparison with your spiritual aspirations, nor must you set your heart upon them, but forget them if you can, and always try your best to attain to a spiritual feeling of God. You would attain to that feeling if you could know and feel God's wisdom, His endless power, and His great goodness in Himself and in the beings He created. For this is contemplation, and the other is not: and St. Paul said this: *In charitate radicati et fundati, ut possitis comprehendere cum omnibus sanctis quae sit longitudo et latitudo, sublimitas et profundum:* "Be rooted and grounded in love, so that you might know", he says, not noises in your ears nor a sweet taste in your mouth, nor any such physical sensation, but so that you might know and feel "with the saints what is the length" of God's everlasting being, "the breadth and the wonderful love and goodness of God, the height of His almighty majesty, and the unfathomable depths of God's wisdom".

CHAPTER 13: *How a contemplative man should be occupied, and in what matters.*

To KNOW and to feel these matters spiritually ought to be the occupation of a contemplative man, for in these four can be understood full knowledge of all spiritual things. This occupation is the very thing which St.

Paul desired, when he said: *Unum vero, quae retro sunt obliviscens, in anteriora me extendam, sequor si quomodo comprehendam supernum bravium:* this means: "It is as if one thing is left to me to desire, that I might forget everything which is behind me, and always reach out beyond with my heart, to feel and to seize the sovereign reward of everlasting bliss". All physical things are behind, all spiritual things are beyond, and therefore St. Paul wished to forget all physical things, including his own body, so that he might see spiritual things.

CHAPTER 14: *How virtue begins in reason and the will, and is finished and perfected in love and delight.*

Now I have told you a little about contemplation, about what it is or ought to be, so that you could recognize it, and set it up as a target in front of your soul's eye, and long all your life to attain to any part of it, by the grace of our Lord Jesus Christ. This is how to conform the soul to God, and it cannot be done unless the soul first be reformed, by the fullness of virtues turned into affection, and this is when a man loves virtue because in itself it is good. There are many men who posses virtues, such as humility, patience, love towards their fellow Christians, and such others; but they have them only in their reason and will, without any spiritual delight in them or love for them. In exercising these virtues they often feel resentment or weariness or bitterness, and still they exercise them, merely because they are impelled by reason through fear of God. Such men possess virtues in reason and in their will, but they have not the love of them in affection; but when, by God's grace and through spiritual and intellectual exercise, their reason is turned into light and their will into love, then they possess virtues in affection. For such a man has then bitten so well on the nut's bitter shell that he has broken it, and he feeds upon the kernel. That is, the virtues which at first were so laborious to exercise are now turned into pure delight and savour, when a man takes pleasure in patience, in humility, in purity, in sobriety and in charity, as he does in any other delight. Truly, when virtues are thus transformed into affection, a man may have the second part of contemplation, and yet, truly, he will not have come to the third part. Now, since virtues dispose you towards contemplation, you must use certain means to attain to virtues.

(CHAPTER 15: *Study of the Scriptures and the Faith; meditation, and constant, devout prayer are the means to contemplation*).

CHAPTER 16: *What a man ought to use and to reject by the virtue of humility.*

Now, if you are to use these spiritual exercises wisely and to labour in them steadfastly, you must begin very humbly. There are three things which you need to have at the beginning, upon which you shall base all your work, as it were on a firm foundation. These three are humility, firm faith and a perfect intention towards God. First you must have humility, in this way. In your will and in your feeling you must, if you can, consider yourself unfit to live among men and women, unworthy to serve God in communication with His servants, useless to your fellow Christians, lacking both the knowledge and the power to carry out the good deeds of an active life in helping your fellow Christians as other men and women do; and that is is why you are shut up in a house alone, a wretch cast out and rejected by all men and women, so that you shall not injure any man or woman by your bad example, since you cannot be of use to them in doing good deeds. Then, further, you must look and see that since you are incapable of serving our Lord by bodily, external works, how much more you should consider yourself unable and unfit to serve Him spiritually in any interior occupation. For our Lord is a spirit, as the prophet says: *Spiritus ante faciem nostram Christus Dominus:* "Our Lord Christ is a spirit before our face", and His natural service is spiritual, as He says Himself: *Veri adoratores adorabunt Patrem in spiritu et veritate:* "True servants shall worship the Father in spirit and truth". You, then, who are so crude, so ignorant, so carnal, so blind in spiritual things, and especially concerning your own soul— which you ought first to know, if presently you are to attain to the knowledge of God—how could you feel yourself able or fit to have the degree and the semblance of contemplative life, which, as I have said, consists principally in the spiritual knowledge and love of God? I say this to you, not so that you should rue your intention and take an aversion to your enclosed life, but so that you should truly feel humility in your heart, if you can; for it is true and not lies, and, even though you do feel so, still you must yearn night and day with all your power to come as near as you can to the state which you have taken upon you, believing steadfastly that that by God's mercy is the best state for you to labour in. And though it may be that you cannot attain to its perfection here in this life, you must yearn to begin that perfection, trusting firmly to have its perfection by God's mercy in the bliss of heaven. Truly, that is my own life; and

I feel myself so wretched and so frail and so carnal and so far from feeling truly what I say and have said that I can do nothing but cry for mercy, and long for it as much as I can, in hope that our Lord in His grace will bring me to it in the bliss of heaven. Do as I do, and do better, as God gives you grace. To feel this humility will put out of your heart unreasonable regard for other men's misconduct and judging other men's deeds, and it will move you to regard only yourself, just as if there were no other living beings but God and you: and you will judge yourself and consider yourself viler and more wretched than any living creature, so that you shall hardly be able to endure yourself because of the greatness of your sins and the filth which you will find and feel inside you. You must feel this sometimes, if you wish to be truly humble, for I tell you in truth, if you wish to be truly humble, a venial sin in you should seem more grievous and more painful, and should sometimes seem to your eyes greater, than the many mortal sins of other men. That thing which most estranges your soul and hinders it most from the feeling and knowledge of God ought to be most grievous and painful to you; but a venial sin which you commit hinders you more from the feeling and knowledge of God than other men's sins, however great, can do. So it seems that within your own heart you ought to be enraged against yourself, and to hate and condemn every kind of sin in yourself which hinders you from seeing God, more zealously than you should condemn the faults of any other man. For if your heart be purified of your own sins, truly the sins of all other men will not harm you; and if therefore you wish to find rest here and in the bliss of heaven, according to the advice of one of the holy fathers, say every day "What am I?", and judge no man.

(CHAPTER 17: *Our right to find fault with others.*

CHAPTER 18: *That the humble should respect others, and consider themselves inferior).*

CHAPTER 19: *What men should do who lack humility in affection: and that they should not be over-anxious because of this.*

NEVERTHELESS, if you cannot feel this humility in your heart with affection as you would wish, do the best that you can: humble yourself in your will and by your reason, believing that it ought to be as I have said, even though you cannot feel it, and consider yourself the more wretched because you cannot feel yourself to be what you truly are. And if you do this, even though your flesh may rebel and will not consent to your will, do not be too anxious, but bear and suffer the false feelings of your flesh as a punishment; and then you will despise and blame those feelings, and quell your heart's rebellion, as if you were well satisfied to be trampled and spurned under every man's feet, as if you were a thing cast out. And so by the grace of Jesus Christ you will greatly reduce the stirrings of pride, and the virtue of humility, which first was only in your will, shall be turned into affective feeling. Without this virtue either in a true will or in feeling, whoever disposes himself to serve God in the contemplative life will stumble about like a blind man, and never attain his object. The higher he climbs through bodily penances and other virtues, if he has not this virtue of humility, the lower he falls; for as St. Gregory says, The man who cannot perfectly despise himself has still not found the humble wisdom of our Lord Jesus.

(CHAPTER 20: *That lack of humility is a characteristic of error*).

CHAPTER 21: *What things men ought to believe by firm faith.*

THE SECOND THING which you ought to have is a firm faith in all the articles of the Faith, and in the sacraments of Holy Church, believing steadfastly in them with all the will of your heart. And even though you may feel some stirring in your heart against any of them, by the enemy's suggestion, to put you in doubt or confusion about them, be steadfast, and not too anxious because you feel such stirrings. But abandon your own intelligence, without arguing or elaboration, and fix your faith generally in the Faith of Holy Church, and pay no attention to the stirrings of your heart which seem to you to be in opposition to the Faith. For the stirrings which you feel are not your faith: your faith is the Faith of Holy Church, though you may never see it or feel it. And then bear such stirrings patiently, as a scourge of our Lord, by which He wishes to cleanse your heart and make your faith steadfast. And you must also love and reverence in your heart the laws and the ordinances made by the prelates and rulers of Holy Church, either in definition of the Faith, or in the sacraments, or in the general government of all Christian men. Assent to them, humbly and loyally, though it may be that you do not know the reason for their ordinances, and though some may seem to you to be unreasonable. You must not judge or condemn them, but accept them and respect them, though they may have little to do with you. Nor must you accept any opinion or fantasy or strange idea which represents itself as a greater form of sanctity, as some foolish people do, whether it be of your own brain or of the teaching of some other person, if it be contrary to the smallest ordinance or to the general teaching of all Holy Church. And furthermore, you must steadfastly believe that you have been ordained by our Lord to be saved as one of His chosen by His mercy: and do not move from this belief, whatever you hear or see, whatever temptation you may be in. And though you may seem to yourself so great a wretch that you deserve to sink down into hell, because you do no good and do not serve God as you ought, still hold fast to this belief and hope, and ask for mercy, and all shall be very well. Yes, though all the devils out of hell, appearing in human form, were to say to you, awake or asleep, that you will never be saved, or if all the men upon earth, or all the angels in heaven—if such a thing could be—were to say the same to you, still you ought not to believe them, or to be moved at all from your belief and hope in salvation. I say this to you because some are so weak and so simple that when they have devoted themselves wholly, as best they can, to serve God, if they feel any stirring, inside themselves by the contrivance of the enemy or from without by some word from the devil's prophets, whom men call soothsayers, suggesting that they will not be saved, or that their order or form of living is not pleasing to God, they are overwhelmed and overthrown by such words, and in their ignorance they sometimes fall into deep melancholy and, as it were, into despair of their salvation. Therefore it seems to me that it is profitable for every creature, who by the grace of our Lord Jesus wishes altogether to forsake sin and who, as well as his conscience tells him, allows no mortal sin to remain in him without confessing it quickly, and who humbles himself before the sacraments of Holy

H

Church, to have faith in his salvation: and even more should they have such faith who give themselves wholly to God and do all that is in their power to avoid venial sins. And on the other hand, it is just as dangerous for a man who is knowingly living in mortal sin to have faith in his salvation, and in that hope to refuse to abandon his sin and to humble himself loyally to God and to Holy Church.

CHAPTER 22: *How a firm intention is necessary to those who would please God, and discretion in their bodily works.*

THE THIRD THING which you must have at your beginning is an intention complete and firm: that is, all your will and all your desire must be only to please God, for that is to love Him, and without it everything that you do would be nothing. You must fix your intention upon always seeking and labouring to please Him as you can, never willingly desisting from good occupations, either worldly or spiritual: for you must not in your heart fix any limit, saying that you will serve God for so long and then allow your mind wilfully to decline into idle thoughts and empty occupations, thinking that you must do this to preserve your health, leaving no guard over your heart and your good works, seeking rest and comfort for a while outside for your intellect, or indulging in worldly folly as if it were for the refreshment of your spirit, to make it keener afterwards for spiritual labour. I do not believe in such things. I do not say that you will always be able to carry out your intention in your acts, because you will often be hindered by physical necessities, eating, sleeping and speaking, and by the weakness of your flesh, and you will be held back however hard you try. But I would wish your intention and your will always to be completely directed towards spiritual labour, never to be idle but always lifting up your heart by desire towards God and the bliss of heaven. Whether you are eating or drinking or occupied in any other earthly business, as far as you can, never willingly abandon your intention. For if you preserve it, it will make you keen and eager in your labour, and if through weakness or carelessness you fall into any idle occupation or into frivolous speech, your intention will strike at your heart as sharply as a hammer, it will rouse you and make you dislike all vanities and turn back quickly to some good occupation. For so far as your health is concerned, you must use discretion in eating, drinking and sleeping, and in every kind of physical penance, or in long-continued vocal prayer, or in any physical manifestation of devotion such as weeping, and also in intellectual exercise concerning spiritual matters at times when one feels no grace. In all these actions it is good to observe discretion, sometimes leaving off, for moderation is the best, except only in destroying sin by guarding your heart, and in everlasting desire for virtues and for the bliss of heaven: and exercise no moderation when you are seeking the spiritual knowledge and the love of God, for the more there is of this, the better. For in your heart you must hate sin and all earthly loves and fears without ceasing, and you must love virtues and purity, and desire them without pausing, if you can. I do not say that this is necessary for salvation, but I believe that it is profitable, and if you observe it, you shall profit more in one year in virtues than you will in seven without this intention.

CHAPTER 25: *How men ought to pray, and where the recollection should be directed in prayer.*

A<small>ND IN</small> your prayer you must not set your heart upon any earthly thing, but all your effort must be towards withdrawing your recollection from every earthly thing, so that your desire may be as it were bare and naked of all things of the world, always mounting towards God, Whom you may neither see in the flesh nor in His earthly likeness by any intellectual effort. But you can feel His goodness and His grace, when your desire is eased and helped, and as it were made powerful and free from all earthly thoughts and affections, and is greatly lifted up by a spiritual power into spiritual savour and delight in God, and kept silent in it for much of the time of your prayer, so that you have no great remembrance of any earthly thing, or, if you have, the remembrance harms you little. If you pray in this way, you can pray well: for prayer is nothing else than a mounting desire of the heart into God through withdrawal from every earthly thought. And this is why it is compared with a fire, which by its own nature mounts from the earth, always up into the air. In just the same way, your desire in prayer, when it is touched and illumined by that spiritual fire which is God, by nature always mounts to Him from Whom it came.

(CHAPTER 26: *The "fire of love" is spiritual, not physical.*

CHAPTER 27: *Of the efficacy of vocal prayer to those who are beginners in contemplation*).

CHAPTER 28: *How dangerous it is for men who at the beginning of their conversion to God abandon too soon the common prayers ordained by Holy Church and give themselves up completely to meditation.*

So BY THIS you can see that these men, if there are any such, who at the beginning of their conversion or soon afterwards, when they have felt a little spiritual solace, either in devotion or in perception, though they have not yet achieved stability, abandon such vocal prayer too soon, along with other simple exercises, and devote themselves entirely to meditation, are not wise, because often, during their repose while they meditate, they imagine and think about spiritual things in the light of their own intellect, and they follow their own inclinations, and they have not yet received the grace which is needed for this. Therefore they often overexert their intellect because they lack discretion, and overtax their physical powers, and so they fall into fantasies and strange ideas or into manifest error, and through such foolish conduct hinder the grace which God gives them. The cause of all this is their secret pride and presumption, so that when they have experienced a little grace they think that this puts them far above others, and so they fall into vainglory and so lose that grace. If they could only know how small their grace is in comparison with what God gives or can give, they would be ashamed to speak of it unless they were absolutely compelled. David in the Psalter says about this kind of prayer: *Voce mea ad Dominum clamavi: voce mea ad Dominum deprecatus sum:* the prophet David, to inspire other men's hearts and tongues, said: "With my voice I cried to God: and with my speech I besought our Lord".

CHAPTER 29: *Concerning the second kind of prayer, which is vocal but not set, but follows the impulses of those who are in devotion.*

THE SECOND KIND of prayer is vocal, but it does not follow any particular sequence. This is when a man or woman feels the grace of devotion by God's gift, and in his devotion speaks to Him as if he were physically in His presence, using such words as best agree with what he then is moved to, and which are habitual with which to express the thoughts of his heart. He may confess again his sins and his misery, or he may speak of the malice and the cunning of the enemy, or of the goodness and the mercy of God: and so he cries aloud the desire of his heart with the speech of his mouth, calling to our Lord for succour and help, like a man in danger amongst his enemies or a man in sickness showing his ills to God, as it were to a doctor, saying: *Eripe me de inimicis meis, Deus meus:* "Oh Lord, deliver me from my enemies"; or else: *Sana, Domine, animam meam, quia peccavi tibi:* "Oh Lord, heal my soul, for I have sinned against You", or other such prayers as may come to his mind. And it will also seem to him that there is so much goodness, grace and mercy in God that he delights in praising and thanking Him with great affection of the heart, in such words and psalms as are fitting for God's glorification and praise. So David says: *Confitemini Domino, quoniam bonus, quoniam in saeculum misericordia eius:* "Glorify and praise our Lord, for He is good and merciful". And let him praise God with such other words as he is moved to say.

CHAPTER 30: *That this kind of prayer is greatly pleasing to God, and sometimes makes a man to behave as if he were drunk, and in his soul to be wounded with the sword of love.*

THIS KIND of prayer is greatly pleasing to God, because it is purely inspired by the heart's affection, and never goes unrewarded by some grace. This prayer belongs to the second part of contemplation, as I have said before. Whoever experiences fervently this gift of God must for the time that it lasts shun the presence and society of all men, and be quite alone, so that he be not distracted. Whoever has it, hold on to it as long as he can, for its fervour cannot last long. For if grace should come in great abundance, it is amazingly exhausting to the spirit, even though it may be delightful, and it is very hard upon the bodies of men who often experience it, for if great grace should come, it makes a man's body to move and turn, here and there, as though he were mad or drunk and could find no rest. And this is one of the heights of the passion of love, which with great violence and force breaks down all earthly pleasures and delights, and wounds the soul with the blissful sword of love, so that the body fails and falls and cannot endure it. This touching has such great power that if the most vicious or carnal man living on earth were powerfully touched only once by this sharp sword, he would for long afterwards be most steady and sober, and all the pleasures and delights of his flesh and of all the earthly things in which he once had greatest joy would lose all their savour[1].

(CHAPTER 31: *The fire of love destroys all fleshly delights*).

CHAPTER 32: *Of the third kind of prayer, which is only in the heart and is not vocal.*

THE THIRD KIND of prayer is only in the heart, it is without words, and it comes through great peace of body and of soul. A man who would pray in this way should have a pure heart, for it is such men and women as have laboured long in body and soul, or have been sharply struck by love as I have described, who attain to the peace of the spirit, so that their affection is transformed into spiritual savour, and they can continually pray in their hearts, and praise and glorify God with no great hindrance from the temptations and vanities of which I spoke in the second part of contemplation. St. Paul says this about this kind of prayer: *Nam si orem lingua, spiritus meus orat, mens autem mea sine fructu est. Quid ergo? Orabo spiritu, orabo et mente, psallam spiritu, psallam et mente.* The sense of this is: "If I pray only with my tongue, if my spirit consents and I labour at it, the prayer is meritorious, but my soul is not nourished, for it does not feel by comprehending the fruit of spiritual sweetness. What shall I do then?" says St. Paul; and he answers and says: "I shall pray by labouring and by the spirit's desire, and I shall also pray more inwardly, in my spirit, without labour, by feeling spiritual savour and the sweetness of the love and the vision of God, and by that

---

[1] *Would lose all their savour*: from the Worde edition as translated by Dom Sitwell: in the manuscript, some words are missing.

vision and by the feeling of love my soul shall be fed". This is how St. Paul knew how to pray, as I understand it. God in Holy Scripture speaks of this kind of prayer in a similitude, saying: *Ignis in altari meo semper ardebit, et cotidie sacerdos surgens mane subjicit ligna, ut ignis non extinguatur.* The sense of this is: The fire of love shall always be lit in the soul of a devout man or woman, who is our Lord's altar, and every day at dawn the priest shall add wood and replenish the fire, that is, such a man, by psalms, pure thoughts, fervent desires, shall replenish the fire of love in his heart, so that it shall never go out.

(CHAPTER 33: *Remedies against distraction in prayer.*
CHAPTER 34: *Meditation for beginners.*
CHAPTER 35: *Meditation on our Lord's humanity and Passion is a gift of God.*
CHAPTER 36: *Why this gift is sometimes withdrawn.*
CHAPTER 37: *Temptations of the devil.*
CHAPTER 38: *Remedies against such temptations.*
CHAPTER 39: *Why God permits His chosen to be tempted.*
CHAPTER 40: *Against idleness and carelessness of grace*).

CHAPTER 41: *That a man ought to know the measure of his gift, and always long for more, and take a better gift when God will give it.*

OUR HOLY FATHERS on earth before us taught us that we ought to know the measure of our gift and work accordingly, not taking upon us by pretending to feel more than we do. We can always wish for the best, but we cannot

H*

always do the best, because we have not yet received the grace. A dog which only chases the hare because he sees the other dogs running stops when he feels tired and turns back for home: but if he runs because he sees the hare, he will not stop because he is tired until he has caught it. It is just like this in the spiritual life. If someone has obtained a grace, however small it may be, if he willingly desists from acting according to it, and sets himself to some other work for which he has not yet the grace, just because he sees or hears of other men doing this, he may indeed run for a while until he is tired, but then he will go back home. And if this man is not careful, some fantasy will make him go lame before he gets there. But he who acts in the grace which he has, and longs for more, humbly and constantly, and then feels his heart moved to follow the grace which he has longed for, he may certainly keep on running, if he preserves his humility. And therefore long to receive from God as much as you can of everything which belongs to His love, and to the bliss of heaven, without any measure or discretion. For he who can best long for God will feel most of Him; but do the best you can, and implore God's mercy for what you cannot do. It was with this idea that St. Paul said: *Unusquisque habet donum suum a Deo, alius autem sic, alius vero sic. Item unicuique nostrum data est gratia secundum mensuram donationis Christi. Item divisiones gratiarum sunt, alii datur sermo sapientiae, alii sermo scientiae. Item ut sciamus quae a Deo donata sunt nobis.* St. Paul says that every man has his gift from God, one this way and another that, for to every man who will be saved grace is given according to the measure of Christ's gift, and therefore it is profitable that we should know the gifts which are given to us by God, so that we may use them, for by them we shall be saved, some by bodily works and deeds of mercy, some by great penance, some by sorrow and tears for their sins all their lives, some by preaching and teaching, some by various graces and gifts of devotion shall be saved and come to bliss.

CHAPTER 42: *That a man should labour to know his own soul and its powers, and destroy the ground of sin in his soul.*

NEVERTHELESS there is one exercise which it is necessary and profitable to labour in, and, so far as human endeavour can achieve this, I believe that it is a straight high road to contemplation. This is for a man to enter inside himself, and to know his own soul and its powers, how beautiful it is and how hideous. When you look inside yourself like this, you will be able to see the honour and dignity which the soul ought to have by its nature as it was first created: and you will see the misery and harm which you have fallen into through sin. When you see this, a great desire and longing will come into your heart to have again the honour and dignity which you have lost. And you will feel horror and loathing for yourself, and a great will to destroy and break down that self, and everything which hinders you from regaining that dignity and that joy. This is a spiritual labour which is hard and painful to begin with: and let no-one hope to advance quickly in it, for it is a labour in the soul, directed against the ground of all sins, little or great. This "ground" is nothing else than man's false and inordinate love for himself; and out of this love, as St. Augustine says, springs every kind of sin, mortal and venial. And truly, until this ground be thoroughly explored and dug deep and, as it were, drained by casting out every carnal and worldly love, a soul can never feel spiritually the burning love of God, nor

see spiritual things clearly in the light of comprehension.
The labour lies in this: a man must draw up his heart away
from carnal love and from awareness of himself, so that the
soul cannot find any rest in any carnal thought or earthly
affection. And if he does this, then because the soul cannot
easily find its spiritual rest in the love and the vision of God,
it will of necessity feel pain. This labour is somewhat straight
and narrow, and yet it is the way which Christ showed to
them who wished to be His perfect followers, when He said
in the Gospel: *Contendite intrare per angustam portam,*
quoniam arcta est via quae ducit ad vitam, et pauci inveniunt
eam: "Strive to enter by the narrow gate, for the way leading to heaven is narrow, and few find it". And our Lord
tells us how narrow this way is, when He says in another
place: *Si quis vult post me venire, abneget semetipsum, et*
tollat crucem suam, et sequatur me. Item qui odit animam
suam in hoc mundo, in vitam aeternam custodit eam. That is:
"Whoever wishes to come after Me, let him forsake himself
and hate his own soul"—that is, forsake all earthly love and
hate all his own earthly life and his own bodily feelings,
however great his intelligence may be, for love of Me—
"and take the cross"—that is, suffer the pains of this for a
while—"and then follow Me"—that is, into contemplation
of Me. This is a straight and narrow way, through which
no earthly thing can pass, for it is death to all sins, as St.
Paul says: *Mortificate membra vestra quae sunt super terram,*
immunditiam, libidinem, concupiscentiam malam: "Slay
your members on earth"—not the members of your body, but
those of your soul—"uncleanness, and lust, and inordinate
love" of yourself and of earthly things. Therefore, just as
your labour until now has been to withstand great bodily
sins and the enemy's open temptations, from without, as it

were, so now in this spiritual labour you must begin inside yourself to destroy and break down the ground of sin in the self, as much as you can. And now I shall tell you how I think you can best achieve this.

CHAPTER 43: *How a man shall recognize the worth and the dignity of his soul, which it should by nature possess, and the wretchedness and misery into which it has fallen by sin.*

M AN's SOUL is a life, made of three powers, recollection, reason and will, made in the image and likeness of the Blessed Trinity, complete, perfect and righteous. As the recollection was made mighty and steadfast by the Father Almighty, to keep itself free from oblivion, distractions or the hindrance of any created thing, it has the likeness of the Father. The reason was made clear and bright, as completely free from error or darkness as is possible for any soul in a yet unglorified body, and so it has the likeness of the Son, Who is Eternal Wisdom. And the love and the will were made pure, burning upwards towards God, without the animal desires of the flesh or for any creature, by God's sovereign goodness, and so it has the likeness of the Holy Spirit, Who is blessed love. In this way man's soul, which may be called a created trinity, was made perfect in its mind and vision and love by the uncreated Blessed Trinity Who is the Lord God. This is the dignity, the degree and the honour of the human soul according to its nature as it was first created. You had this degree in Adam before man's first sin; but when Adam sinned, choosing love of himself and pleasure in himself and in created things, he lost all this honour and his dignity, and you too lost it in him, and you fell away from the Blessed Trinity into a foul, dark, wretched trinity—into oblivion of God, into ignorance of Him and into animal pleasure in yourself. The reason for this is as David says in the Psalter: *Homo cum in honore esset, non intellexit: comparatus est jumentis, et similis factus est illis:* "When man was in honour, he did not know it, and so he lost it and was made like a beast". Now look at the miserable state of your soul. Once your recollection was fixed steadily upon God, but now it has forgotten Him and seeks rest in His creatures, now this one, now that, never finding perfect rest because it has lost Him in Whom rest is perfect. It is the same with your reason. Your love, which once was pure, delighting in spiritual savour and sweetness, is now transformed into foul animal desire and pleasure in yourself, in created things and in carnal delights, delights of the senses such as gluttony and lechery, and of the mind such as pride, vainglory and covetousness. This is so much the case that you can scarcely perform a good deed without becoming defouled with vainglory, you can hardly apprehend with one of your five senses any pleasurable created thing without your heart being caught and infected with a false pleasure and delight in it which drives out your feeling of the love of God from your heart, closes your heart to spiritual savour. Every man who leads the spiritual life knows all this well. This is the misery and harm which the soul has inherited because of Adam's first sin, not to reckon all the other misery and sins which you have willingly added to it. And you can be very sure that even if you had never committed any sin with your body, mortal or venial, but had only this sin, which is called original sin because it was the first sin, which was nothing else than the loss of the righteousness in which you were created, still you would never have been saved, had not our Lord Jesus Christ by His precious Passion delivered you and restored you again.

(CHAPTER 44: *Every man, however sinful, may be saved by our Lord's Passion.*

CHAPTER 45: *Man should recover the honour of his soul, and form again in himself the image of the Trinity*).

CHAPTER 46: *How Jesus must be sought, desired and found.*

SEEK THEN what you have lost, so that you may find it. I know well that if anyone could once have interior vision, however short, of the honour and the spiritual beauty which the soul had by nature and will have by grace, he would in his heart hate and despise all the joy, the pleasure and the beauty of this whole world, as if it were the stench of carrion, and he would never wish to perform any other act by night or day—allowing only for the weakness and the sheer necessities of human nature—than long, mourn, pray and seek how he could attain to that state again. Still, because you have not yet seen it all, because the eyes of your spirit are not yet opened, I shall give you one word to express everything which you must seek and desire and find, for that word comprehends everything which you have lost: and this word is "Jesus". I do not mean the letters "IHS" painted on a wall or written in a book, I do not mean the sounds of the word which you form with your tongue, I do not mean the name as it can be fixed in the heart by the effort of recollection: through such exercises man in love may find Him, but here by "Jesus" I mean all goodness, everlasting wisdom, love and sweetness, your joy, your dignity and your eternal happiness, your God, your Lord and your salvation. Then if you feel great desire in your heart for Jesus, either through the recollection of this name or by re-

membering and saying some word or some prayer, or through
any act which you perform, and if this desire is so great that
it expels, as it were by violence, every desire and remembrance
of the world and of the flesh, so that they can find no place
in your heart, then you are indeed seeking Jesus. And when
you feel this desire for God—or for Jesus, it is all the same—
helped and comforted by a spiritual power so greatly that it
is turned into love and affection, spiritual savour and sweetness, light and knowledge of truth, so much so that for a
time the whole of your intention is directed towards nothing
which has been created, and you feel no impulse of vainglory or of any other evil affection, because they are then
powerless to show themselves, and your spirit is surrounded,
rested, softened, anointed in Jesus: then you have found Him
a little, though not yet Him as He is, but only His reflection.
For the better you find Him, the more you want Him. Then
you will seek Him best and find Him best through whatever
kind of prayer or meditation or occupation gives you the
most desire for Him and the greatest feeling of Him. Therefore if it occurs to you to ask yourself what it is that you
have lost and what you are seeking, lift up the desire of your
heart towards Jesus, even though you may be blind and
cannot see Him at all, and say that it is He Whom you have
lost and Whom you wish to have, and nothing else—no
other joy, no other bliss in heaven or on earth but Jesus. And
though perhaps you do feel Him in devotion or in intellectual
perception or in some other gift, do not take rest in it, whatever it may be, as though you had found the whole of Him:
forget what you have found, and always long more and more
for Jesus, wanting to find Him better, as if you had not
found Him at all. For be certain that however much you
may feel of Him, yes, even though you were transported by

rapture into the third heaven with St. Paul, still you have not
found Jesus as He is. However much you may know or feel
of Him here in this life, He is still far above it; and therefore
if you want to find the whole of Him as He is in the bliss of
love, never cease whilst you live to long spiritually for Him.

CHAPTER 47: *How profitable it is to long for Jesus.*

T RULY I would rather feel and have a true desire and a
pure longing in my heart for my Lord Jesus,
though I were never to see Him at all with my spirit's eyes,
than, lacking this desire, all the bodily penances performed
by every living man, all the visions and the revelations
brought by angels, all the songs and sounds, the savours and
scents, the burnings and the delectable bodily sensations, all
the joys of heaven and earth, in short, which I could have
without this desire for my Lord Jesus. The prophet David
felt what I mean when he said: *Quid enim mihi est in caelo,
et a te quid volui super terram?* "Lord, what is there for me
in heaven, or what do I want on earth, without You?" It is
as if he were to say: Lord Jesus, what heavenly joy can delight
me without longing for You whilst I am on earth, or when
I come to heaven, unless I love You? And the answer is: no
joy at all. So if you want to feel Jesus in your body or your
spirit, long to feel a true desire for Him, so that it seems to
you that your heart can find no rest in any other thing than
that desire. David longed for this when he said: *Concupivit
anima mea desiderare justificationes tuas in omni tempore:*
"Lord, my soul longed to desire your righteousness for all
time". Seek then as David sought, seek desire by desiring, and
if you can feel it, bind your heart to it, so that you never fall

away from it, and find it quickly again, even if you stumble.[1] Seek Jesus, then, Whom you have lost. He wants to be sought, and He can in part be found; for He says Himself: *Omnis qui quaerit, invenit:* "Everyone who seeks shall find". The seeking is burdensome, but the finding is a great joy. So act according to the advice of the Wise Man, if you want to find Him: *Si quaesieris quasi pecuniam sapientiam, et sicut thesaurum effoderis illam, tunc intelliges timorem Domini, et scientiam invenies:* "If you seek wisdom", that is, Jesus, "as though it were silver and gold, and dig deeply for it, you will find it". You must dig deep into your heart, for that is where He is hidden, and utterly cast out every love and pleasure, all sorrows and fears of every earthly thing, and so you will find that wisdom which is Jesus.

CHAPTER 48: *Where and with what Jesus must be sought and found.*

So do as the woman in the Gospel did, of whom our Lord says: *Quae mulier habens drachmas decem, et perdiderit unam, nonne accendit lucernam et everrit domum suam et quaerit diligenter donec inveniat eam, et cum invenerit, convocat amicas suas dicens: congratulamini mihi, quia inveni drachmam quam perdideram:* "What woman is there who has lost a drachma, who will not light a lantern and turn her house upside down and look for it until she finds it", implying that there is no-one who will not do this, "and when she has found it, she calls in her friends, and says to them, Rejoice and sing with me, because I have found the drachma which I lost". The drachma which you have lost is Jesus, and if you want to find Him, light a

_____
[1] In the Worde edition, Chapter 48 now begins.

lantern, which is God's word, as David says: *Lucerna pedibus meis verbum:* "Lord, Your word is a lantern for my feet". By the light of this lantern you will see where He is and how to find Him. If you wish, you may from this lantern light another, which is your soul's reason: for our Lord says: *Lucerna corporis tui est oculus tuus:* "The lantern of your body is your body's eye", and in the same way it may be said that your soul's lantern is reason, by which the soul can see all spiritual things. By the light of this lantern you can find Jesus, if you will lift the lantern up from underneath the basket, as our Lord says: *Nemo accendit lucernam et ponit eam sub modio, sed super candelabrum:* "No-one lights a lantern to put it underneath a basket, but he puts it on a stand". This means that your reason must not be smothered by earthly thoughts or occupations or idle thoughts and worldly affections, but must always be lifted above all earthly things, as much as you can. And if you do this, you will see all the ashes and dirt and dust in your house, that is, all the worldly loves and fears in your soul: or perhaps not all, for David says: *Delicta quis intelligit?* "Who can recognize all his trangressions?", meaning that no-one can. And you will throw out of your heart all such sins, and sweep your soul clean with the broom of the fear of God, and with the water from your eyes you will wash it, and so you will find your drachma, which is Jesus. He is the drachma, He is the coin, and He is your inheritance. It is not so easy to find this drachma as it is to talk about it, for this is not the work of an hour or of a day, but it will take many days and many years, and the sweat and toil of your body and the travail of your soul: but do not give up, keep on seeking, with sorrow and deep sighs and silent lament bend down low and weep tears of anguish and pain, because you have lost your treasure, Jesus. And in the end, when it is His will, you will truly find your drachma, Jesus, and if you only find, as I have said, His shadow or His reflection, still if you wish call in your friends to rejoice with you, because you have found your drachma, Jesus.

CHAPTER 49: *Where Jesus is lost, and where by His mercy He is found.*

SEE NOW how great is the courtesy and mercy of Jesus. It was you who lost Him, and where? Truly, in your house, that is, in your soul. If you had lost Him outside the house, that is, if by your first sin you had lost the reason of your soul, it would never have found Him again. But He spared you your reason, and He never will be lost from it. And though you will not come closer to Him until you have found Him, He is in you, though He may be lost to you, but you are not in Him until you have found Him. This was His mercy, that He would suffer Himself to be lost only where He can be found. You do not need to run off to Rome or to Jerusalem to look for Him there: turn your thoughts into your own soul, where He is hidden, as the prophet says: *Vere tu es Deus absconditus:* "Truly, Lord, You are a hidden God". And you must seek Him there, for He Himself says in the Gospel: *Simile est regnum caelorum thesauro abscondito in agro, quem qui invenit homo prae gaudio illius vadit et vendit universa quae habet, et emit agrum illum:* "The kingdom of heaven is like a treasure hidden in a field: when a man finds it, in his joy he goes and sells everything he owns, and buys that field". Jesus is the treasure, hidden in your soul, and if you could find Him in your soul and your soul in Him, I know that in your joy over it you would renounce pleasure from every earthly thing to have that. Jesus is sleeping in the heart of your soul, as He once slept in the body when He was aboard the ship with His disciples; but they for fear of death wakened Him, and at once He saved them from the storm. Do this yourself: rouse Him with prayer, and waken Him with the cries of your longing, and He will soon waken and help you.

CHAPTER 50: *What prevents man from hearing and seeing Jesus in himself.*

STILL, I believe that it is you who sleep, and not He, for many times He calls to you with His sweet, secret voice, and very quietly He rouses your heart, telling you to give up every other empty argument in your soul, and listen only to Him, to hear Him speak. David said this of our Lord: *Audi, filia, et vide, et inclina aurem tuam, et obliviscere populum tuum et domum patris tui:* "My daughter, listen and see and bend your ear" to Me, "and forget your people" of your earthly thoughts, "and the house" of your carnal and natural affections. Here you can see how our Lord calls you, and everyone else who is willing to listen to Him. What is it, then, which prevents you from ever seeing or hearing Him? Indeed, it is because there is so much empty noise and shouting in your heart, from idle thoughts and carnal desires, that you can never hear or see Him: therefore you must quell this distracting noise, and break down the love of sin and folly, and bring the love of virtues and utter charity into your heart. Then you will hear our Lord speak to you, for as long as He does not find His image formed again in you, He is a stranger to you and far off.

CHAPTER 51: *That humility and love are the special lovers of Jesus, through which man's soul is reformed.*

THEREFORE set about being clothed in His likeness, that is, in humility and love, which are His lovers, and then He will recognize you as one of His own, and will show His secrets to you. This is what He said Himself to His disciples: *Qui diligit me diligetur a Patre meo, et manifestabo ei meipsum:* "Whoever loves Me will be loved by My Father, and I shall show Myself to him". There is no virtue which you may possess, no act which you may perform, which can make you like our Lord without humility and love, for they are the special lovers of God; and that appears very clearly in the Gospel, when our Lord says this about humility: *Discite a me, quia mitis sum et humilis corde:* "Learn from Me"—He does not say, Go barefooted, or retire into a desert and fast forty days, or gather disciples round you, but "Learn from Me, learn humility, because I am gentle and humble in heart". And of love He says: *Hoc est praeceptum meum, ut diligatis invicem sicut dilexi vos. Item, In hoc cognoscent homines quia discipuli mei estis, si dilectionem habueritis ad invicem:* "This is My commandment, that you love one another as I have loved you, because men will recognize you as My disciples", not because you perform miracles or cast out devils or preach and teach, but "if you love one another" in that love which teaches you how to love your fellow Christian as much as yourself.

CHAPTER 52: *How a man shall see the ground of sin in himself.*

Now you have heard a little about what your soul is, and about the honour which it had and which it lost; and I have told you that this honour could by grace and hard endeavour partly be regained, so that you might feel a part of it. Now I shall tell you, as well as I can, though that is not very well, how you can enter into yourself, to see the ground of sin, and to destroy it as much as you can, so that in this way you will be able to regain part of your dignity.

For a time you must desist from all physical activity and from all external affairs, so far as you can, and then you must draw your attention away from your bodily senses into yourself, so that you disregard whatever you hear or see or feel, and so that your heart is not directed towards these things nor fixed on them. After this, draw your attention still further in, away, if you can do this, from every concept about any physical thing, and away from every thought of what you may previously have done on this earth or what other men have done. This is not a hard thing to do when devotion inspires you to do it; but you must do as I tell you, even when you do not feel devotion, because then it is much harder, and you must fix your intention and purpose upon seeking and feeling and finding nothing except Jesus. To do this is a great labour, for empty thoughts will constantly intrude and crowd into your heart, trying to drag your attention down to them; but you must resist them. And if you do this, you will find something. It will not be Jesus, Whom you seek. What will it be, you ask? Indeed, it will be nothing else but a dark and painful image of your own soul, which

has not the light of knowledge, the feeling of love nor its
joy. If you look at this image closely, you will see how it is
all wrapped up in the black and stinking garments of sin,
in pride, envy, wrath, sloth, covetise, gluttony and lechery.

CHAPTER 53: *What the image of sin is like, and what it is
in itself.*

THIS image is not the image of Jesus, but it is an image
of sin, a body of sin and a body of death, as St.
Paul calls it. Wherever you go, you carry this image and
this black shadow around with you. Out of it spring many
great rivers of sin and many little streams, just as, if your
soul were transformed into the image of Jesus in the rays of
spiritual light, out of it should ascend as vapour to heaven
the streams of burning desires, pure affections, wise thoughts
and all decent, virtuous conduct. In the same way, out of this
image there spring the impulses of pride, of envy, and others
like them, which cast you down from the decency of man
into the likeness of a beast. But it may be that you are
beginning to ask what this image can be like; and so that
you should not think too long about it, I will tell you that
it is like no earthly thing. Then, you ask, what is it? Indeed,
it is nothing; and if you will try what I have told you to do,
you can find this out for yourself. Draw your attention into
yourself, away from all earthly things, and then you will
find nothing in which your soul can find rest. This nothing
is merely a lack of love and of light, just as sin is merely a
lack of good. If it were so that the ground of sin within you
were greatly reduced and dried up, and if your soul were
truly transformed to the image of Jesus, then, if you were
to draw your heart into yourself, you would not find noth-

ing: you would find Jesus, you would find the light of understanding and no darkness of ignorance, you would find love and delight and no pain of bitterness and remorse. But because you are not yet transformed, when your soul comes into yourself from all earthly things, and it finds nothing but darkness and grief, it seems a hundred years to the soul until it can get out again, escaping by means of some bodily pleasure or empty thought. This is not surprising, for if someone were to come home and find nothing inside his house but stinking smoke and a scolding wife, he would very soon run outside again. Just so, when your soul finds no comfort in yourself, but only the black stench of spiritual blindness, and the incessant quarrelling of carnal thoughts, shouting at you so that you cannot have peace, it is very ill at case until it can get out again. This darkness is that same nothing and that image of which I have spoken.

CHAPTER 54: *Whoever wishes to find Jesus must wait and labour in the spiritual darkness of this image of sin.*

NEVERTHELESS, you must toil and sweat in this nothing. That is, you must draw your attention into yourself, away from all earthly things as much as you can, and then, when you find nothing but sorrow and pain and blindness, if you wish to find Jesus, you must suffer and endure the pain of this nothing in this darkness for a time, and in your thoughts you must rise up against this nothing by constant prayer and a fervent desire for God, as if you wanted to drag the nothing down and go through it. You must hate and loath this nothing as if it were the devil of hell, you must despise it and break it into little pieces: for deep inside this nothing Jesus is hidden in all His joy; and Him you cannot find, as you seek Him, unless you pass through the darkness of this nothing. This is the spiritual labour of which I spoke; and this labour is the cause of all that I have written, so that if you feel the grace it may move you to the labour. And this nothing of which I speak is the image of the first Adam, and St. Paul knew it well, because this is what he said about it: *Sicut portauimus imaginem terrani hominis, ita portemus imaginem iam et caelestis*[1]: "As we have hitherto borne the image of earthly man"—that is, the first Adam—"so now let us bear the image of heavenly Man", Who is Jesus, the second Adam. St. Paul bore this image, which was often a great load to him, for it weighed so heavily that from inside it he cried out and said: *O quis me liberabit de corpore mortis huius:* "Ah, who shall deliver me from this body and this image of death?"[2]. And then he comforted himself, and others, saying: *Gratia Dei per Jesum Christum:* "The grace of God, by Jesus Christ."[3] Now I have told you a little of how this image is nothing; but still you may be far from understanding how what I say can be true, how nothing can be an image, because nothing is only nothing, so that this will not be easy for you to understand, and so I shall now tell you more plainly how this image seems to me.

(CHAPTER 55: *The "image of sin."* CHAPTER 56: *Pride, and when it is sinful.* CHAPTER 57: *When pride is mortal sin.* CHAPTER 58: *Pride in heresy as a mortal sin.* CHAPTER 59: *Pride in hypocrisy as a mortal sin.* CHAPTER 60: *When pride is venial sin.* CHAPTER 61: *That different states in*

---

[1] This is not the Latin version of I Corinthians xv 49 found in the modern Vulgate editions, but its variants are necessary for Hilton's argument.

[2] The interpolation "and this image" is Hilton's.

[3] In the Worde edition, Chapter 55 begins here.

the Christian life will have different rewards in heaven. CHAPTER 62: *In praise of humility and love.* CHAPTER 63: *How to recognize pride.* CHAPTER 64: *Anger and envy.* CHAPTER 65: *How to love men but hate their sins.* CHAPTER 66: *Different rewards for the same works.* CHAPTER 67: *That whenever possible man's actions should be favourably judged).*

CHAPTER 68: *That no good deed can make a man saved without love, and that love is only obtained through the gift of God by those who are humble: and who he is who is perfectly humble.*

How can any miserable wretch living on this earth, whoever he may be, have pleasure or faith or confidence in himself? Whatever he can do, whatever he may do, with all his physical powers and all his natural intelligence, it is all worth nothing without love and charity towards his fellow Christian. And this love cannot be obtained by any action of his, because it is a free gift of God, sent into a humble soul. This is what St. Paul says: "Who then shall be so bold as to say 'I have love' or 'I am in charity'?" Truly, no man may say this except him who is perfectly and steadfastly humble. Other men may believe and hope that they are in charity, because of its signs, but he who is perfectly humble feels it, and therefore he might confidently say it. St. Paul was such a humble man, and therefore he said this about himself: *Quis nos separabit a charitate Dei? Tribulatio an angustia. . . .?* "Who shall separate me[1] from the love of God? Tribulation or anguish?" And he replies to his question and says: "No creature shall put me out of

[1] Hilton's translation.

the love of God, which I have in Christ Jesus". Many men perform the deeds of love, without having love, as I have said. To rebuke a sinner for his sins is a deed of love, so that he may be reformed in due times; but to hate a sinner instead of his sins is against love. A man who is truly humble can keep these two separate, and no-one else but he can do this, because even if a man had all the moral virtues of all the philosophers he would not be able to do it. He would know how to hate other men's sins because he hates them in himself: but not all his philosophy would teach him how to love the man in charity. And if a man had mastered all the arts and all theology, if he were not perfectly humble he would easily stumble and go astray, and mix up hatred of sin with hatred of sinners. But humility is worthy to receive a gift of God which cannot be taught by human intelligence, and therefore the man who is humble knows how to hate sin and to love men truly. But perhaps you are now beginning to be afraid, because I said that love cannot be obtained by any deed which you can perform, and are asking what you ought to do? To this question I reply that there is nothing so difficult to obtain as love. So far as your own labours are concerned, this is true; and yet on the other hand I tell you that there is no gift of God so easily to be obtained as love, for our Lord gives no gift so freely and gladly and generally as He gives love. If you ask how you should obtain it, be humble and lowly in spirit, and you shall have it. What is easier than to be humble? Truly, nothing is easier, so that it seems that there is nothing which can be obtained so easily as love; and therefore you need not be too afraid. Be humble, and have love. This is what St. James the apostle says: *Deus superbis resistit, humilibus autem dat gratiam*: "Our Lord", he says ,"resists proud men, but He gives grace to humble men", and this grace is indeed love, for you shall receive love according to the measure of your humility. If your humility is imperfect, in your will but not in your affection, you will have imperfect love. An imperfect love is good, for it is enough for salvation, as David says: *Imperfectum meum viderunt oculi tui:* "Lord, with Your eyes of mercy You see my imperfection"; but if you have perfect humility you shall have perfect love, and that is best. We must have the one if we wish to be saved, and we ought to wish for the other. And if you go on to ask me who he is who is perfectly humble, you shall hear nothing more from me about humility at the present time, except for this: the man is humble who truly knows and feels himself to be what he is.

(CHAPTER 69: *How to recognize one's own anger and envy.* CHAPTER 70: *How to know if one loves one's enemy, and how to do this by our Lord's example.* CHAPTER 71: *How to recognize covetousness.* CHAPTER 72: *How to know if one sins mortally or venially in eating and drinking.* CHAPTER 73: *That lust is to be destroyed by spiritual means.* CHAPTER 74: *To overcome all temptations to sin.* CHAPTER 75: *That hunger and physical suffering are obstacles in the spiritual life.* CHAPTER 76: *Remedies against inordinate appetite*).

CHAPTER 77: *That through constant desire and labour in humility and love a man comes sooner to the other virtues.*

THEREFORE obtain for yourself humility and love: and if you want to labour and toil constantly to obtain them, you will be fully occupied until they come; and if you can obtain them, they will secretly rule you and dictate to you, how you should eat, how you should drink, how you should assuage every bodily need. But no-one shall know of this unless you wish it; and it shall not bring to you perplexity or doubt or anger or grief or joy or hilarity, but only the peace of a glad conscience and a solemn rest. I am saying more than I meant to say about this, but still, if you can, do as I say, and I believe that God shall make all things well. From what I have said you can partly see, concerning this image of sin, how much it hinders you. The Gospel says that Abraham said this to the rich man who was entombed in Hell: *Chaos magnum inter nos et vos, ut hi qui volunt transire ad vos non possunt, nec huc transmeare:* "There is a great chaos"—that is, a dense darkness—"between us and you, so that we cannot come to you, nor you to us". This dark image in your soul, and in my soul too, may be called a great chaos, a great darkness, for it hinders us from coming to Abraham, who is Jesus, and it hinders Him, for He will not come to us.

THE SCALE OF PERFECTION

BOOK II

CHAPTER 21: *That a man who wishes to reach Jerusalem;
that is, the city of peace, which is contemplation, must preserve his humility and his faith, and suffer both physical and
spiritual hardships.*

NEVERTHELESS[1], because you wish to have some rule
of life by which you could more quickly attain to
that reforming, I shall tell you, by the grace of our Lord Jesus,
what seems to me to be the shortest and the best help which
I know to achieve this. Let me explain it with this similitude:
there was once a devout pilgrim who wanted to go to Jerusalem, and because he did not know the way, he went to another man, who, he thought, knew the way there, and asked
him how to get to that city. The other man said that he
would never get there without great hardship and much
effort, because it is a long way and the dangers are great,
because of thieves and robbers and many other obstacles
which travellers encounter on the journey. And it seems, too,
that there are many different routes that lead there, but
every day men are killed and robbed and cannot reach the
place where they want to be. None the less this man said that
there is one way which, he could guarantee, would lead any
man who took it to the city of Jerusalem, without his suffer-

---

[1] The previous chapter ends by stressing the impossibility of attaining to a
reforming of the spirit without humility and constant effort.

ing death or murder or starvation, even though he would
often endure robbery and violent handling and great hardships on the journey. Then the pilgrim said: "If it is true that
I can reach the place that I long for alive, I do not care how
much harm I suffer by the way: so tell me what you like, and
I promise to do as you say". The other man answered:
"Look, I shall put you on the right way. This is it: and see
that you follow my instructions exactly. Whatever you hear
or see or feel that might hinder you as you go, do not allow
it to detain you, do not stop to rest because of it, do not look
at it, do not enjoy it, do not fear it, but keep straight on.
Remember that it is Jerusalem that you want to get to, make
that your only object and nothing else than that. If people
rob you, plunder you, beat you, scorn you and despise you,
do not defend yourself if you want to live: but suffer the
hurts that come to you, and go on as if nothing has happened, so that nothing worse may come. And if people want
to detain you with stories and stuff you with falsehoods, to
make you stop and amuse yourself and abandon your pilgrimage, pretend you are deaf, do not argue with them, just
say that you want to get to Jerusalem. And if people offer
you gifts and want to load you with earthly riches, pay no
attention to them, but keep Jerusalem in your mind. And
if you keep to this route and do as I have said, I will guarantee your life. You will not be killed, and you will arrive at
the place you long for". All this we must interpret spiritually.
Jerusalem means "vision of peace", and it signifies contemplation in the perfect love of God. For contemplation is
nothing else than that vision of Jesus which is[1] true peace. So
that if you long to attain that blessed vision of true peace,
and to be a true pilgrim bound for Jerusalem, though I may

---

[1] Or "Who is".

never have been there, still I shall do what I can to set you on the road there. The first steps on the high road along which you must travel are your reforming in faith, humbly founded in the Faith and in the laws of Holy Church, as I have said before. For you may safely trust that though you may have sinned here before, if you are now reformed by the sacrament of penance according to Holy Church's law, you are on the right path. So that now that you are on the safe path, if you want a prosperous journey and to travel well, there are two things which you must always keep in mind, humility and love. Say "I am nothing, I have nothing, and I want nothing except for one thing": and even though you do not always need to be repeating these words in your thoughts, keep their meaning constantly in your intention and in the habit of your soul. Humility says "I am nothing, I have nothing". Love says "I want nothing except one thing, and that is Jesus". These are two strings, and if they are well tuned in the recollection of Jesus, they will make sweet harmony in the harp of the soul, when they are cunningly plucked by reason's finger: for the lower you touch the one, the higher the other will sound. The less that you feel that you are or you have of yourself, through humility, the more you long to have of Jesus in your love's desire. I do not only mean that humility which a soul feels when it sees its own sin or frailties or mortal wretchedness, or the superiority of its fellow-Christians, for though such humility may be genuine and wholesome, it is, comparatively, inferior and earthly, not pure, not gentle, not loving. But what I do mean is the humility which the soul feels through grace in the vision and beholding of the eternal being and the marvellous goodness of Jesus: and if you still cannot see this with the eye of your spirit, believe in it, for it is through the vision of His being,

I

either through full faith or through experience, that you will
consider yourself not merely the greatest wretch alive but also
as nothing at all with regard to the substance of your soul,
even though you never had committed sin. And this is a
loving humility, for in comparison with Jesus, Who is
verily everything, you are nothing at all. And you must also
think that you have nothing, but that you are like a vessel
always standing empty, that in you there is as it were
nothing: for however many good deeds, interior or exterior,
you may perform, until you have, and feel that you have,
the love of Jesus, you have nothing at all. For it is only with
that precious drink that your soul can be filled, and with no
other. And because it is that thing only which is so precious
and so fine, whatever you may have or may do, think of it
as nothing in which to rest, because you have not in it the
vision and the love of Jesus. Put it all behind you and forget
it, so that you might have that which is the best of all, just
as a real pilgrim going to Jerusalem leaves his house and
land behind him, his wife and child, impoverishes and strips
himself of everything which he owns, so that he can travel
light and unhindered. In the same way, if you want to be a
spiritual pilgrim, you must be naked, casting off all that
you have, both good deeds and evil, and put them all behind
you, so that in your own estimation you are so poor that there
is nothing which you have ever done upon which you will
rely, but you will always want more grace of love and will
always seek the spiritual presence of Jesus. And if you will do
this, your heart will be wholly and entirely set upon reaching
Jerusalem and no other place than that. That is, you will
set your heart wholly and entirely upon having nothing
else than the love of Jesus and the spiritual vision of Him, as
He wishes to show Himself, for it is for that alone that you

were created and redeemed, and that is your beginning and
your end, your joy and your bliss. Therefore, whatever you
may possess, however rich you may be in your good deeds,
exterior and interior, unless you possess that and feel that you
possess it, consider yourself as possessing nothing at all.
Have this argument stamped on your heart's intention, and
keep steadily to it, and it will save you from all dangers on
your journey, so that you shall not perish, and it will save
you from thieves and robbers, by which I mean impure
spirits, so that though they steal from you and beat you with
various temptations, your life will always be spared. And,
to sum up, if you travel as I tell you, you will escape every
danger and harm, and you will soon arrive at the city of
Jerusalem. Now that you have your journey mapped and
know the name of the place you are bound for, set off on
your journey. By setting off is meant nothing else than
spiritual, interior exercises, and exterior exercises too, when
they are necessary. You must use these exercises according to
discretion, in this way: whatever deed it may be that you
ought to do, according to your rank and state of life, earthly
or spiritual, if it helps this gracious desire which you have
to love Jesus, if it makes your desire more complete, more
easy and more powerful to seek for all virtues and all goodness, I consider that deed to be the best, whether it be
preaching or meditation or reading or manual work. And as
long as such deeds strengthen your heart and will in the love
of Jesus, and draw your affection and your recollection far
away from earthly vanities, it is good to employ them. And
if it happens that through habit their savour diminishes, and
it seems to you that other deeds have more savour and that
you feel more grace through them, take them on and give
the others up. For even though your desire and your heart's

longing for Jesus may always be constant, still the spiritual
exercises which you ought to practise in prayer and meditation to feed and nourish your desire may be dissimilar and
may well be varied, as you feel yourself through grace disposed to apply your own heart. For deeds and desire are like
sticks and a fire: the more sticks that are put on the fire,
the bigger it is. In the same way, the more different spiritual
exercises which a man has in his recollection, to preserve his
desire whole, the more powerful and burning shall his desire
for God be. Therefore enquire carefully what deed you are
best able to do, and which best helps you to keep your desire
for Jesus whole, provided that you are free to do as you
please and not bound except by common law: and do that
deed. Do not tie yourself down forever to practices which
are voluntary, and which might impede your heart's freedom
to love Jesus if some special grace might visit you. Now I will
tell you what practices are always good and should always
be observed. A practice is always good and should always be
followed if it increases virtue and hinders sin, and such a
practice should never be given up, because you should always
be humble and patient, sober and chaste, if you act well,
and so with all the other virtues. But the practice of one
thing which hinders something better should be given up
at the proper time, if one is free to do so: for example, if one
is accustomed to say a given number of prayers, or to meditate in a certain fashion for a given time, or to watch or
kneel for a given period, or to perform any other such
external work, such a practice should be given up if it is
prevented by some reasonable cause, or else if greater grace
comes by some other way.

CHAPTER 22: *How a man pursuing such a life will have enemies to force him back, and how he shall overcome them by his knowledge of our Lord Jesus, by verbal confession and his heart's contrition and deeds of satisfaction.*

Now that you have set off and know the way you have to travel, beware of enemies who will do all they can to hinder you if they are able. Their intention is to banish from your heart your desire and longing for the love of Jesus, and to drive you back again to the love of worldly vanities, for there is nothing which angers them so much. These enemies are chiefly the earthly desires and the empty fears that spring up from your heart because of the corruption of your mortal nature, which want to hinder your desire for the love of God, so that they could occupy all your heart at their ease. And there are other enemies, some of them unclean spirits which are trying with traps and tricks to deceive you. But, as I said before, there is one remedy which you can use, whatever they may suggest to you: do not believe them, keep on your journey, and desire nothing else than the love of Jesus. Always give the same answer: "I am nothing, I have nothing, I want nothing except the love of Jesus". If your enemies begin by saying to you, suggesting in your heart, that you are not properly shriven, or that there is some sin of long ago hidden in your heart which you do not know about and never received absolution for, and that because of this you ought to give up and forsake your desire, and go to make a proper confession, do not believe what they say, because it is not true and you have been shriven. Have firm faith that you are on the right path, and that you do not need to search your conscience for what is done with.

Keep on your way, and think of Jerusalem. And if they tell you that you are not worthy to have the love of God, and ask you what is the use of your longing for what you cannot obtain and are not fit to have, do not believe them, but keep on, and say "I want to love God not because I am worthy but because I am unworthy, for if I had His love, that would make me worthy. And since I was created to love Him, I shall long for that, even though I may never obtain it; and therefore I shall pray for it and I shall believe that I shall obtain it". If your enemies then tell you that you are beginning to grow presumptuous and complacent in your exercise, they are beginning to fear you. All the same, they will not desist from lurking in your path, whenever they can, as long as you are travelling on your road. On the one hand they will frighten and threaten you, on the other they will cajole and flatter, to make you abandon your intention and turn back for home. Sometimes they will tell you that if you persist in your desire for Jesus and keep on labouring for it as hard as you have begun, you will make yourself ill or brain-sick or mad, as you can see that some do, or else that you will bring poverty and distress on yourself and no-one will help you, or that you will be exposed to secret temptations of the devil against which you will not be able to help yourself: for it is very dangerous for any man to devote himself entirely to the love of God, and to abandon the whole world, and to long for nothing but His love, for many dangers may come which one knows nothing about; and therefore turn back again, and give up what you long for, because you will never achieve it, and behave like other men of the world.[1] This is what your enemies say, but do not believe them, persist in

---

[1] The structure of this long complex sentence has been kept as Hilton wrote it, to show that its various statements are all lying suggestions of the devil.

your desire, and give them no answer except that you want to have Jesus and to come to Jerusalem. And then if they see that your will is so strong that you will not give up, for sin or for sickness, for fantasies or frenzies, for doubt or dread of spiritual temptations, for suffering or poverty, for life or death, but that you will keep on, pursuing one end and nothing else, and that you pretend to be deaf, as if you did not hear them, and that you stubbornly persist in your prayers and your other spiritual exercises without ceasing, using discretion only according to the advice of your religious superior or your spiritual adviser, then they will begin to be angry, and to come up a little closer to you. They will begin to rob you and beat you and treat you as injuriously as they can: that is to say, they will pretend that all your deeds, however well they may be performed, are condemned and detracted by other men, and that everything which you do to help yourself, body or soul, will be stopped or impeded by others, so that everything which you want, however reasonably, will be thwarted. They do all this to inspire you to anger or melancholy or ill will towards your fellow Christians: but against all such afflictions and any others which may come, use this remedy. Call Jesus into your recollection, and neither fight nor argue with them, but remember your lesson: you are nothing, you have nothing, you can lose nothing of worldly possessions, you desire nothing but the love of Jesus; and keep on your way to Jerusalem, doing what you have to do. And if in spite of this you are sometimes impeded by your own frailty, and by such discomforts as are inseparable from your life on earth because of men's ill-will or the devil's malice, as soon as you can, recollect yourself, dismiss all thought of such discomfort, and start again. Do not waste time on such matters, for fear of your enemies.

CHAPTER 23: *A general remedy against evil impulses and grievous hindrances which arise in the heart from the flesh, the world and the devil.*[1]

A ND AFTER THIS, when your enemies see that you are so well disposed that you are not angry or oppressed or enraged or greatly disturbed by any created being, whatever they may do to you or say of you, but that you are determined to endure everything which may happen, comfort or discomfort, praise or blame, and that you will not pay heed to anything, so as to preserve all your recollection and desire for God's love, then they will be much put out of countenance; but soon they will try you with flattery and adulation. They do this when they conjure up before your soul all your good deeds and your virtues, when they din it into you that everyone is praising you and talking about how holy you are, that everyone loves you and respects you for your holy life. Your enemies do this to make you believe that what they are saying is true, to make you take pleasure in this empty joy and find your rest in it. But if you are wise, you will consider all such empty chatter as the lies and flattery of your enemy, who offers you a drink which is poison sweetened with honey. Refuse it, say you do not want it, say you want to reach Jerusalem. You are bound to experience such hindrances or others like them, some of your flesh, some of the world, some of the devil, more than I can tell of now. For while anyone allows his thoughts to roam round the world, contemplating this and that, he will seldom notice these hindrances; but as soon as he concentrates all his

---

[1] This manuscript, originally without these chapter-titles, has had many of them supplied by a second scribe: the titles for Chapter 23 and numerous others are however missing, and are added from the concluding list of titles.

thoughts and his longings upon one thing, wanting nothing but to have it, to see it, to know it and to love it—and only Jesus is this thing—he will indeed then feel many painful hindrances. For everything which he feels which is not the thing which he longs for is a hindrance to him. That is why I have told you in detail about some of them, to serve as an example: but over and above this, I say as a general rule that whatever prompting you feel from your flesh or from the devil, be it pleasant or painful, bitter or sweet, agreeable or terrifying, joyful or sorrowful, that would drag your recollection and your desire down from the love of Jesus towards frivolity, and utterly spoil your spiritual longing for the love of Him, and teach your heart to find its rest in such a prompting, defy it, refuse to accept it, spend no time over it. If, however, it concerns some business of the world which must be attended to, for your benefit or that of a fellow Christian, deal with it as quickly as you can, and get it finished so that it does not hang over your heart. But if it is something else, which is unnecessary or does not concern you, disregard it, do not meddle in it: do not lose your temper, do not fear it, do not take pleasure in it, but thrust it out of your heart at once. And then say: "I am nothing, I have nothing, I am seeking and wanting nothing but the love of Jesus." Join your recollection to this desire, strengthen it and hold it up with prayer and other spiritual exercises so that you never forget it; and it will lead you on the right way, and save you from all dangers, so that though you feel them you will not perish, and I believe that it will bring you to the perfect love of our Lord Jesus. And yet on the other hand I say this: whatever act or impulse it may be which can help your desire, strengthen it and nourish it, and remove your thoughts furthest from the joys and remembrance of the

I*

world, and make them more centred on the love of God and
more ardent in His love, whether it be prayer or meditation,
silence or speech, reading or listening, solitude or company,
walking or sitting, observe that for the time and practise it
as long as the savour lasts. This is always provided that you
use this as a pilgrim uses food and drink and sleep, observing moderation in your conduct as your superiors advise
and order. However great a hurry a pilgrim may be in, he
will still eat and drink and sleep at times, and you must do
the same, for although at the time it may detain you, presently it will help you on your way.

CHAPTER 24: *Of an evil day and a good night, and what
this means; and how the love of the world is compared with
an evil day, and the love of God with a good night.*

IF THEN you want to know what this desire is, truly it
is Jesus, for He creates this desire in you, and He
gives it to you, and it is He in you Who desires, and it is He
Who desires: He is everything, and He does everything,
if you could only see Him. You do nothing but allow Him
to work in your soul, assenting with great joy of your
heart that He vouches safe to do this in you. You, with all
your reason, are nothing but an instrument with which He
works; and therefore when you feel your thoughts, touched
by His grace, taken up by desire towards Jesus, with a
powerful and devout will to please Him and love Him,
think then that you have Jesus, for it is He Whom you
desire. Look at Him well, for He goes before you, not in His
bodily appearance, but invisibly, through the secret presence
of His power. See Him therefore in the spirit, if you can, or
else believe in Him and follow Him wherever He goes, for

He will lead you on the right way to Jerusalem, which is the vision of peace in contemplation. The prophet prayed for this to the Father of heaven, saying: *Emitte lucem tuam et veritatem tuam: ipsa me deduxerunt et adduxerunt in montem sanctum tuum, et in tabernacula tua.* The sense of this: "Father of heaven, send out Your light and Your truth, which are Your Son, Jesus, and He shall lead me by the desire in me to Your holy hill and to Your tabernacles," that is, to feel perfect love and exaltation in contemplation. The prophet says of this desire: *Memoriale tuum Domine in desiderio animae. Anima mea desideravit te in nocte, sed et spiritus meus in praecordiis meis:* and the sense of this is: "Lord Jesus, the memory of You is printed in my soul's desire, for my soul has desired You in the night, and my spirit has longed for You in all my thoughts." And I shall tell you why the prophet says that he desired God in the night, and what he means by this. You know very well that night is a period of time between two days, for when one day is finished it is not immediately followed by another, but first night comes to separate the days. Sometimes it is long, sometimes short, and then afterwards the next day comes. But the prophet was not only talking about this kind of night, for he meant a spiritual night. You must understand that there are two days or two lights: the first is a false light, the second is the true one. The false light is the love of this world which a man has in himself through the corruption of his flesh: the true light is the perfect love of Jesus, felt in a man's soul by grace. The love of the world is a false light, because it vanishes and does not endure, and so does not perform what it promises. This is the light which the devil promised to Adam, when he moved him to sin, and said: *Aperientur oculi vestri, et eritis sicut dii:* that is,

"Your eyes shall be opened, and you will be as gods." And
what he said was true, for when Adam had sinned, at once
his inner eye was closed, and spiritual light was taken from
him, and his bodily eyes were opened, and he felt and saw a
new light of carnal pleasure and worldly love which he
had never seen before; and so he saw a new day. But it was
an evil day, for it was of this that Job warned when he said:
Pereat dies in qua natus sum: that is: "Let the day perish
on which I was born." It is not any day of the calendar year
created by God which Job cursed: he cursed the day made
by man, that is the concupiscence and love of the world in
which he was born, though he did not know it then. He
asked God that this day and this light might perish and last
no longer; but the everlasting love of Jesus is a true day and
a blessed light, for God is both love and light, and He is
everlasting, and therefore he who loves Him is in the light
everlasting, as St. John says: *Qui diligit Deum manet in
lumine:* "He who loves God lives always in the light." So
that if a man sees that the love of this world is false and
failing, and for this wishes to forsake it and seek the love of
God, he cannot feel His love at once, but for a time he must
wait in the night, because he cannot suddenly pass from one
light into the other, that is, from the love of the world into
the perfect love of God. This night is simply when the soul
endures, and withdraws its thoughts from earthly things by
its great desire and yearning to love and to see and to feel
Jesus and spiritual things. This is that night: for just as the
night is dark, and gives concealment to all created beings,
and rest from their physical activities, so a man who applies
himself completely to think of Jesus and to desire only His
love must do all he can to conceal his mind from the sight of
profitless things, and his affections from earthly pleasure in

any created being, so that his mind can be made free and untrammelled and his affections not engaged or forced or disturbed by anything less exalted than Jesus or inferior to Him.[1] And if he can do this, then he is in the night, for then he is in darkness; but this is a good night and a shining darkness, for it excludes the false love of this world and it is the threshold of the true day. And truly, the darker the night, the nearer is the true day of the love of Jesus; for the more the soul by its longing for God can be hidden from the noise and din of earthly affections and impure thoughts, the closer it is to feeling the light of His love, for that love is now near at hand. It would seem that this is what the prophet meant when he said: *Cum in tenebris sedeo, Dominus lux mea est:* "When I sit in darkness, our Lord is my light." That is, when my soul is hidden from every impulse of sin, and as it were is sleeping, then our Lord is my light, for then in His grace He comes close to show me His light. Even so, sometimes this night is an affliction, sometimes it is a comfort: it is an affliction at the beginning, when a man is still defouled by sin and is not accustomed by grace to remain in this darkness often. He wants to force things, and so he sets his mind and his longing towards God as much as he can, wishing to feel or think about nothing but Him, and because he cannot easily attain to this, he is afflicted because of his old habits and familiarity with sin, with the world and with carnal affections and earthly things. His sins in the world weigh down on him so much, always attacking him by violence and dragging his soul down towards them, that he cannot easily hide himself from them as quickly as he wishes. So this darkness is an affliction to

---

[1] "Lower or worse than is himself". The antecedent of "himself" may be "a man", though this seems improbable.

him, and especially when he is not visited by any abundance
of grace. But still, if you are in this state, do not be too de-
pressed, and do not fight too hard, as if by violence you would
drive it out of your mind, because it cannot be done. You
must wait for grace, you must endure it greatly, and do not
drive yourself too hard. If you can, draw your desire and
your spiritual regard up towards Jesus furtively, as if you
were paying no attention to your afflictions: for you can be
very sure that when you want to desire Jesus and think
only of Him but cannot because of the way that such
worldly thoughts crowd in upon you, truly you are escaping out of the false day, and you are entering into this
darkness. You have no rest in your darkness, because you
are unaccustomed and ignorant and impure in yourself:
but exercise yourself often in it, and as you experience grace
you will advance, and it will become gentler and more restful to you. This will happen when through grace your soul is
made so free and so powerful and so concentrated within
itself that it does not wish to think of anything, and is able
to think of nothing without hindrance from any earthly
thing: and then your soul is in a good darkness. When I say
that the soul can think of nothing, by "nothing" I mean
that by grace the soul can be concentrated within itself, and
can stand still inside itself, freely and wholly, and cannot be
driven against its will or dragged down by force to think
or take pleasure or love with cleaving of the affections to any
sin or any empty earthly thing. Then the soul is thinking of
nothing whatsoever: for it is not thinking of any earthly
thing with attraction towards it. This "nothing" is rich,
and the nothing and the night are a great comfort for the
soul which longs for the love of Jesus. It has comfort, because it is free of every earthly thing, but it has not comfort

in Jesus, because though the soul may not think of any earthly thing, still it is exerting itself to think of Him. What is it then which causes this darkness? Indeed, nothing else than a desire by grace to have the love of Jesus: for the desire and the longing which it has at such times for the love of God, to see Him and to have Him, drives every worldly vanity and carnal affection out of the heart, and concentrates the soul within itself, and busies it in thinking only how it can attain to His love. And so the soul is led into this rich nothing: and indeed it is not all darkness, not all nothing when the soul is thinking so, for though there may be the darkness of the absence of false light, there is not the darkness of the absence of love. For Jesus, Who is both love and light, is in this darkness: whether it be affliction or comfort, Jesus is in the soul, He is as it were labouring in desire and longing for the light, but He is not yet as it were reposing in love and showing His light. This is why it is called "night" and "darkness," because the soul is hidden from the false light of the world, but has not yet fully felt the true light, but waits for that blessed love of God which it desires. If you want to know when you are in this safe darkness and when not, all you need to do is to apply this test. When you feel your intention and will wholly directed to desire God and to think only of Him, ask yourself first in your own mind what you want. Do you want anything in this life for its own sake, do you want to use any of your natural senses for the sake of any created thing? And then, if your eye answers "I wish to see nothing," your ear "I wish to hear nothing," your mouth "I wish to feel nothing": and then if your heart says "I wish to think nothing about any earthly thing, or any physical act, I wish my affections to be tied to no created thing but only to God and

towards God, if I can"—if they all give you this answer, and
they soon will if grace touches you, you have begun to enter
into this darkness. Though you may feel and glimpse glim-
mers and hints of idle thoughts and the suggestions of
earthly affections, still you are in this profitable darkness, always provided that these things do not ensnare your thoughts:
for such empty ideas which take the heart by surprise dis-
turb this darkness and afflict the soul a little because it wants
to be hidden from them but it cannot. But they do not
destroy the profit of the darkness, for this is the way that the
soul comes to rest in the darkness. And this darkness brings
rest when the soul is hidden for a while from the affliction
which it feels in all such empty thoughts, and finds its rest
only in the desire and longing which it has for Jesus, seeing
Him in the spirit, as I shall presently describe. Though this
may only last complete for a little while, still, short though
it be, it is most profitable.

CHAPTER 25: *How the desire of Jesus felt in this shining
darkness kills all impulses of sin, and enables the soul to
perceive spiritual light from the heavenly Jerusalem, that is
from Jesus.*

SINCE THEN they are so good and so restful, though
they may only be short, this darkness and this
night which consist of nothing but desire and longing for the
love of Jesus and of a blind thinking about Him, how good
and how blessed it is to feel His love and to be illumined
by His blessed and invisible light so that we may see the
truth. A soul receives this light when the night ends and
the day dawns. I believe that it was this night which the
prophet meant when he said "My soul has longed for You

in the night." It is much better to be hidden in this dark
night from the contemplation of the world, even though
the night be an affliction, than to walk in the false pleasures
of this world, which seem so shining and so full of comfort
to those who are blind to the light of spiritual knowledge.
For when you are in this darkness, you are much closer to
Jerusalem than when you are in the glare of that false light.
Therefore let all your heart be moved by grace, and practise
living in this darkness, and often try to accustom yourself
to it; and soon it will bring rest to you, and the true light of
spiritual knowledge will shine on you, not all at once but in
secret, little by little, as the prophet says: *Habitantibus in
regione umbrae mortis, lux orta est eis:* "To those who live
in the region of the shadow of death, light has risen." That
is: the light of grace has risen and will rise for those who
know how to live in the shadow of death, that is in this
darkness, which resembles death; for just as death kills a
living body and all its physical sensations, so the desire
to love Jesus, felt in this darkness, kills all sins, all worldly
affections and all unclean thoughts while it lasts. Then
you are very near to Jerusalem. You are not there yet: but
by little, sudden flashes of light, twinkling out through the
crevices in its walls, you can recognize it from a distance,
before you arrive. For you must know that though your
soul may be in this restful darkness, untroubled by worldly
vanities, it has not yet arrived at its goal, it is not yet clothed
all in light nor transformed all into the fire of love; but it
feels strongly that there is something, above it, which it
does not recognize and has not yet obtained, though it longs
for it and burns in desire of it. And this something is
nothing else than the vision of Jerusalem before it, Jerusalem which is like the city which the prophet Ezechiel

saw in his visions. He says that he saw a city set on a hill facing the south, which to his sight seemed no more than a rod in length and breadth, though it was six cubits and a palm's breadth long: but as soon as he arrived in the city and looked round about him, it seemed that it was amazingly great, for he saw many halls and apartments, some of them open and some shut up, he saw gates and porticos outside and in, and there were more buildings being made than those which I describe, stretching for hundreds of cubits far and wide. So he was astonished that this city which had seemed so small to him outside could be inside so long and so wide. This city signifies the perfect love of God, set on the hill of contemplation, which to a soul which still stands outside experience of it and is labouring to enter it is visible, certainly, but seems to be only a little thing, no bigger than a rod's length, which is indeed six cubits and a palm's breadth in length. These six cubits signify the perfection of human action, and the palm's breadth the touching of the soul in contemplation. He sees clearly that this is something a little beyond human attainment, just as the palm's breadth is beyond the six cubits, but still he cannot look inside to see what it is. But if he can enter the city of contemplation, he will see far more than he saw at first.

JULIAN OF NORWICH

Revelations

Chapters 50 and 51

These two chapters are found in Julian's second, lengthened version of her REVELATIONS. *We are still awaiting the first definitive critical edition of all the manuscripts, which is to be published by Sr. Anna Maria Reynolds, C.P., and Fr. James Walsh, S.J. This present translation has been made, by kind permission of the Trustees of the British Museum, from two British Museum manuscripts, Sloane 2499 and Sloane 3705, copies of an earlier manuscript made in the second half of the seventeenth century.*

REVELATIONS

CHAPTER 50: *How the chosen soul was never dead in the sight of God: of the writer's astonishment at this; and how three things encouraged her to ask God to make her understand it.*

IN THIS MORTAL LIFE, God's mercy and forgiveness are the road on which we are always led to His grace: and although human, earthly judgement often considers that our souls are killed by the storms and the sorrows which we encounter as our lot, in God's sight the soul that shall be saved was never dead and never shall die. But still this amazed me, and I pondered over it with all the diligence my soul could command: and I said: "Good Lord, I see You, Who are very truth, and I know truly that we sin grievously every day and that we deserve great blame. But on the one hand I cannot deny Your truth, yet on the other hand I cannot see You blaming us in any way. How can this be possible? I know by the general teaching of Holy Church and by what I feel myself that the blame of our sins continually hangs over us, from Adam's day till we shall come into heaven." I was amazed, because I saw our Lord God showing no more blame towards us than if we were as purely holy as are the angels in heaven; and my reason was much afflicted between these two opposites, because I was blind, and I could not rest for fear that His blessed presence would pass out of my life, leaving me

ignorant of how He regards us in our sins. For I should
have been able to see in God either that sin is all done away
or else how God looks upon sin, so that I might truly know
from that how it is my duty to look upon sin, and what is the
nature of our blame. Constantly I beheld Him, and my
longing persisted, and I could not be patient, because of my
great doubt[1] and perplexity. I thought "If I interpret this to
mean that we are not sinners and are not blameworthy, it
would seem that I would be wrong and had failed to understand its true meaning. But if it is true that we are sinners
and are blameworthy, how can it be that I cannot see this
truth in You, my good Lord, my God, my Maker, in Whom
I long to see all truths?" Three considerations gave me
courage to ask this. The first was that this is a humble matter:
if it were exalted, I should have been afraid. The second was
that it is a common matter: if it were extraordinary and
secret, I should also have been afraid. And the third was that
this is something which I thought that I needed to know,
if I were to go on living, for it would help me to use reason
and grace to distinguish good from evil, to love good and
hate evil, as Holy Church teaches. So I cried inwardly with
all my might, calling to God for help, and saying: "Ah,
Lord Jesus, King of bliss, where shall I find comfort and
who shall teach me what I need to know, if I cannot now see
it in You?"

CHAPTER 51: *The answer to these questions, in a wonderful
example of a lord and a servant—God makes us wait for Him,
for it was nearly twenty years before she completely understood this example—and of what it means that Christ sits
at the right hand of the Father.*

[1] Both MSS have *awer:* this seems to be a mistake for *dwere,* "doubt, dread".

A<small>ND THEN</small> our courteous Lord answered me by reveal-
ing to me a wonderful but most mysterious ex-
ample of a Lord who has a servant. As I understood the
revelation, He allowed me to see them both, and to see them
both, and to see them twice: I was shewn a double sight of
the Lord and a double sight of the servant. Then one part
of what I saw was revealed spiritually, but through a bodily
similitude, and the other part was revealed more spiritually,
without any bodily similitude. First I saw two persons who
appeared like human beings—a lord and a servant; and then
God allowed me to understand this spiritually. The lord is
sitting in state, in rest and peace, and the servant is standing
near, in his lord's presence, respectful and ready to perform
his lord's will. The lord looks at his servant in great love
and happiness, and kindly commands him to go to a certain
place to perform his will. The servant does not merely obey,
but rushes off and runs in great haste to perform his lord's
will for love of him; and so he falls into a ravine and is
very severely wounded, and groans and moans and laments
and writhes, but it is impossible for him to get up or to help
himself in any way. And in all this, I saw that his greatest
harm was his lack of consolation, because he could not turn
his face to look upon his loving lord, who was very near to
him and in whom there is every consolation; but like a man
who was weak and distraught, he was at this time entirely
concerned with his own feelings, and he went on suffering,
and in his sufferings he experienced seven great hurts. The
first was the severe injuries which he suffered when he fell;
and this was the physical pain which he felt. The second
was his body's unwieldiness, and the third was the weakness
which followed these two. The fourth was that his reason

was clouded and his mind stupefied, so much so that he was barely conscious that he was still alive. The fifth was that he was not able to rise. The sixth, which was to me the most wonderful, was that he was lying alone; and I looked around, but I could not see any help coming to him, far or near, high or low. The seventh was that the place where he was lying was narrow and hard and painful. I was astonished that this servant could so patiently endure all this suffering there, and I looked at him carefully, to see whether I could discover any defect in him, or whether the lord would impute any blame to him: but indeed I could see nothing of this sort, because it was only his good will and his great eagerness which had caused him to fall, and inwardly he was as prompt and obedient as he was when he stood before his lord, ready to do his will. And still his loving lord goes on looking at him most tenderly, but now with a two-fold expression: one expression is outward, very meek and gentle, full of great compassion and pity, as he did at first; but he also had another, more inward and spiritual expression. When that was shewn to me, I was led towards understanding of the lord, and I saw him greatly rejoicing in his own honorable rest and nobility, to which it is his will and intention to bring his servant by his plentiful grace. This was shown to me as a second revelation; and then my understanding was recalled to the first, whilst I kept both in my mind, and this courteous lord then said in intention "Look, look at my dear servant. See what hurt and injury he has received in my service, for love of me, indeed, and through his own good will. Is it not reasonable that I shall recompense him for his fright and fear, his hurts and shock and sorrow? And more than this, is it not incumbent upon me to make him a gift which will be more good and honour to

him than if he had never suffered like this? If I do not do
this, I think that I should be lacking in generosity towards
him." And at this, an inward, spiritual revelation of what
the lord signified descended into my soul, and I saw that it
must of necessity be so, that the lord's great goodness and
his own honour require that his dear servant whom he loved
so much should be truly and joyfully and everlastingly rewarded, beyond the measure which he would have received
had he not fallen. Indeed, this must be so much so that his
fall and the sorrow which he has experienced through it be
turned into greater honour than he could have had before,
into everlasting bliss. And at this point the revelation of
this example vanished, and our good Lord led on my understanding of this whole revelation to its end. But though
my understanding proceeded through the revelation, my
astonishment at this example never left me, for it seemed
to me that it had been given to me in answer to my desire,[1]
and still I could not at that time find comfort in understanding it fully. For in the servant, who was revealed as Adam,
as I shall say, I saw many different characteristics which
could under no circumstances be attributed to Adam the man.
And so at that time I was placed in great ignorance, because
the full understanding of this wonderful example was not
then given to me: and in this great example there are three
peculiar characteristics of the whole revelation, deeply hidden: and in spite of my ignorance I saw and understood that
every revelation is full of secret matters. So now I must describe these three peculiar characteristics, for I have now
some comfort in understanding them. Its first is that it began
to instruct me, so that I at once understood some of its teach-

[1] Julian's "desire", which she begins her *Revelations* by describing, in chapter ii,
was for three gifts from God: one of these gifts was a more perfect knowledge of
Christ's Passion.

ing. Its second is its interior teaching, which I have learned
from it since. Its third is itself, the whole revelation from
the beginning to the end of this book, which our Lord God
in His goodness often recalls freely to my understanding.
And as I now understand them, these three properties are
so united that I have neither ability nor liberty to separate
them. And it is through these three, united into one, that I
have been taught, and I ought to live and to trust in our
God through that teaching. He revealed it in His goodness
and for His purpose: and in the same goodness and for the
same purpose He will explain it to us, when it is His will;
for it was twenty years, all but three months, after the revelation that I was inwardly taught its meaning, as I shall tell.
God said[1]: "You must pay attention to all the characteristics
and the conditions of what was revealed in the example,
though you may think that they are mysterious, and that
they convey little to you." And I agreed, with all my heart,
and with great desire, and inwardly scrutinized all the points
and the characteristics of what was then revealed, as far as
my intelligence and understanding would serve. I began by
observing the lord and the servant, how the lord was seated,
the place where he sat, the colour and the shape of his clothing, his outward demeanour, his inward nobility and goodness: and how the servant stood, where and how he was
placed, what his dress was like in colour and shape, his
outward behaviour and his inward goodness and his eagerness. I understood that the lord who sat in state in rest and
in peace is God, that the servant who stood before the lord
was revealed to represent Adam; that is to say, one man
and his fall were at that time revealed, to make it understood

---

[1] *God said:* this is the editor's addition, but it is needed to explain Julian's
sudden transition here to direct speech.

how God regards a man and his fall, for in the sight of God all men are one man, and one man is all men. This man's physical powers were injured, and he was made very weak, and his understanding was disturbed, because he turned away from regarding his lord: but his will was preserved unharmed in the sight of God, because I saw God commend and praise his will. But man himself was hindered and blinded, so that he did not know his own will; and this to him is great sorrow and heavy sickness, because he can neither see clearly his loving Lord, Who is so meek and gentle towards him, nor see truly what he himself is in the sight of his loving Lord. And I know well that when these two things are wisely and truly seen, we shall obtain rest and peace, in part here, in full in the joy of heaven by His plentiful grace. This was the beginning of my instruction, which I saw at the time of the revelation, by which I was able to attain a knowledge of how He regards us in our sin. And then I saw that it is only afflictions which blame and punish, and that our courteous Lord comforts and sorrows, and is always well disposed towards the soul, loving us and longing to bring us into bliss. The place where our Lord God was seated was a simple one: He sat upon the desert, barren earth, alone in a wilderness. His clothing was ample and wide and very dignified, as befits a lord: and it was made of an azure blue cloth, most sober and beautiful. His expression was merciful, His complexion was a fine brown, His features were most handsome, His eyes were black, most beautiful and fine, filled with loving pity; and within Him was a high regard,[1] long and wide and all full of endless heavens. And it seemed to me that the love with which He looked upon His

---

[1] Sloane 3705: highward: Sloane 2499: heyward (marked for correction). "High regard" is the conjecture of previous editors, and seems probable.

servant all the time, and particularly when he fell, might
melt our hearts for love and break them in pieces for joy.
This lovely gaze was beautifully mixed, most marvellous
to see: on the one hand it had compassion and pity, on the
other hand joy and bliss. The joy and bliss surpass the compassion and pity by as much as heaven is above earth: the
pity was earthly, the bliss was heavenly; the compassion in
the Father's pity was for the fall of Adam, who is the thing
created by Him which He most loves, the joy and the bliss
were for His precious Son, Who is equal with the father. The
merciful regard of His loving demeanour filled all the earth,
and went down with Adam into hell; and it was by this lasting pity that Adam was preserved from everlasting death.
And this mercy and pity dwell with mankind until the time
when we shall come into heaven. But in this life man is
blinded, and therefore he cannot see God our Father as He is;
and when He in His goodness wishes to show Himself to
man, He shows Himself familiarly as a man, even though I
then saw truly that we should know and believe that the
Father is not man. But this sitting on the barren, desert earth
signifies that He made man's soul to be His own city and His
dwelling place, which is the most pleasing to Him of all His
works; and when man had fallen into sorrow and pain, he
was not then all fit to serve in that exalted office, and therefore our kind Father did not wish to make any other place
for Himself, but He sat on the earth, and waited for mankind, which is mixed with earth, until the time when, by
His grace, His precious Son had redeemed His city and
restored it to its great beauty by His great labour. That
His clothing was blue signifies His steadfastness: the brown
of His lovely face and the handsome black colour of His
eyes was most fitting to show His holy sovereignty: His

ample clothing, beautifully flowing[1] around Him, signifies that He has enclosed within Him all heavens and all joy and bliss. And this was revealed to me in an instant, when I saw how my understanding was led into the lord, and I saw him greatly rejoicing in the honorable restoration to which he wishes and intends to bring his servant by his plentiful grace. And still I was amazed, regarding the lord and the servant, as I have told. I saw the lord sitting in state and the servant standing respectfully before his lord; and the servant has a double significance, one outward, the other inward. Outwardly he was simply dressed, like a workman ready for his work, and he stood very close to the lord, not directly opposite him, but slightly to one side, on the left: he was dressed in a white smock, made in one piece, old and worn, stained with his body's sweat, fitting him closely, short, only a hand's breadth below his knees, looking threadbare, as if would soon be worn out and ready to be cut up into patches. And I was greatly surprised at this, thinking that it was not fitting clothing for a servant so greatly loved to stand in before so honorable a lord. Inwardly, in the servant was revealed an essence[2] of love, the love which he had for the lord, which was similar to the love which the lord had for him. The servant's wisdom inwardly perceived that there was one thing to do which would be for the honour of the lord; and the servant, in love, having no regard for himself nor for anything which might happen to him, sped away and ran at his lord's command to do what was the lord's will and to his honour. By his outward clothing it seemed that he had lived as a regular workman for a long time; and by the inward vision

[1] *Flowing:* a conjecture: both MSS have "flamand", marked in Sloane 2499 for correction.
[2] *An essence:* literally "a ground".

which I had both of the lord and of the servant, it seemed that he was a beginner, beginning, that is, to labour, for the servant had never been sent on an errand before. There was a treasure in the earth which the lord loved: I was amazed, wondering what it could be, and in reply I was made to understand that it is a food, delectable and pleasing to the lord. For I saw the lord, a human being, sitting, but I saw neither food or drink with which he could be served. This was one source of surprise: and another was that this great lord had only one servant, and that he sent him away. I looked, and wondered what kind of work it might be which the servant had to do; and then I understood that he was to perform the greatest labour and make the most difficult journey that can be. He was to be a gardener, to dig a ditch, to toil and sweat, to turn over all the earth, digging deep down, watering the plants when they needed it. He was to go on with this work, guiding the channels of sweet streams, and producing fine, abundant crops, which he was to bring to his lord and serve him with as the lord required. He was never to return until he had prepared this food, as he knew that his lord liked it to be: and then he was to bring the food and carry it with great respect in front of his lord. And all this time the lord would sit in the same place, waiting for his servant whom he had sent out. Still I wondered where the servant came from: for I saw in the lord that he had in himself eternal life and every kind of goodness, except only the treasure which was in the earth. It was rooted in the wonderful depths of love, but it was not altogether befitting the lord's honour until the servant had so finely prepared it and brought it himself into the lord's presence. And except for the lord, there was nothing but wilderness. And I did not understand everything which this example meant, and therefore I was puzzled to know where the servant had come from. In the figure of the servant is comprehended both the Second Person of the Trinity, and Adam, that is, all men: and therefore when I call the servant "the Son" I mean Christ's divinity, which is equal with the Father, and when I call him "the servant," I mean Christ's humanity, which rightly is Adam. By the closeness of the servant to the lord is understood the Son, and by his standing to the lord's left is understood Adam. The Lord is God the Father, the servant is the Son, Christ Jesus; and the Holy Spirit is the equal love which is in Them both. When Adam fell, God's Son fell: for by the true union which was made in heaven, God's Son could not leave Adam, for by Adam I understand all men. Adam fell from life to death, into the ravine of this wretched world, and after that into hell: God's Son fell with Adam into the ravine of the womb of the Virgin, who was Adam's fairest daughter; and this was to excuse Adam from blame in heaven and on earth, and so powerfully He brought him out of hell. By the wisdom and goodness which were in the servant is understood God's Son: by his poor clothing, he standing like a workman at his lord's left hand, is understood the human race, and Adam, and all the harm and debility which follows: for in all this our good Lord showed His own Son and Adam to be but one man. The power and the goodness which we have is from Jesus Christ, the debility and the blindness which we have is from Adam. These two were shown in the servant; and so our good Lord Jesus has taken upon Him all our blame, and therefore our Father cannot and will not assign to us more blame than to His own precious Son, Christ. So He was the servant before He came upon earth, standing ready before the Father

in purpose, waiting for the time when the Father would
send Him to perform that honorable deed by which mankind was brought back again into heaven: that is to say,
even though He is God and equal with the Father, in His
divinity, in His foreknowledge He purposed to become man,
to save man, in fulfilment of His Father's will, and so He
stood like a servant before His Father, voluntarily taking
upon Himself all for which we are answerable, and He then
sped off at once at the Father's will, and fell very low, into
the Virgin's womb, having no regard for Himself nor for
His cruel pains. The white smock was His flesh, and it was
made all in one because there was no distinction between
His divinity and humanity. It fitted closely because He
was poor, it was old because of Adam's sin, stained with
sweat through Adam's toil, short to show that this servant
worked. And so I saw the Son standing and in His intention
saying: "See, My dear Father, I stand before You in Adam's
smock, all ready to speed away and run. It is My wish to be
on earth, for Your honour, when it is Your will to send
Me. How long must I wait?" Without any doubt the Son
knew when it would be the Father's will and how long
He should wait, in His divinity, that is, for He is the wisdom of the Father: so that it was revealed that He asked
this to make us understand Christ's humanity. For all human beings who will be saved by the sweet Incarnation
and the blessed Passion of Christ, they are all Christ's humanity, for He is the head and we are only His limbs, to
which limbs it is unknown when the day and hour shall
be when every passing woe and sorrow shall have an end,
and everlasting joy and bliss shall be fulfilled. All the company of heaven long to see that day and hour; and all who
will ever be under heaven, who will come to heaven, will

find their way there by longing and desire: and this longing and desire were revealed by the servant standing before the lord, in other words by the Son standing before the Father in Adam's smock. For the longing and desire of all mankind who will be saved appeared in Jesus, for Jesus is all that will be saved, and all that will be saved is Jesus, and He is all the love of God, with the obedience, meekness, patience and the virtues which are ours. Also in this wonderful example I have instruction which I can keep, as though it were a child's alphabet, and through which I can have some understanding of our Lord God's intention: for all the secrets of the revelations are hidden in it, even though all the revelations are full of secrets. That the Father is seated signifies His divinity: that is to say, it shows rest and peace, for in His divinity there can be no labour. That He revealed Himself as a lord signifies that He is a ruler to us human beings.[1] That the servant stood signifies labour: that he stood to one side and on the lord's left signifies that he was not altogether worthy to stand directly in front of him. That the servant sped away signifies Christ's divinity, that he ran signifies His humanity: for His divinity sped from the Father into the Virgin's womb, falling to take upon Him our nature, and as He fell He suffered great injury. The injury which He suffered was our flesh, in which at once He felt the pains of mortality. That he stood in fear before the lord and not directly in front of him signifies that he was not suitably dressed to stand directly in front of him, and that to do so could not and should not be his duty whilst he was a workman, nor could he sit in rest and peace with the lord until he had lawfully won his place by his hard

---

[1] *That He is a ruler* is the editor's conjectural addition: some words are obviously missing in both manuscripts.

K

work. That he stood on the left signifies that the Father by His will left His own Son in His humanity to suffer all man's pains without sparing Him. That his smock would soon be in rags and tatters signifies the blows and the scourgings, the thorns and the nails, the pulling and the dragging and the tearing of His tender flesh. As I partly saw,[1] the tender flesh was torn from His skull, falling in fragments until the time that the bleeding stopped, when the flesh began to dry again and to cling to the bones. By the twisting and writhing, groaning and moaning is signified that He could never rise in His almighty power from the time that He fell into the Virgin's womb until His body was slain and dead, and He had committed His soul, together with all humanity, for whose sake He was sent, into His Father's hands. It was then that He first began to show His power, for He went down into hell, and when He was there He raised up the great root from the very depths which was joined to Him in high heaven. His body was in the grave until Easter morning, and from that time on He never lay down again, for then all His twisting and writhing, groaning and moaning was duly ended. And our foul and mortal flesh which God's Son took upon Himself, which was Adam's old smock, narrow, meagre and short, was then beautified by our Saviour, made snowy white, shining and of an everlasting cleanness, wide and ample, lovelier and richer than was the clothing which I saw upon the Father. For that clothing was blue, and Christ's clothing is now of a beautiful, splendid mixture, so wonderful that I cannot describe it, for it is everything which is most glorious. Now the lord does not sit upon the ground in a desert, but he sits in his noblest seat, which He made in Heaven to give Him most delight. Now the Son does not

---

[1] In an earlier revelation, already described.

stand before the Father as a servant before a lord, in fear, meanly dressed, partly naked: but He stands directly before His Father, richly clad in joyful splendour, with a rich and precious crown upon His head. For it was revealed that we are His crown, and this crown is the Father's joy, the Son's honour, the Holy Spirit's delight, and the endless and wonderful bliss of all who are in heaven. Now the Son does not stand on his Father's left hand like a workman, but He sits on His Father's right hand in endless rest and peace: but I do not mean that the Son sits at the Father's right hand, side by side with Him, as one man sits beside another in this life, for as I saw it there is no such sitting in the Trinity. When it is said that He sits on His Father's right hand, it means that He is in the highest nobility of His Father's joys. Now the husband, God's Son, is at peace with His wife, who is the fair virgin, everlasting joy. Now the Son, true God and man, sits in rest and peace in His city, which His Father had prepared for Him in His eternal intention, and the Father is in the Son, and the Holy Spirit is in the Father and in the Son.

Excerpts from

The Book of Margery Kempe

These excerpts have been translated from the edition of the original English of the unique manuscript by Professor S. B. Meech and Dr. Hope Emily Allen (see 69), by kind permission of the Council of the Early English Text Society.

THE BOOK OF MARGERY KEMPE

I. Margery visits Julian of Norwich

AND THEN she was commanded by our Lord to go to an anchoress in the same city [Norwich], who was called Dame Julian. And she did so, and revealed to her the grace of compunction which God had put into her soul, of contrition, of sweetness and devotion, of compassion accompanied by holy meditation and exalted contemplation, and very many holy speeches and marks of His love which our Lord spoke to her soul, and many wonderful revelations, which she communicated to the anchoress to know if there were any fraud in them, for the anchoress was experienced in such things, and knew how to give good advice.

The anchoress, hearing the marvellous goodness of our Lord, devotedly thanked God with all her heart for His visitation, advising this creature to be obedient to the will of our Lord God, and to fulfill with all her power whatever He might put into her soul, if it were not contrary to the honour of God and the betterment of her fellow Christians; for if it were so contrary, then it could not be the prompting of a good spirit but rather of an evil spirit. "The Holy Spirit never inspires anything contrary to the love of God, and if He were to do so He would be contrary to His own self, for He is all love. Also, He inspires a soul to perfect chastity, for those who live chastely are called the temple of the Holy Spirit: and the Holy Spirit makes a soul firm and steadfast in the true Faith and the right belief. And a man who is divided in his soul is always unfirm and unsteadfast in all his ways. A man always in doubt is like to the sea, which is moved and carried about by the wind; and such a man is not likely to receive the gifts of God. Every created being who receives such tokens of God's love must steadfastly believe that the Holy Spirit dwells in his soul. And even more, when God visits one of His creatures with tears of contrition, devotion or compassion, he may and he should believe that the Holy Spirit is in his soul. St. Paul says that the Holy Spirit asks for us with unspeakable lamentations and weepings. That is to say that He makes us ask and pray with lamentations and weepings so plentiful that our tears cannot be numbered. No evil spirit can give these tokens, for Jerome says that tears torment the devil more than do the torments of hell. God and the devil are eternally opposed, and they shall never dwell together in one place, and the devil has no power over a man's soul. Holy Scripture says that the soul of a righteous man is the throne of God, and so I believe, sister, that you are. I pray God to grant you perseverance. Put all your trust in God, and do not fear the language of the world, for the more scorn and shame and reproof which you receive in the world, the greater is your merit in the sight of God. What you need is patience, for in patience you shall preserve your soul."

Great was the holy joy which the anchoress and this creature had, communing in the love of our Lord Jesus Christ for many days when they were together.

II. Margery and Richard Caister

I.

O NE DAY long before, whilst this creature was still bearing children, and when she was newly delivered
of a child, our Lord Christ Jesus said to her that she should
bear no more children, and He therefore commanded her
to go to Norwich. And she said: "Oh, dear Lord, how can
I go? I am both sick and weak." "Do not be afraid: I shall
make you strong enough. I command you to go to the Vicar
of St. Stephen's, and tell him that I greet him, and say that
he is one of My exalted chosen souls, and tell him that he
pleases Me much by his preaching, and reveal your secrets
and My counsels to him as I have revealed them to you."

So she made her way to Norwich, and came into his
church one Thursday, a little before noon. And the Vicar
was walking up and down with another priest, who was
his confessor, and who was still alive when this book was
made. And this creature was at that time dressed in black.
She greeted the Vicar, and asked if she might speak to him
that afternoon when he had eaten, for an hour, or perhaps
two hours, about the love of God. He lifted up his hands,
and blessed himself, and said "Bless my soul! How could a
woman spend one hour or two hours talking about the love
of God? I shall not eat my dinner till I hear what you have
to say about our Lord God which takes an hour to tell."

So he sat down in the church, and she, sitting a little distance away, showed to him all the words which God had
revealed to her in her soul. Then she told him all her manner
of life, as well as she could remember it, from her childhood
on: how cruel she had been towards our Lord Jesus Christ,

K*

how proudly and vainly she had behaved, how stubbornly she had sinned against God's laws, how she had envied her fellow Christians; and then, when it had pleased our Lord Jesus Christ, how she had been chastised with many tribulations and horrible temptations, and how afterwards she was nourished and comforted by holy meditations, and especially by recollection of our Lord's Passion. While she reflected upon the Passion of our Lord Jesus Christ, she heard a melody so hideous that she could not bear it. Then this creature fell down as if she had lost her bodily strength, and she lay still for a long while, wishing to overcome it, but she could not. Then she knew well by her faith that there was great rejoicing in Heaven, where the least bliss surpasses beyond comparison all the joy which could ever be imagined or felt in this life. She was greatly strengthened in her faith,[1] and the more bold to tell the Vicar what feelings she had about her revelations concerning both the living and the dead, and concerning himself.

She told him how sometimes the Father of Heaven held loving converse with her soul, as plainly and as truly as when one friend speaks with earthly speech to another: sometimes it was the second Person of the Trinity: sometimes all three Persons in Trinity, who are in Their divinity one substance, spoke lovingly to her soul, and instructed her in her faith and in God's love, teaching her how she ought to love Him, honour Him and fear Him, teaching her this so excellently that she had never heard a book, not Hilton's book, not St. Bridget's book, not the *Incendium Amoris* or any other which she had listened to, which spoke so exaltedly of the love of God that she had not felt it as

---

[1] It is not clear from the language of the original whether this incident is one which she recounted to Richard Caister, or happened whilst she was talking. The second interpretation seems the more probable.

exaltedly working in her soul, if she had had the knowledge or power to reveal what she felt.

Sometimes our Lady spoke to her recollection, sometimes St. Peter, sometimes St. Paul, sometimes St. Katherine, or any other saint in heaven to whom she had a devotion appeared to her soul and taught her how she ought to love our Lord, and how she ought to please Him. Their conversation was so sweet, so holy and so devout that often this creature could not endure it, but fell down, with paroxysms of the body, and behaved and looked strangely, with violent sobbing and great abundance of tears, sometimes saying "Jesu, mercy!", sometimes "I am dying." And therefore many people slandered her, not believing that this was the work of God, but that some evil spirit afflicted her in her body, or else that she had some physical disease.

Yet in spite of these rumours and complaints by people against her, this holy man, the Vicar of St. Stephen's Church at Norwich, whom God has exalted and showed and proved by miracles to be holy, always took her side and supported her against her enemies with all his might, after the time when by God's command she showed him her form of rule and living, for he firmly believed that she was well instructed in the law of God and endowed with grace of the Holy Spirit, to Whom it is proper to inspire whom He will. And though His voice may be heard, it is not known by the world whence it comes or where it goes.

After this, the holy Vicar was always this creature's confessor when she came to Norwich, and he gave her Holy Communion with his own hands. And when on one occasion she was summoned to appear before certain of the Bishop's officials, to answer to certain charges which had been brought against her through the malice of envious people, the good

Vicar, putting the love of God before any worldly shame, went with her to hear her be interrogated, and he delivered her from the malice of her enemies. And then it was revealed to this creature that the good Vicar should live for another seven years, and should then pass hence with great grace, and so he did as she had. . . .[1]

II.

THE GOOD PRIEST about whom something has already been written,[2] who used to read aloud for her, fell into great sickness, and she was moved in her soul to take care of him on God's behalf. When she lacked what was necessary for him, she went around begging from good men and good women, and obtained such things as he needed. He was so ill that no-one expected him to live, and his sickness lasted for a long time. Then once, when she was in church hearing Mass, as she prayed for the priest, our Lord told her that he would live and be completely cured. Then she was moved to go to Norwich, to St. Stephen's Church, where the good Vicar, who had only died a short time before, is buried, by whose merits God showed His mercy to the people, so that she might thank Him for curing the priest. She obtained leave from her confessor, and set off for Norwich. When she came into St. Stephen's churchyard, she cried, she shouted, she wept, she fell down on the ground, so ardently did the fire of love burn in her heart. Then she got up again, and went, weeping, into the church, up to the high altar, and there she fell down, sobbing violently, weeping and crying aloud beside the good Vicar's

---

[1] The end of this sentence is lost in the original.
[2] See Section V.

grave, completely transported by the spiritual consolations which she had in the goodness of our Lord, Who caused such great grace to come by the merits of His servant, who had been her confessor and had many times heard her confess the sins of her whole life, and often administered to her the precious Sacrament of the altar. And her devotion was so much more increased because she saw how our Lord caused so special a grace to come through the merits of one of His creatures whom she had known in his lifetime. She had such holy thoughts and such holy recollections that she could not restrain her weeping or her crying. And the people were therefore greatly astonished at her, thinking that some carnal or earthly affection caused her to weep, and they said to her: "What is the matter with the woman? Why are you carrying on like this? We knew him as well as you." There were priests there who knew about her spiritual life, and they most charitably took her to a tavern and gave her something to drink and looked after her most hospitably. There was also a lady who wished to invite this same creature to a meal; and therefore, as courtesy required, she went to the church which the lady attended for her, and there this creature saw a lovely image of our Lady, called a "Pity." And as she looked at that Pity her recollection was completely occupied by the Passion of our Lord Jesus Christ and by the compassion of our Lady St. Mary, and this forced her to cry very loudly and to weep very grievously, as if she were dying. Then the lady's priest came to her, saying: "Damsel,[1] it is a long time now since Jesus died." When her crying was over, she said to the priest: "Sir, His death is as new to me as if He had died this very day, and so I think it ought to be

---

[1] People habitually addressed Margery so after she was divinely commanded to wear white, as if she were vowed to a life of virginity.

to you and to all Christian people. We ought always to be mindful of His love to us, and always think of the bitter death which He died for us." Then the good lady, hearing her conversation, said: "Sir, the grace which God sends into her soul is a good example both to me and to others"; and so the good lady spoke up for her and took charge of her, and took her home with her for a meal, and entertained her very well as long as she would stay there. And soon afterwards she returned to Lynn, and the priest of whom we have spoken, on whose especial account she had gone to Norwich, he who had read to her for some seven years, recovered and went about freely, thanks be to Almighty God for His goodness.

III. Margery in Rome

ON ANOTHER OCCASION, as she was passing a poor woman's house, the poor woman called her in and made her sit by her little fire, giving her wine to drink in a stone[1] cup. And she was suckling a little boy at her breast, who sometimes sucked at the breast, sometimes came running to this creature whilst the mother sat, full of sorrow and sadness. Then this creature burst into tears, just as if she had seen our Lady and her Son at the time of His Passion, and holy thoughts came to her mind, so many that she could never tell the half of them; but she sat there still and wept for a long time, so copiously that the poor woman pitied her for her weeping and begged her to cease, not knowing the reason why she wept. Then our Lord Jesus Christ said to this creature: "This place is holy."

Then she got up and went out and about in Rome, and she

[1] That is, alabaster.

saw great poverty among the people; and she gave great thanks to God for her own poverty, having faith that through it she might share in their merit.

Then there was in Rome a lady of high birth who asked this creature to be her child's godmother, and she called it for St. Bridget, because they had known her during her life[1]; and this creature did this. Then by God's grace she had great esteem in Rome from both men and women, and was very popular among the common people. When the master and brethren of St. Thomas's Hospital, where she had previously been refused, as has been written, heard of her esteem and popularity in the city, they asked her to come back to them, saying that she would be made more welcome than before, and that they were very sorry that they had turned her out. And she thanked them for their charity, and did as they asked. When she came back to them they entertained her well and were very glad to see her. Then she found that the woman who had acted as her servant, and who should still have been serving her, was living in the Hospital in great comfort and prosperity, because she was in charge of their wine. And for the sake of humility this creature used sometimes to go to her and ask her for food and drink, and the serving girl was glad to give it to her, and sometimes a groat with it. Then she complained to the girl and said that she had hurt her very much by leaving her, and that after they had separated people had said slanderous and evil things, but that none the less she would be glad for them to be together again.

Afterwards this creature talked to St. Bridget's serving woman in Rome, but she could not understand what she said. Then she found a man who could understand her speech,

---

[1] St. Bridget of Sweden died in Rome in 1373: Margery was in Rome in 1414.

and that man told St. Bridget's maid what this creature said, and that she was asking about her mistress, St. Bridget. Then the maid said that her mistress, St. Bridget, was courteous and humble towards every creature, and that she had a smiling face. And the landlord where this creature lodged told her that he himself had known St. Bridget, but that he had little dreamed that she was such a holy woman, for she was always simple and courteous to everyone who wished to speak to her. She was in the room in which St. Bridget died, and heard a German priest there preaching about her and her revelations and her form of life: and she also knelt upon the stone upon which our Lord appeared to St. Bridget and told her on what day she should die. And it was on one of St. Bridget's feast days that this creature was in her chapel, which previously had been the room in which she died. Our Lord sent such storms of wind and rain and such hurricanes that those who were in the fields and working out of doors were forced to protect themselves by going into houses to avoid such dangers. By such signs this creature supposed that our Lord wished the day of His holy saint to be made a holy day and the saint to be held in more reverence than she was at this time.

And once when this creature wanted to make the Stations, our Lord warned her the night before when she was in bed that she should not go out far from her hostel, for He intended on the next day to send great storms of lightning and thunder: and so in fact it happened. During that year there were such storms of thunder and lightning, of torrential rain and various inclement weather, that very old men who were living in Rome said that they had never seen the like before, for the flashes of lightning were so frequent and shone so brightly inside their houses that they fully expected the houses and everything in them to be burned. Then they implored this creature to pray for them, fully believing that she was the servant of Almighty God, and that they would be helped and rescued through her prayers. When this creature prayed to our Lord for mercy as they asked, He answered in her soul, saying: "Daughter, do not be afraid, for no rain or storm shall harm you, and therefore have faith in Me, for I shall never deceive you". And our merciful Lord Christ Jesus, when it was His will, ceased the storms and preserved the people from all harm.

IV. *Margery in Jerusalem*

A<small>ND</small> so they continued through the Holy Land until they could see Jerusalem. And when this creature, riding on an ass, saw Jerusalem, she thanked God with all her heart, praying Him in His mercy that as He had brought her to see this earthly city, Jerusalem, so He would grant her grace to see the blessed city of Jerusalem above, the city of Heaven. Our Lord Jesus Christ, answering to her thoughts, granted her that she would have her desire. Then, for the joy that she had and the sweetness that she felt in the loving converse of our Lord, she nearly fell off her ass, for she could not bear the sweetness and grace which God caused in her soul. Then two German pilgrims came to her and saved her from falling, and one of them was a priest: and he put spices in her mouth to comfort her, thinking that she was sick. And so they helped her on to Jerusalem; and when she arrived, she said: "Sirs, I beg you not to be angry with me, although I weep greatly in this holy place where our Lord Jesus Christ lived and died". Then they went to the Temple in Jerusalem, and they were admitted in the

evening at the time of vespers, and stayed there until vespers
the next evening. Then the friars lifted up a cross, and led
the pilgrims around from one place to another where our
Lord suffered His torments and His Passion, every man and
woman carrying wax candles in their hands, and all the time
as they went around the friars told them what our Lord had
suffered in each place. And this creature wept and sobbed as
copiously as if she had seen our Lord with her bodily eyes
suffering His Passion then. She saw Him in front of her,
in her soul, truly, by contemplation, and that caused her to
feel compassion, and when they came up on to the Mount
of Calvary, she fell down, and she could not stand or kneel,
but rocked and writhed in her body, stretching her arms
wide, and she shouted with a loud voice as if her heart would
break in two, for in the city of her soul she saw, truly and
instantly, how our Lord was crucified. Before her face she
heard and saw by her spiritual senses the lamentation of our
Lady, of St. John and Mary Magdalene, and of many others
who loved our Lord. And she felt such great compassion
and such great pain to see our Lord's pain that she could not
prevent herself crying and shouting, though she should
have died for it. And this was the first time in any contemplation that she shouted aloud. And from then on this
manner of shouting lasted for many years, for all that anyone
could do, and she endured much malice and much blame
on this account. The shouting was so loud and so amazing
that unless people had already heard it they were astonished,
unless they knew why she shouted. And she had these ac-
cesses of shouting so often that they greatly enfeebled her
physically; and they came especially when she heard about
our Lord's Passion. And sometimes, when she saw a crucifix,
or if she saw a man, or it might be an animal, wounded, or

if a man beat a child in front of her or struck a horse or another animal with a whip, if she saw or heard this it seemed to her that she saw our Lord beaten or wounded as were the men or the animals whom she could see: and this happened in the countryside as well as in the town, when she was alone or in company.

V. *A Priest reads aloud to Margery*

ONCE when this creature was in contemplation, she hungered very greatly for the Word of God[1], and said: "Alas, Lord, out of all the scholars You have in this world, would You not send me one of them, so that he could fill my soul with Your word, and with reading from Holy Scripture, for all the scholars who preach are unable to fill it, for my soul seems to me always to be hungry. If I had enough gold, I would pay a noble a day to have a sermon every day, for Your word is more precious to me than all the wealth in this world. Therefore, blessed Lord, have pity on me, for You have taken the anchorite away from me who was my special consolation and comfort, and who refreshed me many times with Your holy word". Then our Lord Jesus Christ answered in her soul, saying: "Someone shall come from far off who shall fulfill your desire".

And so it happened, that many days after this answer, a new priest came to Lynn who had never known her before, and when he saw her walking in the streets he was greatly moved to talk to her, and he enquired of other people what kind of woman she was. They said that they trusted in God that she was a very good woman. Then the priest sent for

---

[1] Margery could not read.

her, asking her to come and talk to him and his mother, because he had rented a room for his mother and himself and they were living together. Then this creature came to ask his pleasure, and she was well received by them both.

Then the priest took a book and read from it how our Lord, seeing the city of Jerusalem, wept over it, recounting the misfortunes and sorrows that would come upon it, because Jerusalem did not know the time of her visitation. When this creature heard him read how our Lord wept, she wept and cried aloud, and neither the priest nor his mother knew the cause of her weeping. When her crying and weeping was finished, they rejoiced and were very cheerful in our Lord: and then she took her leave and left them. When she had gone, the priest said to his mother: "This woman amazes me, weeping and crying so. All the same, it seems to me that she is a good woman, and I very much want to talk to her again". His mother was very pleased, and advised him to do this.

And in course of time this priest loved her and had great faith in her, and he blessed the day when he first met her, for he had great spiritual consolation from her, and she caused him often to consult many good books and many a good authority which he would not then have read, had it not been for her. He read many a good book of exalted contemplation, and many other books: the Bible and commentaries on it, St. Bridget's book, Hilton's book, Bonaventura, *Stimulus Amoris, Incendium Amoris,* and other such works. And then she knew that it was a spirit sent from God which had said to her, as has just been written, when she complained of her lack of reading, these words: "Someone shall come from far off who shall fulfill your desire". And so she knew by experience that it was indeed a true spirit.

This priest read books to her for the greater part of seven or eight years, to the great increase of his knowledge and merit, and he suffered many an angry word for love of her, because he read so many books to her and took her part in her weeping and crying. Later he received a benefice and had a great cure of souls, and then he was very glad that previously he had read so much.

VI. *Margery is Arraigned as a Heretic at Leicester*

O N a Wednesday this creature was brought into a church, called All Hallows, in Leicester, and there before the high altar were seated the Abbot of Leicester with some of his canons, and the Dean of Leicester, an honorable cleric. There were also many friars and priests, and the mayor of the town with many of the laity. There was such a crowd of people that they climbed up on stools to look at her and stare. This creature was on her knees, saying her prayers to Almighty God that she might have the grace, knowledge and wisdom to give such answers that day as might most please and glorify Him, might best profit her soul and give a good example to the people.

Then a priest came up to her and took her by the hand and led her before the Abbot and his assessors, seated at the altar, and they made her swear on a book that she would answer truly to the articles of the Faith, just as she felt concerning them. And first they discussed the blessed Sacrament of the altar, charging her to say just what she believed about it. Then she said: "Sirs, I believe in this fashion in the Sacrament of the altar, that whatever man has accepted the order of priesthood, however vicious in his life he may be, if he say as is needed those words over the bread which our

Lord Jesus Christ said when He made His Maundy among His disciples as He sat at supper, I believe that it is His very flesh and His blood, and that it is not material bread, and that being once said it cannot be unsaid". And so she went on answering to all the articles, as many as they wanted to ask her, so that they were very satisfied. But the mayor, who was her mortal enemy, said: "Indeed, she does not mean in her heart what she says with her mouth". And the clergy said to him: "Sir, she has answered us very well". The mayor abused her vehemently, and used many injurious and discourteous words which are better hidden than spoken. "Sir", she said, "I call my Lord Jesus Christ to witness, Whose body is here present in the Sacrament of the altar, that I never by deed had sinful commerce with the body of any man in this world except my husband, to whom I am bound by the law of matrimony, and by whom I have born fourteen children. For I would have you know, sir, that there is no man in this world whom I love so much as God, for I love Him above all things, and, sir, I tell you truly that I love all men in God and for God." And she went on to say directly to him: "Sir, you are not fit to be a mayor, and I shall prove it by Holy Scripture, for our Lord God said Himself, before He would take vengeance on the cities, 'I shall come down and see', and still He knew everything. And the only reason for that, sir, was to show men like you that you ought to carry out no punishment unless you are previously satisfied that it ought to be done. And, sir, today you have done just the opposite to me, because, sir, you have caused me great shame because of something of which I am not guilty. I pray God to forgive you for it."

Then the mayor said to her: "I want to know why you go around dressed in white, because I believe that you have come here to entice our wives away from us and lead them off with you". "Sir", she said, "you shall not know from my mouth why I go dressed in white: you are not fit to know it. But, sir, I will gladly tell these honorable clerics, under the seal of confession. Ask them if they will repeat it to you". Then the clerics asked the mayor and the other laymen to leave them; and when they had gone, she knelt on her knees before the Abbot, and the Dean of Leicester, and a Friar Preacher, an honorable cleric, and she told these three clerics how our Lord in a revelation had warned and commanded her to wear white clothes before she came to Jerusalem. "And I have told this to my confessors, and they have therefore enjoined me to dress like this, for they dare not go contrary to my feelings for fear of God, and if they dared they would gladly do it. And therefore, sirs, if the mayor wants to know why I go dressed in white, you may say if you please that my confessors command me to do it, and so you shall not tell any lie, and he will not know the truth".

VII. Margery before the Archbishop of York

THEN the Archbishop said to her: "I have received bad reports about you. They tell me you are a very wicked woman". And she replied: "Sir, they tell me that you are a wicked man; and if you are as wicked as people say, you will never get to Heaven unless you change whilst you are here". Then he said, very violently: "Oh, indeed, what do people say about me?" She replied: "Other people can tell you that quite well, sir". Then an important cleric in a furred hood said: "Hold your tongue: talk about yourself, and leave him alone". Then the Archbishop said to her: "Lay your hand on the book here in front of me, and swear that you will go out of my diocese as soon as you can". "No, sir", she said, "please give me permission to go to York again to say goodbye to my friends". So he gave her permission for one day or two. She thought that this was too little time, so she said to him: "Sir, I cannot leave this diocese so quickly, because I must stay to speak with certain good men before I go, and I must, with your permission, sir, go to Bridlington and talk to my confessor there, a good man who was the confessor of the good prior who is now canonized."[1] Then the Archbishop said to her: "You will swear that you will neither teach the people in my diocese, nor argue with them". "No, sir, I will not swear that", she said, "because I shall talk about God, and reprove those who blaspheme, everywhere I go, until the day when the Pope and Holy Church decree that no-one shall be so bold as to talk about God, for, sir, Almighty God does not forbid us to talk about Him. And it is also said in the Gospel that when the woman had heard our Lord preach, she stood in front of Him and said in a loud voice: 'Blessed be the womb that bore You, and the breasts that gave suck to You'. Then our Lord replied to her: 'Indeed, so are they blessed who hear the word of God and obey it'. And therefore, sir, it seems to me that the Gospel allows me to talk about God". "Ah, sir," the clerics said, "now we know well that she has a devil inside her, because she talks about the Gospel". Straight away an important cleric produced a book, and quoted St. Paul against her, saying that no woman ought to preach. She in reply said: "I am not preaching, sir, I do not get up in a pulpit. I only use conversation and holy talk, and I intend to do that as long as I live". Then a doctor of divinity who had

---

[1] St. John of Bridlington, died 1379, canonized 1401.

examined her before said: "Sir, she told me the worst stories
that I ever heard about priests". The Archbishop commanded
her to repeat the story. "Sir, saving your presence, I only
talked about one priest, and I used him as a kind of illustration. This man, I heard, lost his way in a wood, and this was
by the will of God for the profit of his soul. When night
came on he had no shelter, but he found a lovely arbour in
which he slept that night, and in the middle of the arbour
was a lovely pear tree, all overgrown with flowers and
blossoms, most pleasing to his sight. A great rough bear,
hideous to look at, came up and shook the pear tree and
brought down the flowers. This ugly brute greedily ate and
devoured those lovely flowers, and when he had eaten them
he turned his tail towards the priest and voided them out
again at his rear end. The priest was disgusted at that loathsome sight and much perplexed to understand what it could
mean; and on the next morning he went on his way, sad
and thoughtful, until by chance he met a man of a good
age, looking like a palmer or a pilgrim, who asked the
priest why he was so sad. The priest told him all this story,
and said that he had been seized by a great fear and sorrow
when he saw that loathsome beast spoil and devour such
lovely flowers and blossoms, and then so horribly void them
from his tail end in front of him, and he was unable to
understand its meaning. Then the palmer revealed himself
as the messenger of God, and took him to task: "Priest,
you yourself are the pear tree, at times flowering and putting
out blossoms, when you say your Office and administer the
Sacraments, even though you do it without devotion, because
you pay little attention to how you say Matins and the
Office, so long as you gabble through to the end. Then you
go to say Mass with no devotion and with little contrition for

your sins: and you receive the fruit of everlasting life, the Sacrament of the altar, with little of the proper disposition. Then you waste your time for the rest of the day, buying and selling, dealing and exchanging as if you were a man of the world. You sit in the tavern, giving yourself up to gluttony and excess, and to the delights of the body, in lechery and impurity. You break the commandments of God by swearing, lying, detraction, backbiting and such other sins. And so, through your ill-governed life, just like the loathsome bear, you devour and destroy the flowers and blooms of virtuous living, to your own everlasting damnation, and to the hindrance of many others, unless you have the grace of repentence and amendment". The Archbishop liked this story and praised it, saying that it was a good story; and the cleric who had previously examined her, when the Archbishop was not there, said: "Sir, this story smites me to the heart". This creature said to the cleric: "Ah, sir and honorable doctor, in the town where I usually live there is a good preacher, who speaks out boldly against the evil life of the people, and flatters nobody. Very often in the pulpit he says: 'If any man takes offence at what I preach, mark him well, for he is guilty'. And this is just how you, sir", she said to the cleric, "have acted towards me, God forgive you". The cleric did not know what to say to her: but presently this same man came to her and asked her to forgive him for having so opposed her. And he asked her particularly to pray for him.

INDEX TO INTRODUCTION

INDEX TO INTRODUCTION